The *Little* Girl

L.G.

CHAD TEDDER

To order additional copies of this book, contact:
Bookwhip
1-855-339-3589
https://www.bookwhip.com

Contents

Chapter 1

THE ENCOUNTER

On a Friday night in October a small Texas town fills a college size football stadium with patrons and opposing team's fans. The air has a biter chill and the field has begun to frost. It is more of a family reunion than a football game; most have lived in the area their entire life. Gossip feels the air with the latest rumors from the middle school kids all the way up to the retired ladies of the beauty shop and the old men from the café. Will this be the year for the Coyotes to go all the way? The reporters debate as they unload the equipment on the side lines. The crowd begins to silence just before the home team raids the field. The band gets restless in the stand and starts the schools fight song, the team blitz's the field escorted by coaches and the cheerleaders. Leading the way is, Bratton Lee. Whose accomplishments as the all-state linebacker have been overshadowed by his team's success.

Bratton is kind of quiet but, very rambunctious. He has been raised by his redneck father who had made a name for himself in the rodeo arena some years ago. They still rodeo in the off season to make a little extra money to pay for the extracurricular activities they enjoy from time to time.

Bratton's father Kim or Cowboy as most everyone called him, mingles with the other parents and coaches in the stands stopping to shake hands or hug the ladies much like a politician on the campaign trail. After making his way through the stands he finds his way down the wheelchair ramp to stand in his spot for the game along the fence. Cowboy leaned back against the fence and was talking to a buddy when Mrs. Haygood started down the steps. Mrs. Haygood was getting on up there in age and was a dear friend to Cowboy and Bratton They called her Momma Good. Cowboy had worked many hot summers hauling hay with and for her husband when he was younger. As she came to the bottom or what she thought was the bottom she stumbled and fell to the ground hitting her head on the chain link fence where Cowboy stood. Startled by the sound of her landing Cowboy immediately came to her aid. Another lady walking back from the concession stand saw the traumatic event and came to render aid.

"O my God are you OK?" the lady inquired.

"I am fine I am just old and clumsy" embarrassed by the amount of people who saw her tumble down the steps.

"It looks like you got quite a cut there Momma you sure you are OK?"

"I am fine."

"Why don't you come over here in the light so I can look at you I am a nurse" The stranger requested as she turned to Cowboy and asked, "Is she your mother?"

"No ma'am she is just a good friend I have known most of my life."

"Will you help me get a chair so she can sit in the light and I will clean her up."

"You bet" Cowboy helped momma off the ground and over by the concession stand where the lighting was much better and sat her down. He turned to his friends standing at the fence "Charlie go get Haygood and tell him what happened, so he won't be worried." Charlie scampered up the steps.

The nurse had her cleaned up by the time Mr. Haygood got down to her. He walked slowly toward her to check on her." What happened? Are you OK?"

The nurse could tell he was worried but not panicked he was just concerned about her. "I think she will be fine but she had a good fall so you might want to keep an eye on her for the next few hours and if she has any trouble at all take her to the doctor."

"Yes ma'am" the elderly gentleman replied.

Cowboy helped her up once again and they used the wheelchair ramp to get back in the stands. Cowboy looked back at the nurse and hollered out "Miss, Miss" until she turned to look at him. "Thank you for your help."

"It was nothing" she replied with a smile and waving him away with one hand.

When the nurse had turned around, her cousin was hollering at her "Jessica come on you are gonna lose your seat." She hurried back up the steps with her drinks in hand and walked with her cousin Jack Barrett up to their seats. "Who was that guy?"

"That is Kim Lee everybody calls him Cowboy" he sharply answered

"He is sweet"

"Jess he is a long way from sweet. He got his name riding in the rodeo and fighting in the bars. He is not sweet I have known him all my life. He is just a player."

"Well he sure seemed nice down there when that lady fell. That is all I am saying."

The game started shortly after they made it to their seats. The kickoff and the crowd cheering made the game go by like a ping pong match. The coyotes won and everyone was excited. Most of the adults and parents made their way to a small bar in town after the games for a drink, because it would take the boys at least an hour to get back to the locker room and get dressed. Jessica and Jack went up there to wait and to meet up with Shelly, Jack's wife. The three of them sat and had a beer talking and laughing. Shelly and Jack got up to dance and left Jessica at the table alone. She sat and looked around the bar watching people come and go. She would turn and look toward the door each time it opened, thinking *I hope none of these rednecks ask me to dance.*

At that time the door swung open extra wide and she could hear chairs moving back and people walking toward the door. She turned to look once again, and it was Cowboy making his way through the bar everyone congratulating him on how well Bratton had played in the game. The whole bar met him at the door, and he pushed his way to the bar to order a beer. He took the beer from the bar slowly turned his back to the bartender and took a drink. A tall handsome man with rough hands, salt and pepper hair and slightly weathered shin. Jessica knew he was not a lawyer like her cousin. She could see he was a hard worker and most everyone liked him.

Cowboy glanced around the bar and saw Jessica sitting alone. He nodded his head at her and slowly strolled her way. "I wanted to thank you again for helping out Mrs. Haygood. She is getting old, but she is still tough as nails."

"It was really nothing. I just washed her up is all."

"It was still a nice thing to do. What is your name?"

"My name is Jessica."

"Well it is nice to meet you there Jessica." His boyish smile, rough voice and Texas draw made her smile.

"Let me guess you are Kim? Is that right?"

"Most ever…"

"Everybody calls you Cowboy I know" She razzed him. "Who talks like that anymore?"

"What do you mean?"

"You know Yaaaa'lll and Maaa'aaam"

"So now you are gonna pick on me cuz the way I talk?"

"NO, it is kind of cute, I guess. So, what do YA'LL do around here?"

"Me I have a little piece of property outside of town I run cattle and horses on. You said you were a nurse where do you work?"

"I work at Cook's Children Hospital"

"Wow educated city girl I feel a little threatened." He joked "What brings you all the way out here to redneckville?"

"We had a family reunion at my cousins place and his boy plays on the varsity with I am assuming your son from what I figure"

"Who is your cousin?"

"I AM" Jack boldly interrupted

"Jack" Cowboy greeted him with disappointment. "Mrs. Shelly! How are you doing these days?"

"I am doing good Cowboy how are you"

He nodded his head and turned back toward Jessica," Would you like to dance?"

"We were just leaving" Jack interrupted.

"Well I guess not they are my ride"

"Well give me your number and we can do lunch if you want, I am sure you got more jokes about the way I talk."

Jack and Shelly walked to the door and Jessica followed close behind them looking back at Cowboy and waving. He raised his hand about waist high had gave her a halfhearted wave to show his disappointment in her early exit from the bar.

Chapter 2

RED QUIT BARKIN'

You may think this is another Friday Night Light's, but it really has nothing to do with football or rodeo at all, but rather a beautiful little girl.

See after football was over and Christmas had passed. The trees were beginning to bud and the fields were turning green. On a ranch just north of town paid for by the blood sweat and tears of their great grandparents. The ranch had been in the family for more than a hundred years and had just recently been labeled with a historical marker. This is where Bratton and his father Kim Lee lived. Very few called him Kim, as a matter of fact his own son Bratton called him Cowboy. We all thought it was strange; no one had ever met the boy's mom. He was born when he was out on the road and no one ever saw him around town till he was almost 2. They said that Cowboy took a bad spill and it messed him up pretty bad so he decided to cash in while he could still walk. Some say the boy's mom got messed up on drugs and abandoned him and his dad at a rodeo never to return. Personally, I think he quit for the boy so he would not have to grow up on the road. No one really knew except Cowboy's mom and dad and they had passed away when the boy was 5 or 6.

Cowboy raised Bratton by himself from that time on with help from me, Cross, an old family friend and ranch hand who lives on the property with them. He treated the boy more like a side kick than a son and all the girls just adored that little cowboy and his daddy knew it. See Cowboy would use the boy to meet women a lot of times and on the weekend, they would spend most of their time at local roping or out hunting. As Bratton got a little older, he was just like his dad with the ladies, a real charmer, if you know what I mean and never really kept them around for long. A senior in high school and a sure thing for a scholarship to almost any college he was ready to get out of this sleepy little rumor mill of a town.

That spring the two of them were getting things ready for the big hunt they go on each year. This year they were headed to Colorado and Utah to hunt bear and Elk, they had begun gathering things up several months in advance in between their night life and social activities. This Saturday was the county fair and rodeo in town, and they had entered the team roping event, which they were a sure in to win. Not real sure why they did not get back on the circuit and go pro, but I think they looked at it as relaxing and a meat market. There were always a few ladies who would come into town, who were oblivious to their reputation. When the rodeo was over, and they got their prize money and the 2 loaded up the horses to return home for a shower and get back to their newfound lady friends. Bratton got in the shower first, it was an old 5-bedroom 2 story house with only 2 bathroom they saw no reason to change it. Cowboy was 15 minutes behind him because the water had too warm up and there was no since getting in a hurry because Bratton would need an hour or so to get dressed. Cowboy never took too long "What you see is what you get with me" that is what he always said to the ladies. They had finished getting ready and drank a few beers. They did not want to be early. It just was not their style. They also had to argue over who was driving. They always ended up driving their own vehicle because neither of them liked being stranded and it had happened every time they rode together aside from the rodeos or hunting trips which there was no women involved in. Bratton opened the door and pushed on the wood framed screen door that led to the front porch. The door seemed much heavier than it should, so he hollered out "Move out of the way red". Red was their red healer who would lie in front of the door from time to time just to get some attention. Red didn't move so Bratton turned on the light to see what he was doing. It wasn't Red this time it was a pink cloth bag a little larger than a purse but smaller than a suitcase. Bratton yelled at his dad "Cowboy what the hell is this?" He thought maybe his dad had gotten him an early graduation present and put it in a pink bag as a joke, so he carried it in

Cowboy came to the living room buttoning up his shirt with is pants undone and asked "What is what boy"

"This pink bag, I found it on the front porch what did you do? I am not taking this thing on a hunting trip. What is it?"

He thought it might be the new pistol he had wanted to take on the trip, so he started going through it. When he unzipped it there were diapers?

"ha ha very funny what kind of sick mind do you have?"

Cowboy just laughed and said, "I didn't do that maybe one of your high school buddies done that."

"Come on now where is the gun".

"I am telling you I had nothing to do with this. What else is there?"

"Well there is a small blue turkey baster, some Desitin toothpaste, God that smells awful, baby wipes, and bottles." Before he could finish, they heard a sound like a peacock cry out on the front porch.

Cowboy said, "that damn red I'm gonna kill him if he don't leave them birds alone". He went out on the porch shouting at red "Damn you dog I'll whip your ass--- WHAT IN GOD" S NAME IS THIS? Son you got more to your present out here."

Bratton thinking his dad was hamming it up goes to the front porch and there is a little alien in a plastic crate.

"Do you need to tell me something?"

Bratton replied "ME??? Do you need to tell me something?"

"Well it ain't mine"

"It sure is hell ain't mine."

Cowboy told him "Watch your mouth around the little one son".

"Let's see whose it is there is a note here."

Bratton opened the note and it said, "Please take care of her dad".

"What the hell dad you don't need no more kids"

"Well I don't think it is mine and you are just as bad with the ladies as I am."

"Well what are we gonna do"

"I don't know pick her up and bring her inside."

7

"How do you know it's a she? I told you it was yours."

"It was a guess you idiot she is wearing pink."

"Ok I'll give you that one."

Bratton carried the baby inside and sets it on the floor. Both the men paced back and forth as they debated whose child it could be and what they were going to do with it. Finally, Bratton decide he would leave, and Cowboy said, "now hold on you're not going anywhere you're gonna stay here and take care of your baby."

"My baby?"

"Yea that is what I said"

"How do you know that?"

"I don't but I got stuff to do to night, so you stay with your baby or (gulp) little sister"

"Well I don't know what to do with a baby"

"Me neither"

"You raised me"

"But you're a boy and that was a long time ago"

"You're not leaving me here alone with this thing"

By the time they had finished arguing it was already too late to go so they both sat down and stared at the baby in the carrier. Both men unsure what to do or how this happened, decided they would take it to the Doctor in Ft Worth so no one would know about it until they had proof who the baby belonged to. The baby cried all night and Cowboy had put some real milk in a bottle and fed it to the girl it would appease the little critter for a few minutes, but she would start up again shortly after the bottle. Then she spit up and the 2 avid hunters and wilderness boys suddenly turned and ran.

Cowboy told Bratton to clean up the mess and he would wipe the baby up.

"Oh my god what the heck is this stuff it is nasty. Is this normal?"

"I'm sure it is" said cowboy as he tried to figure out the complicated locking mechanism on the carrier.

Chapter 3

COWBOYS AND HOSPITALS

Neither of them got much sleep that night and in the morning, it started all over again with the same thing. They put the baby in the seat and were unable to figure out how to buckle her in so the tied her down in the middle with a lariat rope so she could not get away. They got to the hospital and were checking in and realized they did not know the babies name. The nurse found it odd that they paused when she asked and then Cowboy replied "Her name. UHHH. It is Elgie"

The nurse said, "That is an odd name is it a family name?"

"Why yes, it is after my great grandmother on my dad's side"

Bratton looked at him with a bewildered look, trying not to ruin anything because Cowboy was good at making things up on the fly. After the nurse left Bratton asked him "Elgie? What kind of name is that? Why didn't you just say Olga or Bessie? That is awful"

"It was all I could come up with. Little Girl popped in my head, so I went with the initials."

"Well thank God you had a rhyme or reason to it. It is still terrible. If it is mine, I'll name her Katherine, no I think Maddie. What if she is yours?"

"She aint mine!" Cowboy snapped

The nurse returned and asked, "What was wrong with the baby?"

Bratton said, "she won't quit crying."

The nurse said, "Well I'm just guessing but you could try changing her."

"What can we change her for" said Bratton, followed by a stiff arm to the chest from Cowboy and a stern "Shut up and let me talk to this nice lady." As he leans down and reads her name tag. She was not quite sure what he was doing so she was feeling a little violated because, Cowboys eyes are not as good as most, so he got pretty close to her and she thought he was looking down her shirt.

"I'm gonna be square with you Jessy or do you prefer Jessica?"

"Jessica is fine" annoyed by his antics

"We just found this little girl on our steps with this note."

"Excuse me before you finish why don't I get you a diaper and you can clean her up?"

"Yes ma'am"

His slow draw kind of made her snicker as she walked into the other room both of them sat silent being careful not to bring up the subject of who was going to actually do the changing they both knew it was going to be an argument but wanted to assume the other was going to step up to the plate and perform the unwanted task.

She returned with diaper and baby wipes in hand and much to Bratton's surprise His dad manned up and took the diaper from her but it did not last long because he turned to him and said "just pull that one off son and we will get this one on her." Bratton sighed in discussed and proceeded to pull the diaper off without unfastening it. His illustrious leader began making a play on the nurse Jessica.

"Would you like some help with that?" She asked

"No, I think I just about got it as he tugged away at it"

She gently took Elgie from him and unfastened the diaper as she talked real soft and quite to her

I'm guessing neither of you know how to clean her up or put the new one on.

Cowboy said, "I did it with him once, but he is not no girl", and let out a laugh trying to make light of the situation.

Jessica finished and handed the baby to Cowboy. He hesitantly put his long-fingered hands around her and held her out away from his body like he was going give her back to her. She gave him a stern look and he turned at the waist and gave the baby to Bratton and said, "Hold her boy so me and Jessy can settle up on the bill."

10

She said, "you have not seen the doctor yet."

"Well we don't need to. You done fixed her. So, what do I owe you", as he reached and grabbed his wallet out, full of 20- and hundred-dollar bill (it always impressed the women at the rodeo to see that)?

She said "Well she probably needs to be checked out just for precaution and we will notify CPS in the event the child has been kid knapped or something"

Cowboy said, "What is CPS?"

Bratton said, "It is an abbreviation for cops dummy."

Jessica giggled and said, "well I guess it could be, but it stands for the Child Protective Services."

"Hell, we can protect her we got plenty of guns" Cowboy said.

"Well we have to notify them when something like this happens. So, you are the father of the girl? What is your name?"

"How do you know I'm the father?"

Bratton barked out "I told you" as he gleefully bounced in his seat.

Jessica said "I just assumed"

"Well we don't know who the dad is. We are hoping the mom will return to let us know"

"We have test now that will determine the father"

"Are the tests hard?"

"No, we draw blood and compare the DNA to the babies, and it will tell us whose baby Elgie is."

"Well let's do that."

"Ok we can do that but first let's finish the paperwork. Do you have insurance?"

"Nope don't need it"

"Where do you live?"

"We are about 80 miles north west of Ft Worth just past Weatherford"

"I meant what is your address?"

"Oh well I'm sorry it is PO box 455, Graham, Texas I sure appreciate all your help Nurse Jessica I bet all them other people are jealous you giving us all this special treatment and all."

"Well that is my job I did same for all of them when they came in there is nothing special about it."

"Well your pretty special to me", Cowboy said with a smile and a wink

11

"HUH I bet I am mister. Umm and what is your name?"

"I apologize I am Cowboy, and this is my boy Bratton"

"OK Cowboy we will use your real name?"

"That is, it"

"No, it is Kim Lee if I remember correctly"

Bratton said "You are right. He just hates it", as Cowboy glares at him.

"It is true that is my birth name, but everyone calls me Cowboy. I got that name cuz a China Man delivered me in my grandma's Living room. He owned the cleaners in town it is still there, Kim's cleaners, only Kim is dead."

"I never knew that. Are you lying to her?"

"No that is the truth your granddad gives them a steer for doing that for them and they were real good friends you used to call him papa Kim, but you were really young."

"Guys! Can we get back to the paperwork?"

"Sorry what else did you need? Now I know where I know you from you are Jack and Shelly's Cousin ain't ya?"

"I was beginning to wonder if you would remember me or not."

"How could I forget after you turned me down for the dance. I almost cried myself to sleep that night."

"I bet you did. Can we get back to the paperwork and we can talk about that later?"

"I guess so, man you are tough row to hoe". Her eyes got wide and her lips flattened into a thin line. "NO, it is a saying farmer's use I was not calling you a Hoe"

"Well that is good to know."

They proceeded with the paperwork and examined the baby. The doctor estimated her age to be about 6 months old and she was in excellent health. Both the men pondered the question why would anyone leave a perfectly healthy baby with them. They each examined their past and the women they had been with to try and figure out which girl would do such a thing. Even though they had both been around the block a time or two the women they had been with never seemed to be the type to just up and leave a baby behind more especially get pregnant without wanting something in return. It was a mind-boggling experience for the 2 of them but neither would let on to the other that it had crossed their mind, because none of them wanted to admit the kid could be theirs.

When the doctor cleared the baby's health, Nurse Jessica had to break the news to them that the CPS (Child Protective Services) needed to discuss a few issues with the 2 of them. She introduced them to Shirley a retired nurse who now worked for the CPS. Shirley greeted the gentlemen and figured by the way they had been dressed that they were not her typical clients. Most of her clients in the past had been Drug attics, alcoholics, or family violence cases, all the things associated with a big city. She had never been involved in a case with a healthy baby left on a doorstep like Moses, just found in the river. She was at a loss. She did not know what to do so she just started to ask questions off the top of her head. The first question she knew the answer to: "who is the mother?"

Bratton and Cowboy looked at each other with a strange look and replied simultaneously "We're not sure"

Shirley asked, "Which of you is the father?"

Cowboy piped up without delay" We are not sure of that either"

Shirley then replied, "I tell you what why don't the 2 of you tell me what you know, and we will go from there."

Cowboy and Bratton began to tell the story about how the little girl had been left on their doorstep like some movie filmed back in the depression and then showed her and Nurse Jessica the note left with the girl. Shirley was at a loss. She asked Cowboy and Nurse Jessica to leave the room so she could talk with Bratton alone, if that is OK with Cowboy.

Cowboy said, "That is up to him!"

Bratton said, "I got nothing to hide from my dad."

Cowboy was proud and a little misty eyed when he said that but told him it would be fine. Nurse Jessica noticed the admiration in his and his son's eyes for one another. When she saw Cowboy's glossy eyes after Bratton's response, she knew that the 2 of them were very close and made her feel a little jealous for her own son who never really knew his dad much less bond with him.

After they had left and shut the door Shirley took a little time to get to know Bratton. Shirley smiled at him and asked, "Are you or could you be the father of the baby?"

Bratton" Am I? Could I be? Wow I have been pondering that question since I read the note. Am I the dad? I guess I could be. Do I think I am? Maybe that is the question. I don't feel like I am. I do not honestly feel like the girls I have been with wouldn't do something like this but I guess you really never know women do crazy things after having a baby that is how I ended up with my old man and no mother."

Shirley cleared her throat and lowered her glasses and came back with an" Excuse me Women do what?"

He said, "not to offend you or talk bad about women hell I love women."

"So, I gathered" She muttered sarcastically.

"No, I am not like that. I am not a womanizer or nothing I respect women it is just that my mom left me with my dad when I was 6 months old and left him a note about she just could not handle this and she knew I would be fine with him and his family."

Shirley was puzzled about the whole situation and was curious about the relationship with him and his dad, so she asked how he liked being raised by his father. Bratton looked at her and said "I wouldn't have it no other way. When dad and I got back to the farm Cross told me dad was scared to death, but my Oma and Papa helped him a lot, but for the most part he did everything just a little help from them."

"So, you live with your grandparents?" She asked

"Well we did up until they both passed away. Oma had a heart attack when I was 7 and Papa died 6 months later, we don't know why. He never had any problems and always checked out just fine with the doc. We just woke up that day and found him in his recliner not breathing."

"I am sorry to hear that"

"Don't be if you're gonna go that is the way, laid back in your chair, no suffering just don't wake up. They said he died of a broken heart and I believe it cuz he tried to get past Oma's death but just always moped around he never slept in their bed again after she died and he had complained about that mattress for years but she would not let him go buy another one when she was around. You would think after she died, he would have but he never did and would hear nothing of us doing it for him. Cross was almost as bad after papa passed; they had been friends since they were in grade school back in the depression. All of Cross's family had pasted away from small pox's or something and he was raised like a lot of the kids during that time by my great grandmother and granddad. I am sorry I got kind off track there. What else did you need to know?"

"Wow you seem to know a lot about your family except your mom's side. Do you know anything about her?"

Not really. Her and dad met at the finals in Vegas and she left me. We don't really discuss her much dad don't really like it."

"Well tell me how you are doing in school?"

"Oh, I am doing good we have a deal dad and I so long as I make an 80 or above, he don't mess with me. I aint got perfect attendance or nothing but I have only made 3 "b's "this year and I have a partial scholarship to TCU for football and academics."

"That is impressive. What do you do in your spare time?"

"Dad and I work on the ranch, rodeo, and we hunt a lot. We do almost everything together."

"Sounds like you and your dad are really close."

"Well we are more like best friends, I guess. Every once in a while, he will put his pants on and get on me but, we get along really good and Cross is always there to help out if he has to be outta town."

"Well Bratton if you are the father who would you think is the mother?"

"I have been going through my mind this whole time asking myself that question I guess if I was put on the spot and had to say someone, I would say Susan."

"What would make you think it was her?"

"Well? She and I had been friends for? Well since I can remember we did everything together but never really dated. Her dad got a job with an Oilfield company and was getting transferred out to Odessa. She came over to tell me and let me know that she always had a crush on me. I kind of had one on her but never wanted to tell her cuz our families were so close, and I did not want to lose my best friend cuz I am an idiot with women. We went down by the river that night and talked forever. I guess you can figure out the rest."

"Is that the only girl you have been with?"

"No ma'am it is just that she moved away about a year and a half ago, so she was my best candidate. If she is mine, I hope she is the mother, but she better has a damn good excuse for telling me this way."

15

"That is kind of sweet Bratton. Thank you for being honest with me."

"As he was leaving, she asked him to send his father in so she could speak with him."

After he left, she definitely realized this was not going to be the normal case. When Bratton was in the room with Shirley, Cowboy was in the waiting room by himself. Nurse Jessica had noticed he was very uncomfortable and decided to take an early lunch break to sit with him and try to make him a little more comfortable. They talked the entire hour Bratton was in the room with Shirley and never even realized that she was late clocking back in from her lunch. As Bratton exited the room, she realized the time and frantically returned to her duties at the hospital. Cowboy apologized for keeping her and she replied, "I enjoyed the conversation. It is hard to come by these days with a guy". Walking back to the clock she realized the guy she thought to be a player and a womanizer was really more of a front and she found herself thinking about him and the genuine conversation they had engaged in but brushed it off as a freak coincidence.

Bratton told his father in a joking manner "The principle wants to talk to you."

His dad said, "great what did you do this time?" It was their way of making light of stressful times to crack jokes and lighten the mood although most people saw it as them never taking anything serious, but it was the way they coped with their problems.

Cowboy entered the room with a little anxiety not knowing why he felt this way because he had done nothing wrong but somehow felt he had. Shirley asked him to sit down but he felt like a prisoner being interrogated and said he would feel more comfortable standing up if it was OK with her. She said that would be fine with her as she fed him the same questions as she did Bratton and to her amazement got almost the same exact answers as she had when interviewing Bratton, except for the questions regarding Bratton's mother. Cowboy did not elaborate much and seemed to be a little closed off when the query came about.

Shirley brought them back in the room and Nurse Jessica with them to let them know what all was going to happen. As they all sat down Shirley began to go through the protocol of the CPS regarding child custody of an abandoned child. She thanked both men for allowing her to interview them and being honest about the situation with the baby. She said the baby is healthy and since neither of you know if you are the father and no one can determine the mother of the child we will have to perform a paternity test on the two of you and the baby, that will tell us who the father is, and we can work from that point forward. They each gladly surrendered their arms to Nurse Jessica for the blood sample and then she took a sample from the baby. It was a little emotional for each of them seeing the baby in pain. Shirley was a little tickled at the fact that both men were fine having a needle stuck in their arms but seemed to be in pain when the baby was crying. When the blood work was sent to the lab, she released the 2 men to go home. Cowboy started to gather up the baby to place her in the car seat and Shirley stopped him. "The baby will have to stay here until the results are back from the lab" She told them with an authoritative voice.

Both men replied sternly "well we will wait."

By this time both had come to grips that whether the father was determined the little girl was their flesh and blood. Nurse Jessica softly replied to lighten the rapid building tension in the room "That will take about a week"

Each of the men began to bicker and complain how stupid it was and that they should have never brought her there. They tried to do the right thing and it backfired the system was messed up and against the innocent.

Shirley was getting vocal as well speaking loudly to drown both the men out and saying, "I don't make the rules if you don't like it take it up with a judge." and even threatening to call security.

Everyone was defensive in the room except Nurse Jessica who after few minutes regained some resemblance of order to the room. The 2 guys bowed up like roosters ready to spar and Shirley red faced and biting her lip. Jessica told them all to calm down. "I am sure there is a way we can all get along. Now everyone set down and let's be civil."

Everyone in the room obliged the nurse and sat down to hear what she had to say. The nurse asked Shirley what their options were. She said they don't have any. Cowboy chimed in that whoever the mother was knew that the baby would be safer their than in the "System" and whether or not the baby was his or Bratton's that she was theirs one way or the other and they would see to it that she was taken care of anyway they could.

Nurse Jessica hearing the sincerity and concern in their voices offered up a suggestion. "OK let Shirley and I talk for a second and see what we can work out."

Cowboy muttered, "Well someone had better figure it out cuz she is ours and she is going with us" as he left the room again.

They stood in the hallway with their backs to the door in complete silence each of them in a huff. They each tried to pretend they were not listening, but both had a keen ear to the jumbled conversation in the room on the other side of the wall. Nurse Jessica was to quite to hear but Shirley's voice carried through the walls as if she was in the hall with them. That was all they could make out

"Well yes a childcare professional would have to stay with them", followed by the pause of Jessica speaking "Are you crazy?" Another pause for a lengthy period while Jessica spoke "Yea it would work but you are crazy you don't know these two what are you going to do with your kids?" They endured another long pause of what seemed to be silence. After that the door was opened and Jessica asked both the men to come back in." I think we have a solution that we could run by you. You would be able to take the baby with you if you have a licensed childcare professional stay with the child at all times until the results are back from the lab."

"Well where the hel… I mean heck are we gonna find one of those on a weekend?"

Shirley cut him off and said, "if you will let her finish, she has a proposition for you."

Jessica continued "I would be willing to stay with you this weekend until you are able to find someone else. I am off this weekend and my kids are at their grandparents, so I have nothing to do. I could use a change of pace. I could stay at my cousins at night with Elgie and bring her over in the mornings you would just have to cover any expenses but that is all I would ask for."

Shirley loudly cleared her throat and said, "of course you could tip her or pay her for trouble."

"I would never ask that" Jessica said. "I understand your situation and you both seem to be good people aside from your rough exterior. Would that work for you? Shirley has already approved it."

"Yes, ma'am that would be great."

Cowboy had realized that this was the only way the baby would be able to come home with them and was getting the vibe from Shirley that this was the only way she was going home with them. So, he agreed to the deal.

After the paperwork was done and the baby was in the car seat, Cowboy told Jessica she could follow them. He needed to get fuel for his truck and would go ahead and top her car off so she would not have to worry about it. As they pulled away from the parking lot and she had time to think. She wandered what she was doing. This was crazy. I don't even know these people. Even with all the questions in her mind it just seemed like the right thing to do. The thoughts ran through her head and yet she could not talk herself out of the blind commitment she had made to these total strangers.

Chapter 4

WEEKEND STAYCATION

When they stopped for gas Bratton started to pump fuel in her car and then went to fuel up Cowboys. Cowboy made his way to her car and started some small talk. During their discussion the topic of the hotel came up and he would pay for her to stay there but, the local motel was not all that nice and if she wanted, she could stay at their house. We have a big enough house that you can have the whole upstairs to yourself. I will just need to clean it up but for tonight you can have my room and I can stay in the bunk house with Cross he has enough room and he could use some company. She said she would give it a try, as they passed the motel in town, she was glad. She figured he could not afford the hourly rate for all weekend and even though she loved Shelly, Jack was kind of creepy cousin.

They continued to drive through town and the road began to narrow from a 2 lane hi-way to a single lane road then to a dirt road and finally they pulled through the gate to the property. A sigh of relief they were there or so she thought. The winding drive was about 3 miles long and was not easy for a car to pass. Now she saw the purpose of the big truck they were driving. The lights of the homestead could finally be seen in the distance thru the foggy night air. It was dark and eerie like a scary movie. The lights grew bigger and separated into several lights as they neared the structures on the property. As the figures started taking shape, she could see a large 2 story house, a huge barn with an arena, and a nice sized guest house. When the picture became clearer to her she was almost awe struck by the natural beauty of the panoramic view, even at night. The huge Pecan trees accented by smaller mesquite trees, peach trees, a big porch and balcony that wrapped the entire house and shrubs that outlined each habitat. She was impressed with the place. It was nothing like she had envisioned Her first impression of the guys was old broken down cars lining the driveway with trees growing through the bumpers and dogs tied up on chains barking as you approach the front door but, it was almost completely opposite. This did ease her conscious a little. She opened the door on the car and popped the trunk to get her bags to find Bratton was already getting them for her. She told him "I can do that" but he said, "no I already have them you just get that lil' girl inside so she don't get cold."

Cowboy escorted her in the house. "I apologize I am sure you are used to a lot nicer place than this, but it is better than the whoretel in town he snickered."

"I saw that place I am glad I am not staying there."

"Well I just want to thank you for doing this" he said "I don't know nothing about her except she is my daughter or grand daughter and I could not live with her being in a foster home or stuck in a hospital if she did not have to."

"You two seem nice enough and I needed to get away and this is definitely away."

"The house ain't normally in this bad a shape but we had a heck of a night and left first thing this morning and this day has worn me out. Come on I'll show you the room you will be in tonight."

Cowboy showed her his room and asked her if it would work. She was astonished at the overall beauty of this house it was at least 100 years old and was a little cluttered but aside from that it was real nice and after a coat of paint and new furniture could be a dream home. Cowboy took her on the abbreviated tour of the house and retired with his bed roll to Cross's house. She readied herself for bed and then got the baby to sleep. She lay in the bed awake wondering what it would be like and what her kids would think of living in this place. Then she thought this is crazy I'm gonna be here for 2 days and I am already fantasizing about it. No doubt about it she had not seen much but she loved the place. She kicked her feet and squirmed about in the king size featherbed with the tall corner post and squealed like a little girl at a sleep over. Just then she heard a knock at the door and a voice call out.

"Miss Jessica, are you alright?" It was Bratton. "I was heading to get some water and heard you scream thought I would check on you."

She said "I am fine I just got in bed and the sheets were cold" trying to cover up the truth.

He told her he would start a fire to warm it up and she replied, "that would be nice". It made her feel even more secure than she already did. Which was weird considering she was in a strange house were 3 guys lived that she did not know and a baby no one even knew anything about.

She awoke the next morning to the crow of a rooster at dawn but, it was the shrill of a peacock that caused her to jump out of bed and scamper to check on the baby. *So, this is what it is like to wake up on a farm* she thought to herself. She made her way to the kitchen area where she had found a note from Bratton. There is hot coffee on the stove and some biscuits and bacon in the oven. It aint much we will go shoppin later if you will make us a list of what you need.

"Coffee on the stove? Do they not have a real coffee maker?" She poured a cup of the warm familiar liquid but today it smelled so much better than normal she almost did not drink it, it smelled so good. She was hungry after skipping dinner the night before to ease Cowboy's mind at the hospital, so she thought she would try the biscuits and bacon in the oven. She was not sure why it was, but everything smelled more pungent and fresher here. She must have really needed a break from here normal life to feel this good in the morning. She was worried about the days to come everything had gone without a flaw last night both the men were very nice and polite, but most men are when you first meet them.

She fed the baby and put her down for a nap. Then she made her way to the front porch and sat in an old wooden porch swing made for 2 that was hung from the ceiling by rusty old chains. To the side of the house she heard the sounds of a rusty old gate open and whistling "come on now hep hep yeyaw" She peeked around the red tipped shrubs by the porch to see the men bringing in some cows to feed. Just then she had thought "*how long have they been up before me? Do they think I am lazy for sleeping in?*" So, she scurried back inside to get dressed and check on the baby. After her shower she began to pick up some things lying around the house and tried to do something useful just by tidying up a little. She felt bad that they had been up for hours and were working while she just lay around. Not long after she picked up the living room Cowboy came in followed by Bratton and a tall skinny grey headed older man, she assumed to be this Cross fellow they had talked about. Cowboy greeted her with a "good morning"

She answered sheepishly "good morning" She felt very awkward her stomach was dancing. It felt as if she just woke up from a one-night stand and came out to see the whole family looking at her.

"Did you sleep good"

"Yes, quite well thank you"

"I see you found the coffee OK and the living room looks nice. You did not have to do that we were gonna get it but them cows get pissy if we are late feeding"

"Oh no it kept me busy and I felt bad sleeping in like that". As if she would not normally do that.

"Well it was kind of a crazy day for all of us and that is a long drive getting here if you're not accustomed to it" said Cowboy.

Bratton questioned if she had time to make a list of things, she would need but she had not. He asked her if she and the baby might want to go with him to town so he got the right stuff and Dad and Cross could clean out the upstairs while they were out. She said that would probably be the best and asked how long before they would leave.

"Whenever you are ready just holler and I'll go." Bratton always did the shopping Cross and Cowboy would not go to town during the daylight because everyone gossiped about them. Cowboy always said the paper went out of business when he quit going to town because they had nothing else to write about.

Bratton and Jessica head to town with the baby. When they got there Bratton ask her if it would be alright if he dropped her off at the store. So, he could go to the feed store and come back and get her. He told her to just charge whatever you need to our account. She was OK with that since the feed store was only a block or so down the road.

She was shopping in the small store for an hour or so getting diapers, formula and all the necessities for an infant. As she entered the checkout, she could see the truck in the front with Bratton talking to some friends.

The clerk an attractive 27 to 30-year-old woman asked if it was cash, check, or charge?

She replied, "O charge it to the Lee Ranch account."

The clerk Debbie said, "Whose account?"

"The Lee Ranch"

"So, I guess you are telling me you are staying out there? I knew this would happen sooner or later."

Jessica could tell really quick where this conversation was heading and knew better than to keep it going but she could not resist by the attitude the young lady had.

"Yes, I am staying out there"

"Well you must just really be something. Almost every woman in town has been trying to get out to that ranch for as long as I can remember."

"I guess you would be one of those women too since you live in this town and all"

She snarled and said "uh yea I guess"

"Well sorry for your luck" and went to the truck. As she made her way out the door, she heard a familiar voice speak out from behind her "So how long have you been out at Kim's place?" She rolled her eyes before putting on her best fake smile "Jack??? How are you? I was going to call you today."

"Really? Why?"

"I needed to ask you some legal advice for Kim"

"He doesn't need my advice"

"Jack don't be that way. This beautiful little girl was left on their door step and they don't want her to go to a foster home so I volunteered to help them out and I wanted to know what legal problems they might have so I can get back to town."

"So, some low life he was sleeping with left a baby on his doorstep? It proves that the women he runs around with don't know nothing about him. Probably a crack whore"

"Jack they did the right thing by bringing the baby to get it checked out and she is perfectly healthy so don't be like that and put whatever it is between you two aside and do this for that little girl."

"OK I will look into it for you and her, but I don't want you running around with that low life."

"There is nothing between us I promise. Thank You. Maybe you and Shelly can come over and eat lunch with us tomorrow or Sunday."

"We will see, in the meantime take care of yourself and call me if you need me to come get you."

Chapter 5

LOOKING OUT FROM
THE INSIDE

*A*s she entered the truck Bratton loaded the groceries while Jessica loaded the baby. Bratton climbed in the cab and smiled just short of laughing. "I am sure that went over well" he said with a chuckle. "I am sorry if I had known she was working I would have went with you."

Jessica said "That is OK she did not bother me. She is a gold digger, isn't she? I know her kind, so I just let her think what she wants" she said with a smile. "She was the least of my worries. Running into my cousin Jack was awkward."

Bratton said "oh boy school will be fun on Monday. I can hear that old printing press firing up at the Epigraph as we speak. Headlines will say "What have them Lee boys done this time"".

They laughed and joked about it all the way to the house about the media and the news cameras with helicopters buzzing overhead. It seemed like it was just minutes before they were back at the ranch.

While they were in town Cross and Cowboy had a chance to talk about the situation and work on a game plan. Cross could see something different in the way Cowboy was moving today and was not sure why. Was it the little girl or was it Jessica? Hell, it was probably just sleeping on the hard couch in the bunk house last night combined with all the drama of the last two nights. They worked on the dusty old upstairs and had one of the 3 bedrooms and the bathroom clean. Cross did not understand why they did not just stop there. So, he quizzed Cowboy on what he was doing. Cowboy just grumbled under his breath about this has needed to be done for years.

"She aint gonna want to stay in no pig sty." Cowboy said.

"Who LG or Jessica?" Cross smarted off without hesitation.

"Either one"

I have been around Cowboy since he was born and loved to get him riled up. I knew there was something he wasn't saying, and I also knew that I would never get it out of him, but I love to razz him when he gets this way. "I just don't understand why we can't just shut the doors on the other 2 rooms up here. She don't need but 1 room and 1 bath. No one else is gonna use it. Hell, I've lived here for damn near all my life you never cleaned it out for me. What makes her so special?"

"She is a girl. They are different"

"Which one you talking about Jessica or the little one"

"Can you just shut up and work? We got other stuff to do."

"Then let's just shut the doors and do them" I said as I laughed.

I could tell that Cowboy was interested in Jessica because he was avoiding the questions and never talked about her. Normally he would come home from meeting a woman and just go on and on and boast about the whole date and how all the women loved him but, not a word since she had been there.

By the time Bratton and Jessica had returned we had all the junk out and just needed to dust and clean up a bit. All of us went to the truck to bring in the supplies Cowboy told Bratton to go unload the feed and he and I would be there shortly after they cleaned the last 2 rooms up. Jessica without hesitation told them she would be happy to clean them up so they could get their chores finished. Cowboy assured her she did not have to do that, she had done enough already but, she insisted.

He thanked her numerous times and each of us grabbed our worn-out cowboy hats hung by the door and returned to our normal duties on the ranch.

She had noticed that the guys were all very polite and never wore their hats in the house. She thought at first they were just trying to impress her but after watching them it was a habit all the little things opening the doors, carrying the groceries in, and always letting her go in first made her feel special and now that she had realized it might not have been just an act, it made her feel like she was really special. She had never been around a man with manners before and was almost tearful to experience it. She smiled at Cowboy and put her hand on her chest almost like she was catching her breath and told him it was the least she could do since they had been so polite to her. Cowboy tipped his hat and smiled. The baby began to cry and they both had paused for a second. No one existed but the 2 of them, at that moment in time the world stopped turning. It was a moment neither would soon forget. The baby whined once again. She regretfully said, "I better check on her" and Cowboy replied, "yea I gotta get this stuff done we are running out of daylight."

Bratton and I witnessed the whole thing. I whispered to the young hand "looks like He is in trouble with this one."

Bratton snickered lightly "yea I think your right I never seen him act this way before. She seems to be nice but, we will see"

Cowboy hollered out "quit standing around yapping your jaws and let's get to work" almost like he was aggravated to have to leave the house. That was real weird because all they ever did in the house was eat, shower, and sleep. Cowboy was embarrassed that we had seen the encounter and knew we were going to give him hell over the way he had been acting.

We were hard at it, working the rest of the morning and had not even stopped to get a drink. Around 12 o'clock Jessica thought she would be nice and fix us all a light lunch. She made up some sandwiches but, we were too busy working to realize the time. She waited a little to see if we would come up, but we never did so she put the baby down for a knap and meandered out around the barn and slowly made her way toward the noises of men working. She could hear all of them raising their voices cursing at one another and yelling at the cattle in the pin. None of us knew she had been watching and did not even realize she was standing by the barn until she began to laugh at Bratton slipping in a pile of cow manure and busting his butt. I yelled at him "you dumb Son of a >>>> you can't even stand up on your own much less get these damn cattle in the pin". Cowboy chimed in with a few words of his own and Bratton barked right back. When we heard her laugh, we all got quiet, and Cowboy apologized for our language. She said "oh it was cute. I hear that stuff all the time."

"Well you shouldn't hear it around here. We are just under the gun to get this place cleaned up by the end of the month. So, we are a little stressed out right now."

"Well I just wanted you to know I made some lunch for ya'll if you want." She told us.

Bratton started to say "we don't"

Cowboy cut him off and said "well thank you we'll get washed up and be right in."

Me and Bratton looked at one another in disbelief. Cowboy had always followed in his dad's footsteps. He would always say "we ain't got time for lunch. You only eat when the sun ain't up"

Cowboy gave each of us the evil eye as if to tell us, we had better keep their mouths' shut and eat. "Then he told us let's get these in the pin and we will come back and finish moving the rest of them."

It was not long before we finished, washing up in the barn and dusted our pants off. When we were heading inside Bratton looked at me and said, "he is definitely in trouble."

Cowboy without turning around or missing a step barked out "I heard that and I'm not in nothing. I'm just trying to be polite"

When we entered the house, it looked different I said, "did you rearrange the furniture or something?"

"No" she said "why?"

"It looks different" I replied

"I just washed the curtains and dusted the furniture and swept the floor."

"Well it sure looks different cleaned up. You done a good job. Hey Cowboy, she is a keeper" and snickered a little. Bratton almost fell over when I made the remark. Jessica asked what was so funny. Bratton Said it was nothing just something I had done. As we enter the kitchen I said "ya'll still have this table?" with a cheesy grin and said "I ain't seen flowers on this table since Maw passed. It is kind of nice."

"I guess Maw must have been a good lady" Jessica said, "I think the flowers make everyone feel better." Each of us got silent when she said that. "Did I say something wrong? I am so sorry I should be quite."

Cowboy answered with a deep voice "No you didn't do anything wrong. That is just exactly what she always said to my dad about the flowers. He always complained about her flower gardens, but he always made sure they got watered and she always had plenty to pick."

"Your dad sounds like a sweet man"

"He would roll over in his grave if he heard you say that, but he was always good to her like that. And she never wanted for anything."

"I remember one time she wanted this new cook ware that had come out. It was pretty and she had seen it advertised on TV and she really liked it. She made mention of it one time about liking it in front of him and he said our stuff works just fine. The very next day we went to get feed and he run off to the department store and got it. He wrapped it up so we would not know. We got home and he gave it to her. He told us he was tired of hearing about it, but we knew that he was just an old softy. You remember that Cowboy? We give him the dickens over that but that is how he was."

Cowboy said "he was always a sucker for kids and women"

"Just like someone else I know" I shot a wink to Jessica.

"That is enough talk boys we need to eat so we can get back at it before it gets dark"

"I'll leave you boys alone and let you eat. Kim is there anything else you need me to do around here? The baby is sleeping, and I don't mind helping out."

When me and Bratton heard "Kim" we both swallowed hard and looked surprised at one another.

"No Jessy you have done enough." He said Jessy because at the Hospital she had gotten kind of defensive about it and he wanted to make a point. "I guess if you see something that needs doing you can do it. There aint nothing you can tear up around this old place that is worth anything and we aint got nothing to hide so just make yourself at home."

The boys had finished eating and went back to their chores outside.

Jessica had made a cup of coffee and went to sit on the porch swing while sitting there she could hear the guys working but could not see through the red tipped shrubs that surrounded the porch. So, she quietly asked Bratton, as he walked by, where some clippers were. Bratton told her not to worry about that stuff they would get it. So, she went to the barn to look herself. While she was in the barn and milling around looking for some yard tools, she came across a saddle that Cowboy had won back 18 years ago from the Nationals in Las Vegas It was beautiful and looked like it had never been used. She cleared some of the dust away with her shirt sleeve pulled over her hand as if she was trying not to leave any fingerprints. The Saddle said All Around Cowboy World Champion 1990. As she was taken back by the beauty and the writing on the saddle, I must have come in and startled her.

She nervously said, "I am looking for hedge clippers."

"They're over there on the wall.... You know he won that the last year he rode. The next day she left, and he came home and never really competed again."

Jessica did not want to pry to much so she just said" Well by the looks of it he must have been pretty good"

"YEA he was, He was the best and was still getting better"

"Wow that is impressive." She said still unsure of Cross' quite mystique "well I guess I better get back to the house Thanks for your help"

"You're welcome"

She went back to the porch and began to work on trimming the hedges. She had them cleared on one side before Cowboy had seen what she was doing. He stopped to watch her work. He could tell that she was not accustomed to manual labor by the clumsy and awkward way she handles the clippers, but he could also tell she was enjoying it by the big smile on her face. While he was watching her finish up the one side, she stopped to wipe the sweat from her brow. He saw her gloves on her hands were 3 sizes too big and she was getting tired but looked like the work was rewarding. She had a sense of accomplishment about her. She sat on the steps worn out and she looked over at Cowboy and smiled a girlish smile. Then she poked her bottom lip out like she was pouting and blew a puff of air out to clear her hair from her face and stood up trotted up the steps and leaned over the handrail, smiling at Cowboy again and said" now don't you think that this better? You can see everything isn't it beautiful?

Cowboy said "it sure is" but he was not talking about just the porch. The site of her up their covered in dirt with a glowing smile softened his hardening heart just a little that day.

Not long after that I came by and said you want to go for a ride and see the rest of the property?

She told me that would be nice and wanted to know how long they would be gone. I told her about an hour. She wandered how this was going to turn out since I never really said much and when I did talk it was always just a deep quite grumble and she only understood bits and pieces of the conversation. She agreed because she had only really gotten to see the house and barns so far.

I told her we could leave whenever she wanted to. Of course, being a woman, she had to clean up a little first. She went to the restroom to wash her face off and freshen up and came back outside to see a 4-wheeler waiting on her and another one with me on it. She said I don't know how to ride that thing. Don't you have a truck or something we can take?

"Well I guess we could saddle up some horses; I did not picture you as much of a horse person. You can always ride on back if you want to however, a truck won't make it through some of the trails and you will want to see the whole picture." She climbed on back with me and as we passed by Cowboy and Bratton. Cowboy hollered out "Cross try not to flip it this time. Take it slow" as he and Bratton were laughing hysterically. Her heart began to race, she swallowed hard and latched on to me.

"They are just jealous that you are going with me I aint never really flipped one with just me on it at least" as I chuckled and pulled away. She was scared as I sped down the drive laughing and asked her "you alright back there?" She nodded in acknowledgement. Then I said let me know if you get scared. "I'll slow down if you want."

"That would be great. My eyes are tearing up from the wind *and it* is going to make my mascara run." She sniffled as she wiped her eyes. We stopped and opened a gate that led into the front pasture. As I opened the gate, I told her "during the winter we keep the livestock up here. The winter rye comes in good and we can keep an eye on them, so the cats and coyotes don't get them."

"Cats what kind of cats?"

"Mountain lions and bobcats."

"There aren't any mountains around here"

"I know that, but you might wanna tell them that because they are here."

She began to reconsider her decision to go on this tour after hearing about the predators in the area. We went thru the pasture and into a tree line that ran across the back of it. The trail was rough, and he was right the truck would not make it through there. After about a half mile back in the woods to a stream of water and then turned to go up stream. I took her to the fishing pond where we always took the kids to entertain them. It was a spring fed pond and was surrounded by trees about 50 yards away from the water. The willow trees shaded everything around the pond. We even have a pick nick area set up off one side and a homemade dock out to the middle with a small john boat. "Wow this is nice how do you keep it mowed like this?"

"We trained the cows to eat grass" I replied in jest "We can come back here if you want but I wanted to show you the rest of it before dark." We swerved our way through the trees and across numerous pastures each of them had cattle and horses on them and were green like the yards in a ritzy neighborhood back home. He took her to an area fenced off under a large pecan tree. As they neared, she realized it was a graveyard. It was unusual because it seemed peaceful there; it was not depressing at all. Jessy never cared for grave sites or anything like that, they made her nervous but this one was beautiful. None of the graves were new and the grass was well kept with flowers growing on some and beautiful painted head stones. I explained to her that my wife and both Kim's parents along with his little sister had been buried there. She was speechless but managed to say, "this is really nice."

I hopped back on the quad and said, "come on to the finally and it is the perfect time we have to hurry." She jumped on the back and I hollered "hold on" and hit the gas she grabbed me tight around the waist and held on for her life through the winding trails and the rough terrain. Then we went up a really big hill "Hold on tight now. I don't want to lose ya" I hollered over the noise from the 4 wheelers engine.

She cinched up tight as we climbed the hill. The 4-wheeler was rocking side to side and the wheels were spinning. Her heart was racing, and her adrenaline was pumping through her veins, she was elated and scared at the same time. She really thought they were going to flip over at one point and then they topped the hill. I let off the gas and coasted to a stop. When I killed the engine, she heard nothing complete silence it was crazy and hard for her to wrap her mind around it. She had been at home without the kids by herself and thought it was peace and quiet until now. This was the real deal. No sirens, no horns honking, no traffic just quiet. She could feel a gentle breeze blowing in her face and heard a limb creek on the hillside. I dismounted the vehicle and stood still not saying a word so she could absorb the moment.

She cracked the silence with 2 little words "OH My" she said in a meek whisper.

"I know it is almost a religious experience being here at sundown." In a deep whisper

We sat there on a log looking at the view of the ranch. You could see the house and barn in the distance. The sun setting on the horizon right behind the windmill. It was the most picturesque sight she had ever seen. The sun rays bounced off the meadows and fields and reflected a rainbow of colors. The trees gently swayed in the breeze and the birds all began to make their way back to the nest. While all the varmints scurried the ground for a place to sleep.

She looked to me and said, "Do you realize how lucky you are to be able to see something so beautiful?"

I looked at her and said "Well I think I am just lucky in general. I have been here almost all my life on this place. Since high school I reckon."

"Wow that long" she asked? "Are you and Kim related?"

"No, me and his dad went to school together. He was 2 years older than me and my parents owned the property right there where the sun is setting. When we was in school, he would come by and pick me up take and bring me home. We would always find stuff to do to make extra money on the side, but we always helped each other out when it was hay season or in the winter with the cattle. I guess we just got along. He always gives me a hard time until Kim come along. He and momma where like big brother and sister to me and I guess I am like Bratton's grandpa but don't tell him I said that. The 2 boys are all I got anymore but I would not trade them for the world even though they are a pain in my backside a lot of times."

"If you don't mind me asking what happened to your place?"

"After I graduated from high school me and my dad had a little argument and well, I run off to live in the big city. Not long after that he had a stroke and when I found out and came back to tend to the place and be with him to help. The doctor bills and the taxes just got too much so after dad passed away, I had to sell off the place to get caught up on the bills. We kept the house for a bit and I got married but mom only lasted a little over a year without dad around she died of a broken heart is what I say but doctor said she had a heart attack in her sleep."

"How sad. I am so sorry!!"

"No don't be. It was tough then when it happened, but I know she did not suffer a day in her life, never had a health problem one until that day. I know she was happier being up there with him and it is where she was supposed to be."

"You are too sweet. So why don't you live in the house?"

"Well I started working on this place after I sold everything off and it was all going good until my wife come down with the cancer and pasted away so I had to sell it to settle up the bills again and I was pretty tore up. I had nowhere to go and Kim's mom and dad where the only family I had so his dad asked me to come out here and live and help him out no rent or nothing. Those 2 are angels in my book they helped me through some rough times. Kim is the same way he don't like to see no one suffer. When he was on the rodeo circuit after he would win, he would always see some broke down cowboy and give him a little something to help him get on his feet. I think that had a little to do with him not staying with Bratton's mom."

"Who is his mom?"

"I ain't never met the woman. Momma and pop met her at a rodeo once when she was pregnant and Kim had plans on bringing her to the farm but she was too much of a city girl I reckon and from what I am told just up and left him when Bratton was about 3 months old. So, Cowboy just retired a little early and came back to raise the boy."

"So, he quit because of Bratton? WOW that must have been a tough decision for him if he was really good."

"I don't think he even had to think about it to be honest with you. He was more than good in the rodeo but that boy came first and he could not raise him by himself on the road so he did what he knew was best for the boy and the next day they were here with everything they owned."

"Kim sure is much different than what I imagined him to be when I first saw him walk in the door at the bar. I figured he was a real player and I guess kind of an obnoxious, conceded, nice looking sweet talker."

"Well he is all those things but not really in a bad way. He has been known to be a ladies' man, but he has calmed down quite a bit in the past few years. That life gets old after some time and you want to find someone to come home to eventually."

"Does he have anyone special? I mean is he seeing anyone?" As she blushes and smile

"Not that I know of. There has not been a female on this property since Susan moved off to Odessa."

"Is Susan Bratton's mom?"

"No, she was Bratton's best friend. They are the ones that bought the house from me. Them 2 was raised together. I guess these 2 houses are meant to be together somehow. But them 2 was like the 3 stooges you never saw one without the other. Her dad worked in the oilfield and got transferred out a little over a year ago and they aint seen each other since."

"So, his high school sweetheart moved off?"

"No, I don't think it was like that (she figured she did not meet up to the physical standards of Bratton's reputation) I am not sure, but they never dated. Who knows how that works with kids these days? I know he aint had a steady girl since and you are the first woman on this ranch since that day. It took me back when I seen you get out of the car."

"That is the 2nd time I heard that about me being out here what is the big deal with me being here?"

"There have been more women than I can count trying to get on this property. Some for the money, some so they don't gotta work and some just to say they are hooked up with one of them 2 knuckle heads but none for the right reasons they all want something."

"Well I had no idea they were celebrities or something?"

It made me Chuckled lightly and said "I reckon they are around these parts. They rodeo, hunt, fish and do what they want. What guy would not want to be them and what woman would not want to be with them and live on this property?"

"I guess I see what you mean it is pretty impressive and all of you are very handsome, polite and chivalrous men. I thought it just might be for show at first but when I went to town with Bratton and saw him acting the same way with everyone else I knew it was not an act but I also liked thinking I was being treated special. That is real silly I guess"

"No, you are special. You are the only woman on the ranch aside from Susan in 15 years. See you are special."

"Well thank you for making me feel better"

"Well I hate to but we better get on back down this hill before it gets to dark and I can't see." we both mounted the SUV and I fired it up and turned around to face down the hillside we had climbed earlier and it looked much worse from the top side than from the bottom and now she was definitely scared. She grabbed me so tight I thought she was giving him the Heimlich maneuver. I let out a cough and a sigh as she apologized and closed her eyes. Then I revved the engine and asked, "are you ready?" I felt her nod and heard her whimper a little. Then I turned the SUV to the right and began down another trail nowhere near as bad as the hill we climbed and when she realized that we were not bouncing and being tossed around she opened her eyes and saw a road big enough for a truck like the driveway she came in to the property on. She swatted me on the shoulder and giggled out loud "you are an ASS" I just laughed and continued down the road.

We made to the house by the light of the moon and went inside. Cowboy was making dinner and Bratton was playing with the little girl. Cowboy told us "I am glad you made it back we were gonna eat without you."

She looked in the kitchen to see him cooking and thought to herself "O my God I wander what he is making." She figured they would eat some kind of trail food like beans or chili. So, she told him "I will cook" trying to keep from having to eat what she envisioned to be heart burn in a pot.

"No, you just set back and relax I got this". He could tell by the distress in her voice she did not know what was in store for dinner and so he started clanking pans and slamming doors on the cabinets mumbling to himself. He would holler ever so often things like "where is that hog lard? Do we get any jalapenos? And is this pot in the sink dirty or did we just use it this morning?"

She was getting concerned and we realized what he was doing so we would just nonchalantly reply to his question and keep doing whatever we were doing. She was very concerned so she said, "I think I will give the baby a bath."

Cowboy said, "well dinner is ready can't that wait?"

"Well I am really not hungry after that big lunch."

"Non-sense you set down and eat. I made dinner for ya'll someone is gonna eat it."

As they made their way to the table Bratton looked at me and said "I hate when he gets in the kitchen and does this. I sure hope he did not make that Mexican surprise crap again."

"Oh God me too" and looked at Jessica and told her he thinks he knows how to cook but he don't and he gets mad if you don't eat.

They all eased into their seats slowly staring at one another in dismay. Cowboy brought out a bowl of what looked like chili out of the can that had not been heated up with a slice of cheese and walked toward Jessica. Her eyes got as big as the bottom of a coke bottle and Bratton muttered yep that is it as he turned away like he was getting ill. She began to fidget in her seat and was trying to think of something to do to get out of this but couldn't come up with anything. She looked at Cowboy and said "well thank you for cooking me dinner. It looks real good" with uncertainty in her voice. "What is it called" she asked?

"Well I call it dog food. This is Red's dinner but, if you like I can make him more and you can have this we are eating hamburger steak smothered in mushrooms, onions and brown gravy" He said with a smirk trying not to laugh.

I started to laugh out loud and Bratton almost fell out of his chair laughing. Cowboy could not hold back the laughter anymore and started laughing with us.

She looked at them and smiled taking a swing at Cowboy with her napkin and saying "you 3 are awful" as she laughed with them.

After delivering Reds food Cowboy made his way back to the kitchen to feed everyone else. We enjoyed the conversation and the food. Much to her surprise the food was excellent. She had never known a straight man that could cook.

After dinner was over Jessica began to clear the table and Cowboy stopped her "You are not here to be a maid for us I appreciate the help and all you are doing but we can clean up. Why don't you get that little girl in the bath and get her to bed?"

She knew by the way he had said it that he was being nice but meant what he had said. She already had a good feel for when he was joking and when he was serious. So, she conceded and took care of the baby. She figured that Bratton or I would clean up or at least help but, as she was bathing the baby she overheard him tell us to go on you 2 have done enough for the day just go sit down and relax and then throw a sarcastic shot at me "I know you are probably wore out old man after that exhausting tour you took her on."

Cowboy cleaned the kitchen and she heard the screen door slam behind him. She finished rocking the baby to sleep and put her to bed and left the door open so she could hear her if she woke up. She made her way back into the living room and no one was there so she peeked into the kitchen and could not see anyone there but she could hear the rusty chains on the porch swing squeaking and she walked to the porch to see who was out there. Cowboy sat on the swing alone drinking a beer and smoking on a cigar. She said "I guess you got the kitchen taken care of and I got her to sleep for now. I think she is getting used to be out here. She seems to like Bratton pretty good and I have already seen you spoiling her to" she said with a grin as she made her way to the handrail beside the swing on the porch to sit down. She made a little hop to get on the rail

Cowboy slid to the side of the swing and said "you can sit here if you want. I won't bite right now I just ate."

She accepted his offer because that is what she wanted to do anyway. She still felt like a little schoolgirl with her boyfriend around him and was somewhat embarrassed by the crazy emotions she was feeling when he was near her. After sitting down, she asked where the other 2 had gone

"The old one was heading to bed he had a rough day."

"I heard that when I was giving the baby a bath" as she gazed toward him and with a stern but jokingly look.

"And Bratton is well going somewhere I am not real sure where."

"Well they are both good guys I guess you don't have to worry too much about them getting into trouble. Bratton is one of most well-mannered teenage boys I have met. It says a lot about the person who raised him."

Cowboy cut in and said "Cross sure has helped me a lot with that boy but he is a good kid I don't worry about him getting in too much trouble nothing serious anyway. He did get caught painting the water tower with a friend of his Susan who claims to be my adopted daughter. If that is the worst thing, he does then we done pretty good in my book."

"Cross told me about Susan. She must have been a real sweet girl. What was she like?

"She is a beautiful girl. I always thought they would end up dating or getting married something like that, but they moved off and she would call from time to time but we aint heard from her in 9 month or so. Ever so often Brat will ask if she has called and I guess he could call her, but he don't."

She was taken back to hear she was pretty, the gears in her brain engaged. The timeline and the baby she quit calling she knew now that the little girl was Bratton's

Cowboy asked her "what else did Cross tell you?" As he took a puff on the cigar.

Jessica coughed lightly to express her displeasure for the cigar and said, "Oh he told me a lot of things."

Cowboy snuffed his cigar out and said, "I am sure he did for a quite old man he sure lets a lot of stuff get out." He stood up and started to walk off. She thought she had upset him when he turned to her and asked if she would like a drink?

"No thank you."

"I could put some coffee on if you want."

"That sounds nice."

He moseyed his way to the kitchen and was making coffee as he was speaking loudly to stay engaged in the conversation. "So, what else did ole gabby and you talk about?"

"Oh, nothing really, we mostly just sat and watched the sun go down. He told me about his ranch and what had happened with it and that was pretty much all."

"He is worse than them ladies in the beauty shop downtown I tell you."

"I like him. He isn't as tough as he acts is, he?"

"Cross?? No, he is a big softy for women and children, but don't tolerate anyone being disrespectful to him."

Kim walked out of the house with 2 cups of coffee and sat down on the swing beside her. He handed her one of the cups and said "I guess I should have asked if you wanted cream or sugar. Well do you?"

"No, I drink it black I don't usually have time to doctor it up. I am always in a hurry to work or pick up the kids, cook breakfast. It has been real nice being out here. It is so peaceful and relaxing."

"Well you have not relaxed much since you got here waiting on us boys' hand and foot, cleaning up the house and the shrubs. After you leave, I'm gonna have hell breaking the boys back in, you got them so spoiled" As he looked at her with a grin. "I think they like having you around here and the little girl too."

"Well what about you?"

"Oh, I am a sucker for babies too she is a sweetheart and won't stand a chance finding a man in the real world with the 3 of us spoiling her all the time."

She said, "Oh so you like the baby" as she raised her eyebrows and nodded her head "I see HUM !!"

"No now don't go taking it out of context I kind of like having a woman around that I aint got to baby sit or hold her hand all the time. I am just not that kind of person. I really appreciate what all you have done this weekend. I bet you will be glad to be back home."

"Well I do miss my kids, but I am glad for the break. As far as getting back home I like it out here it is quiet."

"Well you don't have to be a stranger. You can come back anytime you like"

She was a little bit flabbergasted by his offer but took as him just being polite. Until he finished what he was saying

"You ought to bring them kids out so they can run a little and stretch their legs. We might even get them up on that old gray mare over there for a ride if she don't kill over before you come back with them. How older are your kids anyway?"

"Well Dylan is 11 and Cassie is 7. They are a handful." This was the first time that any of them had asked about anything personal, so she did not want to talk his ear off about them.

"Well what do they like? Do they play sports? What do they do for fun?"

"Dylan plays baseball and he is OK I guess I try to help him but I don't know anything about that stuff and Cass well she is a girl and by that I mean a girly girl she likes to dress up and is always wanting a new pair of shoes every time we go to the store. I guess she gets that from me."

"There aint nothing wrong with that" they both smiled at one another and took a sip of coffee as they let their cups down their elbows collided and the hot liquid spilled on Kim's knee they both giggled and went to wipe it off at the same time. Then they butted heads as they leaned over and as they drew their bodies back up, she was a little faster than him and elbowed him in the eye. Both of them were laughing like a couple of teenagers. She reached up and rubbed his eye still snickering from the whole situation and said "I am so sorry" with a smile on her face "are you OK"

He turned to her, their faces not much more than 3 inches apart their noses were almost touching, the mood became real somber as their eyes met for the first time and he said in a soft voice "it is OK, I am fine." Each of them leaning a little more toward the other and slightly tilting their heads just before their lips touched the baby cried, they simultaneously jumped up and both started saying "I got go huh"

She said "me too I think I need to check on her"

"Yea I got to get the horses put up. I'll be back in a bit"

Each of them out of breath from the anticipation of the kiss scurried away to calm their heart beats and gather their thoughts.

They both went their own way and when he returned to the house, she was washing the coffee pot and cups along with sterilizing the bottles.

He said "you don't gotta wash that"

"Oh, it is fine I was in here anyways"

"No, I mean it is a coffee pot it sterilizes itself"

"Yuck" she said.

"Come on that is boiling hot water everyday"

"That is nasty" she said.

"I am just funnin' with you"

Every time he said that she would just melt on the inside. There was something about that slow southern draw and the way he did not pronounce the g on the end that just made her brain swirl and heart stop working for a split second and caused her to gaze in his direction with those big brown eyes. When she did that he was defenseless to anything she said or did, that look in her eyes was the kryptonite to his macho man, I don't need a woman attitude and neither of them even had a clue what the other was thinking or doing during this time. She could have been dancing on a pole naked for that split second and he would have never seen it. There was something electric between the 2 of them but neither would admit it and, it was obvious to me and Bratton just not to the 2 of them. From that moment on they would never forget the color of each other's eyes.

She looked at him and said "I really enjoyed talking with you on the swing"

And he told her "yes ma'am that was nice to just sit and talk we should do that again sometime."

"I would like that"

As she passed between him and the stove he was backed up to the table and their bodies brushed one another. He reached for her shoulder to help steady himself and she said "excuse me I did not mean to knock you over" and kept walking with her head turned towards him and their eyes locked on one another she took a few steps and reached out with her left hand and felt for the wall, that she knew was there but could not see because she was looking at him, to keep from running into it. Neither of them blinked for what seemed an eternity. She felt the wall and slid around it shyly as she cleared the corner her back to the other side of the wall their eyes broke contact and she could no longer see him she slid down the wall almost going to her knees. She could hear him set down and heard him "wew "with a sigh he could still hear her movement on the other side of the wall. They could almost hear one another's heartbeat. It was a spiritual experience but, with a pure feeling more than a sexual one. They were just shy of embracing and ravaging one another but somehow, they dodged another close encounter.

Each of them retired to their rooms and lay awake for some time convincing themselves that they were incompatible on so many levels. She was making a pro's and con's sheet:

Pro's	Con's
He is good looking	I am really not his type I am older
He has his own place	other girlfriends
HE CAN SUPPORT HIS SELF	lives to far away
He is a gentleman	he is not ready to settle down
He is good looking	He is set in his ways
He is good looking	I have kids to think about
He is good looking	He likes the night life
He is good looking	

43

Her list continued like this for some time not really wanting to admit to herself that they really were not compatible and trying to outweigh the con's with pro's she just kept repeating the same thing. She finally got frustrated and gave up she crumbled the paper up and threw it at the trash can by the dresser and turned over to try and sleep.

Meanwhile downstairs he was muttering to himself. She is independent and don't want no man like me. She lives in the city. She would not make it a week out here. She sure is pretty. She aint no bimbo. She probably won't like to camp or hunt or fish. But man, she is pretty and smart and would be a good woman for someone to settle down with. This went on until he finally just fell asleep.

The baby woke up early in the morning just before 5. She got out of bed and put her robe on over her PJ's, went to make a bottle and put on some coffee. When she entered the kitchen, Bratton was there standing at the sink drinking water.

"I did not expect anyone to be up this early" she said.

"I am not up early I am getting in Late" he said with a smile

"Oh well I guess you had a long night then"

"Yea and a long day ahead of me. Is dad up yet" he asked

Kim rounded the corner and with a stern voice said, "yea I have been up almost all night. Where have you been?"

"Where have I been? I was at the rodeo waiting on my partner who never showed up. So, I had to rope with old man whiskers cuz his grandson did not show either."

"Well sorry bout that I was too tired and decided not to go. How did ya'll do?"

"Well we got third. I guess it was OK someone else won the team roping for a change"

"Yea we want to make sure we have competition next year that is why I did not go" as he turned to her and smiled and said, "how did you sleep?"

"I slept good. How do you feel?"

The whole time they were talking Bratton was just standing there he had it in his mind that they had slept together and said, "well I guess I better leave you 2 alone."

Kim looked at him and said, "what time was the rodeo over with?"

"I guess it was over around midnight by time we got everything loaded collected the check it was almost 2 and we went to Whataburger for taquitos. You know how it works. The same thing we always do"

"Next time you need to call so I'm not worried about you."

"Yes father" he replied sarcastically

Then Kim turned back to her and said, "I really enjoyed last night that was the first time I have done that in a while" and gave her a wink

She caught on to his idea and said "Oh I really liked it I am wore out though. Maybe next time it will last a little longer"

Bratton's jaw dropped and he stood there astonished by what he was hearing. It was funny when he was assuming that they had slept together but just like any other kid he did not want to hear about his dad's rodeo in the bedroom.

Kim looked her in the eyes and told her he would try to work on that for her and the next time it would be better. "Maybe I can read up on some topics on the internet, so you won't get bored so quick next time."

When Kim made that comment Bratton just looked disgusted and hurried out of the room. After they heard his door slam, they both started to laugh.

Jessica told Kim he was mean, and he looked at her and said you did not have a problem going along with it and aging it on, so you are just as mischievous as me. It was just one more thing to add to the list of why they should get together.

Chapter 6

LONG LEGS AND SMALL CARS

Jessica went to tend to the baby and Kim whipped up some biscuits and gravy for breakfast. They sat at the table and talked for some time. They really enjoyed talking to one another and shared common interest in things like politics and religion. They would bicker back and forth over a few of the minor issues but for the most part they solved the troubles of the world sitting at the table. I came in about 5:45 and sat down to eat and have coffee. Jessica tried to bring me in to the conversation but never got more than "yeah" and "huh" out of me.

Kim told her the old man aint much on talk this early in the morning.

"Especially after you two were on the porch yapping and laughing all night." As I took a sip out of his coffee shot Kim a look of approval over the rim of his coffee cup.

Jessica got up from the table and rinsed her dishes off. She made it clear that none of them were to do the dishes today that she would handle cleaning the kitchen before she left. It was at that point that Kim realized she was going home today, and he felt a little remorse that she would not be there to talk with him anymore. He had enjoyed her company so much that he did not realize the weekend was over. So, he had to think of something fast to get her to stay. So, he said to her "You can't go yet we don't have the results of the test.

Jessica said I know. I will call and see if they have gotten them in yet if not, maybe we can work something out.

Well I guess that will have to do.

She wandered out the kitchen and Kim kind of hung his head low as he drank his coffee. I looked at him and said, "What is wrong with your boss?"

Kim said "Well that means the baby will have to go to foster care that is what I am worried about. I wanna know if she is ours or not."

"You sure that is all?"

"What else would it be" he said as if he was getting aggravated

"I don't know you tell me."

"That is, it. Don't go making nothing out of it" and stormed out of the house.

The guys went about their daily duties and around lunch time she came out to the barn to talk with them. She explained to Kim and Bratton that there was a problem with the results, but they did get them back. The CPS agent wanted to talk with them again and wanted them to come back in today if possible. Kim and Bratton agreed to follow her back into town to meet with the CPS. Jessica went back into the house to gather all her things and to get the baby ready. She returned outside and loaded the car with her things and strapped the baby in the back seat. She shut the back door and in one continuous motion spun around and lay back against the car and sighed. Talking to herself she muttered boy it is hard to leave a place this beautiful as she took in all the natural beauty of the property for one last time. After a few minutes of just enjoying the afternoon air she rounded up Kim and Bratton to head to the big city. Bratton hopped in the truck and pulled it around to unhook the stock trailer from it and hollered "out you go ahead we will be right behind you."

Jessica was not real sure how to get back to town much less how to get to Ft Worth from here so she kind of giggled and said "That is fine but I am really not sure where I am out here, can you tell me an easy way to get to town".

Kim said to Bratton "I guess I could ride with her and we will meet you there"

Bratton told him that would be fine with him he wanted to shower up anyway before going in case they happened on to a few HOTTIEs.

Kim meandered over to the car and said" I'll just ride with you, so you don't get lost. That way I don't have to drive or ride with the crazy teenager." Kim fold his long thin body into the car and looked much like an accordion in its case. He moved the seat all the way back, but the car seat was in the way, so it really did no good at all. Jessica was trying to help him and leaned over in his lap trying to get the latch between his legs to release she was jerking on it with all her might and her head was bobbing up and down Kim was laying his head all the way back in the seat and just happened to look to the side of the car and see Bratton and me standing there with the most mischievous smiles on our faces It took no time at all for Kim to figure out what was going through our perverted minds and he quickly put a halt to her actions by grabbing her head and pulling her back up telling her he was fine but it was too late when Bratton saw him put his hand on her head and lean forward in the seat and we started laughing . When she heard us and then saw us laughing, she said "what are they laughing about."

Kim said, "me being in your car" and by this time he was trying not to laugh because he realized how it must have looked to the others. And then it dawned on her what it was, and she slapped him on the shoulder and said "ya'll are awful" her face was bright red from the embarrassment.

Kim looked at her smiling and all but holding his breath and said, "they started it and you have to admit it probably looked really bad." She said, "I am sure it did ya'll are sick" and then laughed with them. Kim liked that about her a lot she could take a joke and not get upset she could laugh at herself and with them. She never got offended by things like that she just found the humor in the situation and went with the flow. He also realized she had the most beautiful smile.

They drove off down the long windy driveway and every bump she would hit Kim would grimace. She asked him numerous times "are you sure you are alright"

Every time she got the same answer "I'm fine" but in his head he was saying who in the hell would build a car this small?? Damn foreign cars."

Finally they made it to the end of the drive and she asked him if he would like to drive because she was unfamiliar with the roads, but the real reason was her seat would move all the way back so he would be more comfortable and she was considerably shorter than the long legged cowboy.

This took no time for him to answer and he said "well I recon I can drive if you want" so they jumped out of the car and ran the fire drill after both of them got settled in he turned to her and said this is a little better but you need a truck. She smiled in humor and just said "I know, but I am usually not on these kinds of roads"

He said, "I really do appreciate everything you have done for us this weekend and having you out there was kind of a nice."

"Oh, there is no need to thank me. I needed that little get away. It was so nice to be away from all the hustle and bustle of the city, where it is quite and all you can hear is nature. I wish I didn't have to leave. You boys are such gentlemen I never see that where I live so I should be thanking you."

"Well you know you could always come back out here and help with LG. We can fix up Cross' place for you and you could just live there or something like that. I can pay you"

"I wish it were that easy, but I have kids to think about. I'm honored that you suggested that, and I would love to be out there, but I can't just up and move the kids."

"Well then at least bring them kids out here to meet me on a weekend or something I am sure they will have fun and you can relax like you want. All 3 of us are good with kids. I won't promise you they will stay clean, but they will have fun."

The whole time he was talking she was daydreaming in her head about living on the ranch and the kids there with her, but Kim had not mentioned bringing the kids back with her to stay. She would volley back and forth the idea of moving kids out there and how ridiculous it is for a grown woman to be so smitten by a man she hardly knew but she was, and she was almost positive he felt the same way. Unsure how to bring the elephant out of the closet she just kept quiet and listened to him ramble on every so often she would mutter an "UH HU."

It was strange to her that he was talking her ear off he had said more in that first 5 miles to her than he had said since the day they met. Kim would talk because he was nervous and really wanted to get to know her better. Even though he was a charmer with the ladies he had never wanted to get to know any of them so, he was in unchartered territory and it made him a little nervous. He kept talking and she kept pretending to listen. Then she heard him say "we are here"

She said "what we are already here? I must have fallen asleep"

"You can say that you may want to wipe the drool of my shoulder. I never picked you for a snorer either I'd never be able to sleep in the same bed with you."

"I don't snore"

"Yes, you did" as he smiled

"No, I didn't, and you would not sleep with me in the same bed anyway I'm not your type" she razzed him

"Well what is my type?"

"You know the blonde bimbo type"

"Now that aint fair you don't know that"

"Well I know one of them finally graduated to be a cashier at the grocery store"

"OH, OK so maybe you do know my type that was low, but she is pretty much a blonde bimbo. Well what if my taste had changed and I wanted someone I could sit and talk with and someone to settle down with what about that?"

"HA you settle down? That is funny. I haven't known you very long, but I am sure that is a long way off from happening."

"Maybe not maybe that is what I've been waiting on. Someone to fit the job."

"Then why all the other women?"

"I was just doing interviews" he said with a naughty grin

"You are awful Kim Lee!! OOPs?? I guess it is Cowboy now that we are in public?"

"That is right JESSIE" he said and laughed because she had acted like that name bothered her and normally it did except when he said it. It was different. Not Jessie like a gunslinger from the OK corral but, Jessie like a foreign mistress. Again, he made her blush and she just could not figure out why she was so wrapped up in him. "OK let's not talk about the past and you quit being mean to me" as he chuckled lightly

"OK I will but you have to behave."

"I promise I'll be good"

They grabbed the baby and all her things from the car and made their way into the hospital. As they entered the front door, he looked to her and with a serious face said, "I hate these places."

"Are you nervous?"

"NO, I just don't like being in a hospital"

"Well it will be fine I will stay right here with you and make you feel better"

Cowboy never cared much for hospital after spending time in there during his rodeo days. They made their way to the desk and checked in with the receptionist. She asked them to have a seat and they would call when it was time to go back for the results meeting.

"I wonder why they could not tell on the phone who the dad is?"

"Normally they make you come down to the facility for legal issues it is standard procedure"

"I don't understand why we both have to be here"

"Well if they only told one of you to come then you might decide to run off to Mexico or something."

Jessica knew he was nervous and decide to change the subject, so she asked him "why are you afraid of hospitals?"

"I aint afraid of them I just don't like them. I spent about 3 weeks in this one around 20 years ago"

"What happened to make you stay that long?"

"That long they wanted me to stay longer but I got tired of being here and just left"

"Well what happened why were you here?"

"AHH hell I got hung up and busted a few ribs and some stuff"

"You don't stay in the hospital for a few ribs being busted. It had to be more than that"

"I was at the Stock Show rodeo and I made to the finals. I already wrapped up the all-around cowboy for the whole deal, but I was riding for 1st in the bull riding. I got hung up on my exit and the bull decided he wanted me off too. That was the only thing we both agreed on, so he rubbed me off with the fence. I reckon he got upset cuz I rode him out, so he came back and rubbed his nose in my back. Then he stepped on my arm and broke it and even with the bull fighters trying to get him off me he hooked me and threw me and the two bull fighters about 20 feet in the air. That finally satisfied him I guess cuz he just turned and strutted to the gate. The bad thing is when I drew that bull for the finals I was pissed because he was not a very aggressive bull and I knew he would hurt my score. But I guess I got a little more than I bargained for on that one. When I got here, I had a broke arm, busted ribs, a punctured lung, 2 cracked vertebrae, and a few other little things."

"Oh, my goodness that is bad"

"Not as bad as being cooped up in this place with nothing to do."

"Why did you leave you had to have been in pain?"

"Well I had a sponsor at the time, and I was known as the Iron man cuz nothing could keep me from making a rodeo and Cheyenne was that week, so I had to go to keep money coming in."

"That is awful I would have died. I can't even stand getting a shot."

"It hurt but there wasn't anything they could do to make it quit so you just deal with it and go on. It was going to hurt just to lay there too."

"Well I am sorry you had to go through that."

He could hear the sincerity in her voice and it made him feel a little better about talking with her he had never spoken about the numerous wrecks to anyone in any detail like that, usually when people or the press would ask him about something like that his comment was "it is a rodeo and wrecks happen you can deal with it or cry about it and quit." And he would smile and walk away. She had a tendency to bring stuff out of him without even trying. He just wanted to talk to her about anything just to hear her talk and have her sit by him."

They both agreed not to talk about the Hospitals or the accidents of the past anymore. She could see it brought out the tougher side of him and he would get quiet, so she started talking about the property and the house and all the things they had. It always brought out a sense of pride in him because he had put in endless hours and continued to put a lot of blood, sweat and tears into the property. Not long after they had been there Bratton came in and sat down with them. She listened to the 2 of them banter back and forth to one another and Kim rag on Bratton about not getting things done around the place. She could hear him telling him "Boy when I was your age, I was working 4 jobs and going to school."

Bratton would say "yea yea and you had a parent that would feed you. I am so weak from lack of food."

It was funny to hear. They would get loud every now and again and she would have to tell them to be quite like all moms do and finally she told them both "if you two don't stop I am going to separate you." That was the last straw she made Bratton sit on one side and Kim on the other then the fun began. Kim pulled the old stretching the arms move and placed his arm on the back of her chair and leaned in to whisper something in her ear about that boy is just unruly as he hit Bratton in the back of the head with a slap. Bratton grabbed his hand and they started play fighting and she said, "you two stop it."

Kim said well "he started it"

Bratton said "he hit me. Isn't there a number I can call?"

She just rolled her eyes "quit it!!" in a stern voice. They both knew that they had better stop. They looked just like they were a family that had been together for years.

The receptionist received a phone call and after she hung up, she spoke out to the three of them. Mr. and Mrs. Lee, you can come with me. Kim looked at Bratton and raised his eyebrows and said, "yep we stopped by the JP on the way surprise" and they started laughing.

Then Bratton hugged Jessica from behind her and said, "I love my new mommy."

She was giggling by that time "you two are awful now shut up and come on." She could not figure out what had gotten into the two of them, but it was a stressful situation and that was way they dealt with, cutting up and acting like it was not bothering them. She got a good laugh out of it and they made their way to the back room where they sat down and waited a few minutes for the Doctor to come in.

When the doctor came in and sat down, he said "hi to Jessica what are you doing here?"

Jessica said, "they are friends of mine and they asked me to come up with them since I work here."

The doctor whose name was Dave was not a bad looking guy and he struck Kim's nerve right off the bat when he started nonchalantly flirting with Jessica in the room

Dave said, "I missed you this weekend I thought you were supposed to work but I never saw you."

"Well I had to take some sick time"

"Are you ok or was one of the kids sick?"

"No one was sick I just took some time off to be by myself"

"I wish I had known we could have gotten together over the weekend"

"I was out of town"

"Where did you go" he said picking for information

"I went to Graham?"

"Where is that?" he said with bewildered look?

And Kim had heard enough "It is where I live can we get on with this?

"OH, I see ya'll are"

She interrupted him and said, "no I just went to help them out."

Bratton could tell his dad was none too happy about this guy flirting with Jessica he had never seen his dad get pissy over a guy talking to any of his previous flings. He politely said "can we get on with this I have some things to get done. Just tell us who the dad is, and we can head back home."

The doctor cleared his throat and explained" that is the problem. We are not sure who the father is."

Kim stood from his chair and said, "you mean to tell me neither of us is the dad?"

"Well no not exactly" the doc cried out raising one eyebrow in disbelief of his own research. "I have been in this business for some time now and I have screened the DNA samples of at least 1000 people, and I have never had this happen before. We are not sure which of you is the dad, but we know one of you is the father of the baby."

"WHAT?" both men yelled out "what do you mean?"

"Hang on just a second and I will explain. Like I had said before I have been doing this for quite some time and I have never seen this before. Usually we determine the father by a match of 99% and we have that, but it is both of you. I know it is crazy, but it is probably because you are father and son and your DNA are already a match. I have never had a case with a father and son before."

Cowboy looked at the doc "OK well that makes a little sense why did you not just tell us on the phone?"

"We are not allowed to discuss these things on the phone because we cannot be sure that we are talking to the right person."

"Well what happens next?"

"Typically, we will take the child to foster care until the paternity test is resolved"

"NO, that little girl is going with us" Cowboy sternly explained "whoever this babies momma has trusted us enough to leave the kid with us and she obviously belongs with us, so she is going home with us end of story." Cowboy stood to his feet and grabbed his hat. Then he looked at Bratton and said "Come on get the baby and let's go"

At this point the Doc was a little worried but was still trying to do his job so he told the men in a shaky voice "I can't let you do that I have to follow procedure"

"You don't have a choice" Kim said.

Jessica knew Kim was plenty upset and stood up in between the men and said "everyone calm down no one is leaving right now we can work this out. Dave why don't you go get the CPS agent on duty and we will see if we can work something out. I don't think it right that the child be placed in foster care at this point. I will stay here with them to make sure they don't make a break for it."

"Ok I will do that I will be right back. And for what it is worth I don't think she needs to go to foster care either if she has someone who cares about her like they do but I have a job to do. That is our protocol. I am just following the rules."

She smiled at him and said"

I know you are so let's see what we can do."

After hearing the Doc say that it eased the tension in the room some and the 2 Lee boys sat back down. Still in a huff both sat silent and Jessica could tell the 2 were obviously not going to leave without the girl. They sat in the room in complete silence both men with their arms crossed, legs stretched out, crossed at the ankles and a scowl on their face. Like to kids waiting to see the principle for fighting in the school yard. Jessica tried to break the silence with small talk several times but was unable to strike up more than a yes or no answer. These 2 were really disgruntled at this point and she was worried what would happen. So she turned to Kim and Bratton and in a serious tone said" Look I know the 2 of you are not happy at this point and I would not be if I was in your shoes but, when CPS gets in here and the 2 of you are being hard asses like you are now sitting here pouting they are not going to let her go with you. So, I suggest that the 2 of you change your attitudes and get happy really quick." And she turned back around in her seat and looked straight ahead.

Bratton's Jaw hit the floor as he said, "Yes Ma am ". He knew she was serious, and she must have been a little upset herself. Plus, he was waiting to see what his dad would say.

Kim looked at her and said "I am sorry you are right"

Bratton looked at his dad with his eyes wide open and was amazed his dad never said I am sorry. As a matter of fact, he hated that phrase all together. Every time he had heard "I am sorry" used around his dad. Kim would say "Sorry my ass that is just; words prove it to me then I will believe it. People use that about like I love you they just say it cuz they think they are supposed to."

Kim turned to Jessica" what do you think we need to do to get her back out to the house? Do I need to call my lawyer and have him come up here?"

"I am not sure at this point let's see what CPS says and examine our options we may be able to work something out with them."

"OK I'll trust you on this one, but we are not leaving without that little girl."

For some reason Kim had a soft spot for this baby and neither Jessica nor Bratton could figure why. Bratton loved the little girl, but his dad was fighting mad at just the thought of her not coming home with them.

Jessica looked at him and said "let me handle it and it will be fine" as she winked and smiled at him. That eased his conscious even more and he gave her a half smile. Then he put his arm on the back of her chair and gave her a one arm hug patting her on the shoulder and said "You are a good woman. I like you. I really appreciate everything you are doing."

Again she got cold chills and fought off the urge to wrap her arms around him and just squeeze him as close to her as she could but, instead she looked at him and said "Well I like you two also and I think you are a good group of guys just a little rough around the edges" as she rubbed Kim's 5 o'clock shadow on his face and smiled wantonly at him. This led into a verbal exchange of bantering and flirting back and forth between the two of them and Bratton getting sick to his stomach listening to them.

When the CPS agent knocked on the door and announced herself it was an all too familiar voice to them. Kim knew it was Shirley once again and rolled his eyes. Jessica saw the look and grabbed his knee and squeezed. He giggled and said stop it, so she squeezed again, and he started to snicker and wiggle away from her, she had found a ticklish spot on the mean old cowboy.

Bratton said, "will you two behave this is serious and you're embarrassing me." So, they stopped but the quite giggles would continue for a few more minute.

Shirley said, "people usually are not this happy to see me." As she turned around and said "Well we have familiar faces here today. How are you doing Jessica? Did everything go well??" She said with a smile. Then with a smirk she said "Mr. Lee, Bratton what are we gonna do with you two? I thought we had all this worked out and here you go making my job harder than it already is."

"Well ma'am we" Kim started to say and just about the time he started talking Jessica loudly and intentionally cleared her throat.

Kim looked at her and told her "I'll just be quite I guess."

Jessica turned back his way and smiled. Then she began to speak "I guess you know by now that there is a problem with the paternity test because they are testing a father and a son or whatever but Dr. Dave said that one of them is for sure the father just not sure which one at this point."

Shirley looked at her with a smile and said, "Dr. Dave huh?" Shirley and some of the other women at the hospital had been trying to get Jessica and the good doctor together for some time. Jessica thought he was a nice guy and would be great for someone just not her. They continued to push her to go on a date with him and he always seemed interested in her. She would tell him when he asked her to go or do something that she did not like to date people from work.

Jessica looked at Shirley and said "Don't start that again"

"Well OK" she replied "but you should think about it. So back to the child what are we going to do? I understand you 2 don't want the child going to foster care but I cannot allow her to go to a home that is not certified by the state so what are we going to do?"

"How can we get them certified by the state?" Jessica asked

"Another representative from the CPS or myself would have to come out and perform a case study and evaluate the home and all the individuals that habitat the establishment."

"How long does that take?"

"We cannot get out there until possibly the middle of the week. Until then she would have to stay with a childcare professional."

"No that is no good for us" Kim said.

"Well I am sorry you feel that way Mr. Lee but it is not what is good for you that concern me it is what is good for that little girl in your lap that I am worried about."

Jessica looked at Kim with a stern look and he knew he was not supposed to be talking so he sat back in his chair and held the little girl not to speak again. Jessica asked if she could talk with Shirley in the hall, so the 2 left the room and continued their conversation in the hallway. Shirley asked her a few questions about the weekend that had just passed and how it went. Jessica told her it was great and went on and on about the property and how nice everyone was and how she enjoyed the time out there and even slipping up a little and saying she would love to live there.

Shirley could tell by the way she was talking that she was falling for Kim and the whole idea of living out on a ranch. She grabbed Jessica by the arm and told her "girl you better get a hold of yourself. You don't need no broke down old cowboy and his problems"

"No, he is not like that at all. All of them are true gentlemen and really nice what you see is what you get they are the real thing, besides there is nothing going on between us. I am not his type and he is not my type. But you have to admit there is something about him that just does something for you or at least for me there is."

"Oh boy you done went and got to deep I have seen that look before and I know what it is. Now what is it you want to do this time?"

Well I was thinking that the next 2 weeks are spring break for the kids and well I will have to talk with Kim but we could stay out there just until you can get out there and do the case study on the house."

"Now hold on listen to yourself. It is one thing for you to go out there and stay which, I thought was stupid, but to take your kids to a stranger's house for a week girl you are crazy."

"These guys are harmless. Everyone in town knows them and loves them. I have not heard one bad word about any of the 3 guys that live out there."

"Whoa Whoa there is another one?"

"Oh, yea he is an older guy his name is Cross, and he is a great guy real soft spoken and quite but funny and can out work any young guy I have ever seen around here. They are great with this little girl. I hate to leave her with them because she will be so spoiled rotten and I know when she gets older there will never be a man who could measure up to their standard but, they really are great people."

"You are crazy girl you actually want to go back, there don't you?"

"Oh, I love it. It is so quiet and beautiful. The scenery changes every second by the way the light hits it. It is gorgeous."

"Well I guess it is OK as long as you are there. The department won't have a problem, but I still think you have gone Looney. I MEAN THAT." Shirley said with a chuckle and sour look at Jessica.

"Thank you. If you are the one who comes out there you will see."

"I am not coming out there them boys look like they live in the KKK area I might get Kilted or sumthin like that." With her Ebonics accent

"No, you won't. Now you are talking crazy."

"Well you go and have fun with your new cowboy boyfriend, and I will try to get out there to see the place."

"He is not my boyfriend"

"Uh HUH!!" Shirley mouthed as she turned and exited the hall to re-enter the room.

When she walked through the doorway she said "Boys it is your lucky day the girl can go with you, but I am going to let Jessica explain the rest. Go ahead girl tell them!"

Jessica was nervous to tell them her plan because she had not spoken with them prior to talking to Shirley. So she stood in front of them fidgeting like the teacher had called on her to answer a question she did not know the answer to and in a shaky small voice she started to speak "Well if it's OK with ya'll I was thinking I could come back out there and stay with you and the baby until the audit was done."

Before she finished Kim stood up and told Bratton to get the girl, we are done here with a no emotion on his face she was scared almost to tears thinking he was not keen to the idea. She looked at him and squeaked out "did I do something wrong?"

"NO what makes you think that?"

"You said you we're leaving."

"Cuz you said the baby and you were coming back to the ranch hell I love that deal"

"Well you don't even know the DEAL!! Yet", with her hand making air quotations.

"I figure there is more, but we could talk about it outside this place." Showing his hatred for hospitals which she had completely forgotten about but then she got a little aggravated at him not letting her finish and she sassily remarked

"well you need to sit down now and let me finish THE DEAL before you get all wound up and ready to go."

He sat down and Bratton turned back to his seat, laughed, and told his dad "You better sit down, shut up and listen before you get on her bad side she looks like she is pretty tough."

"Now as I was saying before I was interrupted" She looked his way and grinned and he hung his head and made pouty lips like he was in trouble "The baby and I are going to come out there but I had already taken this 2 weeks off for the kids being out on spring break, so I f I do this the kids will have to come with me. If that is a problem, then we can't do it."

"Your gonna bring the kids? That is even better I got a lot of work to get done around there. We could use the extra hands." As he laughed "I already told you to bring them out why would you think that was gonna be a problem? Can we leave now?"

She was liberated by his attitude towards the kids coming out, before she thought he was just being nice about the invitation to bring them out and now she knew it was no joke and for the first time she thought he might be interested in her and it made her feel like a million dollars, a man with a reputation of young Twinkie blondes and in the fast lane might actually like her. This was a first; she normally attracted the opposite of him, more of the nerds and the Brainiac's, never the cool and popular type like him.

She smiled lovingly towards him and she said "Yes we can leave and work the rest of it out on the way outside. I have to go pick the kids up"

Chapter 7

MEET THE FAMILY

*T*hey vacated the hospital and talked out the details on the way out. They had come to the conclusion that Kim would go with her in the truck to get the kids and all their clothes Bratton could drive her car back to the property and not be out so late since he had school the next morning. It was also away for Kim to not have to drive or ride in that little car again.

Bratton took off in what he called her go cart while Kim, the baby and Jessica left in the truck to get the kids and all their stuff.

Jessica's parents' house was not too far from the hospital so they pretty much just chit chatted between her giving directions and him asking her how do you drive in this stuff every day. By the time they had reached the house he was so stressed out he wanted a beer but would never ask for one. They stopped in front of the house and she looked his way and said, "do you want to come in?"

"Well do you want me too?"

"It will make it a little easier to explain. I am probably going to catch hell from my mother for doing this."

"Why would she care?"

"I am her daughter but the grandkid taking them to stay with me and at a stranger's the whole nine yards. She is very protective."

"Well if it will make it easier on you, I will go meet them I am sure they can't be that bad if they raise a sweet and beautiful girl, like you. I just don't want you hollering at me no more"

"Ok I won't holler anymore but I appreciate you meeting them."

"It is the least I can do after all you are doing."

"As they walked up the sidewalk side by side, he could tell she was a nervous wreck wondering what they were going to think. So, he threw his arm around her, pulled her in tight to his side. With the baby in a carrier on one arm and her on the other he said "it will be fine Jessie don't worry about it"

When they reached the door, she could hardly breathe from the excitement in her and from the energy spawned by a side hug. She was flushing hot and almost blushing. Her parents answered the door and she was no longer nervous, but she was giddy again. She tried to introduce Kim to her parents but all that came out was laughing and she knew she had to get away from him so she pushed her way through the door past her dad and grabbed her mother by the arm and headed straight for the kitchen to get her bearings about her. Kim stood at the door with the baby at hand, towering over her father who was a shorter stocky guy and still in good shape for his age. Kim said, "I think she was trying to tell you that my name is Kim and stuck his hand out."

"How are you doing Kim I am Jerry" and shook his hand firmly. Jerry told Kim to set the baby on the couch next to Cassie if he wanted. Kim judged a man on his handshake and could tell he had worked all is life and was a very confident man. Jerry was the same and was unsure why Kim was there, so he invited him to come in. Jerry was cooking on the grill in the back yard, so he made his way out there and Kim just meandered about the living room looking at photos while the 2 kids slept on the couch. Jerry returned after a few seconds and asked him if he would like to come out on the patio while he cooked. With no hesitation Kim headed for the porch and sat in an old wooden rocking chair. His eyes lit up when her dad asked, "would you like a beer?"

Kim said "that is the best offer I have had all day" as Jerry reached in his cooler and pulled out 2 beers and passing one to Kim, popping the top on the other and taking a drink. Kim broke the silence by telling him "after driving in the city all day I needed that" and sat back in the chair.

Jerry turned and said tell me about it. I hate that damn traffic it wasn't always like this. That struck up the conversation and they both were a lot alike and got along great. It was hard for Jessica and her mother to believe. Her father had never really cared for any of her past boyfriends no matter how successful or how manly they were he never really talked to any of them other than when he just had to. In the 4 years she was married he might have said 20 words the whole time to her husband and now he was sitting out there rambling like a schoolgirl. It was crazy and neither of the two women understood it.

Jessica sat in the kitchen answering fifty million questions from her mother about what was going on and how she met Kim. She went into the Living room to check on the kids and said, "oh what a beautiful baby who does she belong too?"

Jessica said, "we are not sure she was left on his doorsteps, so I am helping him out until we get it all sorted out." Her mother removed the baby from the carrier and began playing with her while continuing to drill her about Kim. Jessica repeatedly denied the accusations that they were dating, and her mother continued to pry. Jessica told her the story of how they met, and her mother's jaw dropped to the ground.

Her mother worried "I just cannot believe you went home with a man the first night you met him. Especially one who lives that far away? What were you thinking and now you want the kids to go with you? And you are not even a couple? This sounds fishy to me. I don't like it at all. I think you do like him and that is why you are trying to make an excuse to go back out there."

Jessica denied allegations that she fancied the older cowboy even when her mom told her "well at least he is a clean-cut handsome man for a change and not one of those young thugs you usually date".

Jessica just squealed out "MOM"

"Well it is true he is good looking. You could do a lot worse. Even your father gets along with him. And he is really good looking "she added once more. "I saw him with his arm around you when you walked up. You cannot tell me there is nothing going on between the 2 of you. I also saw how you were looking at him coming up the sidewalk and I have not seen you this giddy since your prom date came to the door to pick you up for your first real date. Another winner You brought home."

The conversation became redundant as her mother kept prying away at Jessica's conscious and subconscious to get her to talk and Jessica repeatedly denied the allegations that the two of them were dating or a couple, even though she knew there was a connection between the 2 of them and her mother knew it as well.

Gayle, Jessica's mother made her way outside with a platter for the meat Jerry was cooking and sat it on the table between the 2 men. She turned to Kim and said I guess ya'll will be staying for super since the kids have not eaten yet.

Kim looked to her and said "well I don't want to be a bother"

"You are no bother. We have plenty."

"Well that would be fine with me if it is no trouble. By the way I am Kim. I don't think we have been introduced." As he stood towering over the small framed older woman and stuck his hand out.

She immediately felt a little overwhelmed by his stature and said "OH my!! Well I am Gayle, and this is my husband Jerry."

Jerry piped off "We have been out here talking for an hour don't you think we have met enough?"

Kim snickered and said "yes ma'am we have already met, and it is a pleasure to meet you. I really appreciate your hospitality."

She turned toward the door and made her way back inside. After the door shut behind her Gayle looked to Jessica" boy he really is a tall drink of water"

Jessica surprised and embarrassed to hear her mother talk like that. She had but one reply again "Mother! Stop that!"

"You sure are a lucky girl to have a man like that. Tall good looking, manners, oh my." Fanning her face as if she were getting hot

"Mother for the last time he is not my man. Can we just drop the subject? Please."

Shortly after Gayle came in, the two men entered the room. Kim holding the door for Jerry who was carrying the grilled pork loin he cooked for dinner. Jessica saw them come in and looked to Kim with the come on let's make a break for it eyes. Then she told everyone "I guess we will get out of here and let you eat I have to get the kids' stuff packed and ready to go."

"Why are you leaving why not stay and eat?" questioned her dad. Knowing she was a little nervous

"Well Kim probably has to get up early in the morning and it is a long way to his house, so we better go"

"I don't have to get up it is fine by me"

Gayle said, "I already asked him if he wanted to stay and eat and he was fine with it."

"OH Ok" she replied with the voice of uncertainty "I will go wake the kids so they can eat."

"We already fed the kids they were tired, and the meat was taking too long, so I fed them left over's just before you got here."

"So, it is just going to be us I guess?? Great!" she muttered lightly as she clapped her hands together "well let's eat and get this over with"

They sat at the table and began to talk and have just a casual conversation. Kim looked to Gayle and Jerry and said "man this is some meal. I should hire you 2 to cater the big dog and pony show we are having in a couple of weeks."

"What is a dog and pony show?" Gayle inquired

Jerry told her "it's what people call a big event that they really don't what to go to with their boss or some other important people"

"You can say that again" Kim remarked

"What is going on in a couple of weeks?" Jessica asked

"Oh, nothing big the Governor is coming out to claim our property a historical marker for the state. I don't really care for the big ceremony and all the press but, I won't have to pay taxes no more."

"Hell, I want to claim this property as a historical site then."

"I wish it was that easy the family has to own the property for 100 years or more before they will do that."

"Well we only have 70 years to go looks like we are out of luck on that."

Jessica said, "why did you not tell me about that?" Sounding disappointed

Kim looked to her and said "well it is not that big of deal. I am sorry"

"Well don't you think I would want to know something like that"

"I am sorry next time I get a piece of property historified or whatever; I will call you" he said sarcastically

They picked back and forth at one another for a few minutes like a couple that had been together for years. Gayle and Jerry just sat there snickering at the two, playfully bickering at one another.

After dinner was done the ladies began clearing the table and Kim once again thanked them for the meal. Jerry and Kim sat at the table and talked of the way things used to be while Gayle and Jessy cleaned up the kitchen.

Gayle looked to Jessy and told her "I really like him he is a nice guy; too bad you are not dating." Then Jessica went into the whole story about how she was not his type and finally confessed to her mother that she was smitten by the older cowboy and told her that he was always this way with everyone. She had not seen him meet a stranger. When they were done with the kitchen the women sat at the table with the guys and joined in the conversation. Gayle suggested they play dominoes and Kim said well" I am good if ya'll want".

Jessica knew they would not be able to get out of there if they started the dominoes so she declined and said "we can play later but we really need to get home and pack. It is getting late."

"Are you sure" they said.

"Yea it is already late enough"

"Well we are gonna hold you to that playing some other time" Jerry said as he looked toward Kim

"You are on and I am not gonna take it easy on you either" he said as he stood to his feet and extended his hand in Jerry's direction. "It was really nice meeting the two of you and thank you for all your hospitality the food was great. Ya'll are gonna have to come see the place sometime. Maybe you can make it out for the dedication ceremony."

"It was nice meeting you too. Glad to see Jessy find someone with a little bit of manners for a change" Jerry told him as he glared at Jessy.

Jessy squeaked out with a shrill "Daddy" and said "come on Cowboy let's get you home" smiling at Kim

Kim liked the way that sounded so he told her "yes ma'am", looked at Jerry and said "looks like she is making me leave I guess we will just embarrass her more some other time. Gayle it was so nice meeting you" as he stooped down wrapping his arms around her and gave her a hug. Her eyes barely cleared his shoulders and she was looking right at Jessica and moving her lips. Jessica made out the words "He is a keeper."

Jerry stood beside them and said "hey ease on my wife she is taken "in a joking manner.

Kim laughed and replied, "well I would hug you, but she is way better looking and smells better." They all laughed as they made their way to the living room to get the kids.

Jessica tried to wake them up, but they were dead to the world, so Kim grabbed the boy up in his arms and said, "I'll get them." Then he swooped down and snatched the little girl up with the other arm and headed for the door with the 2 kids. Together weighed about 130 pounds and he could sling them around like sacks of feed in a barn. He headed for the truck and the little girl wrapped her arms around his neck to hold on and snuggled up to him closer. It brought back the days of when Bratton was that size and he just melted on the inside. He lay the boy down in the back seat on the passenger's side and then eased around to lay the little girl down on the driver's side and buckle her in. Jessica buckled the boy in and sat their bag in the floor.

Gayle insisted on carrying the baby out and placed her in the truck. Taking special care of buckling her back in and kissing her good night. "You better take care of this little angel she is a beautiful little present you got here"

They each said goodbye one last time then loaded up in the truck to get the bags packed for the next week. As they drove down the road Jessy broke the silence by telling Kim how much she appreciated him being so nice to her parents. Kim said he was not being nice to them he was just being himself, but he really enjoyed talking with them. When they arrived at the house it was about 11:30 at night and she still had not packed anything for her or the kids. Kim suggested they just stay the night there and make their way to the ranch in the morning. Jessica was glad to hear him say that because she was tired and did not want the kids to wake up in a strange house.

They put the 2 kids in bed and Jessica kissed them good night. She made her way in the living room and sat on the opposite side of the couch from Kim. Who was holding LG.? "I really had a good time tonight I have not been able to sit and talk with my parents like that in a long time. You are a good ice breaker."

"Why do you not talk to them?"

"Well to make a long story short they have not liked my selection in men here lately, so we have not seen eye to eye on a lot of things. Mom thought I was crazy for taking the kids to your place at first but I am sure she is fine with it now that she has had a chance to get to know you." As she pulled LG from his grasp and carried her away "I better get her a bed made." She went into her room and laid the baby in the bed and surrounded her with pillow. As Kim continued the conversation from the living room

"Well your mother and I agree we both think you are crazy" he said to her.

"Kim" she yelled out and slapped him on the shoulder as she came back in the room. "That was not nice." She slapped him again and they began to wrestle a little on the couch. Before she knew what was going on, she was on top of him with her hair in her face, the two of them laughing. She called for a time out to pull her hair from her face, while he held her other arm. Both of them were breathing hard and when she cleared the hair away, again they were nose to nose. She is not quite sure why but she leaned in and kissed him softly and even though it only lasted a second or two everything was in slow motion she told herself not to do it and she thought she could stop but the magnetic energy was too much and it happened. Immediately after she jumped up off his lap and apologized. Kim just lay there slouched down on the couch dumbstruck. He had never been kissed like that before it was soft and moist, it meant something. Even Stacy had never made him feel the way she did with that one brief touch of the lips. He was breathless and speechless. He managed to mutter the words "what are you sorry for?"

"I just should not have done that I know I am not your type I am sorry"

"Hold on just a minute not my type what is that supposed to mean?"

"I know you are not looking for a relationship you like the young blondes and I am neither of those." Scampering away, "I need to go do laundry."

"Wait a second" he blurted out as she turned to do the laundry. "I like all women I am a guy. As far as me not wanting a relationship how do you know that? That maybe exactly what I need and furthermore I am not sorry for you kissing me I enjoyed it."

"Me kissing you. HUH? I think it was you kissing me. I am not your type I have kids I am too old, and I am nowhere near as pretty as all those other girls you run around with. But I did not kiss you"

"Wow Jessica you are crazy" he said with a smile as he grabbed her by the waist and pulled her to him. "You did kiss me, and you did like it and you are a beautiful woman. I love kids and you are right about one thing you are nothing like those other women I have run around with before. But you are gonna kiss me again and then tell me you did not like it." He leaned down and pressed their lips together and they held the embrace for some time. When they released the hold he said "how was that? Did you still not like it?" As she stood in front of him with her legs feeling like over cooked noodles and her face glowing with Joy

She shook her head yes and said with a whimpering voice "no. Maybe you should try again."

So, they did, and they were kissing and stammering to the living room and fell over the couch but, continued to kiss as they fell both of them caught up in the moment and loving every minute of it. Kim finally said "wait let's not do this? Not now let's wait."

She took it as a sign of rejection. "I knew it you are a pig."

"NO, I just don't want to do this right now. I am tired of the fly by night relationships I want something more. I want someone who wants me for me not for my status. I like you a lot and I don't really know you I want to spend more time with you."

She looked like a puppy dog waiting for a treat but, still felt a little rejected. No man had ever told her anything like that before and she was not real sure how to take it. The thought haunted her mind. Is he serious or his he just trying to be nice and not hurt her feelings? Does he really want a relationship or is she just not his type like she had said? She deliberated the whole scenario for the rest of the night and decided to just play it by ear and see how things would go. Each time they came in contact the unsettled energy in the air made for an awkward feeling.

He was not real sure how she felt, he was trying to be honest and that was not something he was used to doing. He spent the rest of the night evaluating his past relationships thinking about the entire night and fly by night relationships that had no future. The only one true relationship he has had was with Stacy and he often wondered what he did to run her off. Was there something wrong with him that he could not keep a woman around? Was he really that bad of a guy? All these thoughts randomly running through his brain and still he had no answer. The only thing he was sure of was that he did not want to die old and alone he wanted a woman to take care of and spoil like his dad did with his mother. After many hours on the couch pondering the past, he decided to Play it by ear and if she acted like she wanted to embark on this endeavor with him then he would give it a go.

She brought out some blankets and a pillow and told Kim he could sleep in her bed because she normally slept on the couch. The living room was a small room with only a couch, love seat and a TV. Her house was not big or lavish it was a small house built in the late 70's and only had 1 bathroom but it was all she needed and all she could afford. It was not a big deal to Kim because he never put a lot of stock in a house or car if it kept the rain off his head, he was fine.

Kim refused to take her bed from her and she refused to sleep on the bed as well so she curled up on the love seat with the blanket and he stretched is long thin frame out over the arms of the couch and kicked his boots off. They sat in silence for a few minutes and Jessica told him he could watch whatever he wanted to on TV. He just replied I don't normally watch TV when I am sleeping so this show is fine whatever it is if you like it.

She finished watching the news and watched him toss and turn trying to get comfortable on the couch. He finally got settled in and dozed off with his legs from the knee down hanging off the arm and his head on the other arm and arms almost to the floor. She really did not want to wake him up, but she knew that he could not be comfortable and that in the morning he would be sore. So, she woke him up and told him. "I am going to the bedroom if you would like to sleep in the bed, we can split it down the middle. You, on your side and me, on mine. I know you have to be uncomfortable and I don't want you falling asleep while you are driving tomorrow."

Kim was a little groggy and half asleep, but he obliged her and they each retired to her room. The queen size bed was still a little short for Kim but was much more comfortable than the couch and he was so tired he did not even realize he was sleeping in a bed covered with flowered comforter and pillows. He fell back to sleep almost instantly. She lay awake beside him and just watched him sleep for a few minutes. She was always too stressed out to fall right to sleep and normally read a book to take mind off all the stress that surrounded her. Tonight, she did not read but lay in bed still pondering what to do about Kim should she tell him how she felt? Or just let it be and whatever happens, happens? She was afraid of being rejected but she also knew that she had some extremely strong feeling for him. She fell asleep with this still in her head and even dreamed about it that night. Her dream was of them two together back on the ranch with him and all the guys working with the livestock and her and her daughter Cassie working in the flower beds on a beautiful spring day. Then it turned into a corny dream like the sound of music and her running thru a field of flowers twirling around like a little toddler running after butterflies.

Chapter 8

THE LONG RIDE

The sun began to rise over the houses and penetrated the window Kim awoke first to find Jessica sleeping with her head on his shoulder and wrapped in his arm. At first, he was a little startled. He had woken up with many different women beside him in bed but this time he still had clothes on. He started to get out of bed, when he saw her sleeping so good and looking so peaceful, he just let her lay there and for a little bit longer. He took the time to observe how beautiful she really was with no makeup and her hair in a mess he still thought she was very attractive. Her long flowing dark hair and her soft tan skin, He normally would be chomping at the bit to get out of bed before the sun but today he was in no hurry to move he just laid there with her on his arm and enjoyed watching her sleep, occasionally laughing real lightly so not to wake her when she would snore a little. Not long after that she woke up and saw him next to her with her sleepy eyes and her brain not functioning right just, yet she smiled at him and hugged up to his chest. Then she realized what she was doing and popped up really quick and wiped her mouth off just in case she had been drooling and said "ooh I am sorry. Did I drool on you?"

Kim laughed "a little" and said "no you didn't but your snoring woke me up. You were sleeping good and I figured you could use the rest, so I just lay there and let you sleep"

"Well should have woke me up"

"You did a good job of that on your own you snored so loud you woke yourself up" he said with a mischievous grin on his face,

"No, I did not you are terrible! Are the kids up?"

"I am not sure that is another reason I did not get outta bed I figured I might scare them some strange guy walking around the house"

"Oh, they would have been fine"

"Do they wake up to a lot of strange guys walking around the house?"

"KIM LEE!!" she squealed and slapped him on the chest, "you are awful" she got out of bed and asked if he wanted some coffee and breakfast. He said he would love some coffee, but he thought they could get something on the road. He needed to make sure to get home or Cross and Brat would be loafing around not doing anything if he was not there.

"I am gonna run grab my shaving kit out of the truck would it be OK if I used your bathroom to clean up and brush my teeth?"

"Well sure you can. I will get the coffee on and finish up packing I 'll be ready in about an hour so. Is that OK"

"Yea take your time no big rush."

Kim walked to the bedroom door and turned to see her making the bed. It reminded him of his mother she hated to see a bed not made and that was the first thing she would do after she woke up the bed had to be made. He smiled and turned around to go to the truck as he walked down the narrow hall, he passed the kids room to see Dylan playing with a deck of cards on his bed. Not knowing what to do he said "Hey" and Dylan replied sheepishly " Hey".

Kim walked to the truck and grabbed his bag. When he got back in both the kids were awake and, in the kitchen, talking to their mother. He decided to let her field any questions they had, and he would get cleaned up. He went into the bathroom to brush his teeth and to shave. In the middle of shaving he heard a cry in the room which scared him enough that he cut himself shaving. He let out a yelp and turned around to see what it was, but nothing was there. He thought it might have been one of the kids running down the hall. He faced the mirror to finish shaving and heard the scream once again. Again, he cut himself and turned to see what it was and again nothing was there. Then he saw in the bathtub was a baby with pillows under her like a bed. Kim loudly said "Jessica" with uncertainty in his voice "will you come here please?"

She hurried her way in the bathroom after hearing the distress in his voice. "What is wrong?"

"The baby is crying."

"O well I will get her"

"Will you please tell me why she is in the bathtub? With pillows all round her and a blanket on her?"

"It was all I could think of I did not want her to roll off the bed or anyone to step on her so I made her a pallet in the bathtub so I could hear her if she woke up and she would not get hurt. It was all I could come up with at the time."

"Well I have to have a picture of this for when she gets older. Also, as black mail on you."

"You would not do that!"

"No, I wouldn't but I find it hard to believe they trust you more than me with her after this" he said jokingly

"That is not nice at all. I am very good with kids."

"I am just funnin" with you. After you explained yourself it makes sense to me, but it was a little bizarre at first."

Jessica picked up the baby and went into the room to change her and Kim made his way to the kitchen to get a cup of coffee. Kim sat with her two kids striking up conversation. The kids asked him why he was there, and he just told them he was picking them and their mother up and taking them for a little vacation on his ranch. They asked him every question imaginable about the place and he gladly answered each one of them with a smile. Jessica had walked by the kitchen and had seen Cassie sitting in his lap and Dylan leaned over the table listening to the old cowboy intently. The kids really took to Kim and she was glad. He seemed to be a gentle giant when kids were around, he had a whole different demeanor. When Jessica was done tending to the baby Kim asked if she was ready to go and she told him I got the baby ready now I must pack all our stuff.

Sarcastically he started to razz "Good Lord woman could you hurry up? Me and these kids are ready to get to the ranch and all you are doing is lolly gagging around!!! Aint that right kids?" as he turned to Dylan and Cassie.

Who chimed in their 2 cents worth?

"Hurry up mom we want to go"

"Gosh you always make us late for everything."

"Well if you kids would help, we would be on the road quicker" she barked back "and if you would quit stirring up trouble this would go much smoother" she told Kim

"Ahh I was just funnin" you" he remarked with his slow Texas draw. "What do you need me to do? I can start hauling stuff to the truck if you want. I aint used to all this waiting around, so I get a little antsy. When we go somewhere it is all guys we just load and go no makeup no kids, so don't get offended I will get better at it."

"It is OK I can handle you giving me a hard time. I don't get offended easy or I would not be a nurse. If you want, you can take these bags to the truck I am almost done."

He grabbed 2 of the bags and told Dylan to grab the other one by the door and they made their way to the truck cutting up and joking around, they finished loading all the bags and waited in the living room for Jessica to finish.

She hollered out from the bedroom to Kim "will you put the baby in her car seat and get the kids in the truck I will be right behind you; all I have left is my make-up. He put LG in the seat and grabbed her up off the floor by the handle "Come on kids lets load up"

They all made their way to the truck. Kim strapped the baby in and helped Cassie into her seat, the truck was a little too tall for her to get in without getting dirt all over her and being the girly girl she is, she would not get in the truck without help. Kim was tickled by her refusal to get in the truck without help.

"I am not getting in that dirty thing!!" she stated boldly. So, Kim picked her up with a gentle swoop and tossed her in the truck.

"Now is that better? "He asked

"Yes, thank you kind Sir" as she smiled at him innocently.

He just snickered to himself and smiled back at the prissy little girl. This little girl knows how to butter up a guy that is for sure. He wondered how Cross was going to hold up his grumpy old man routine with her cute little face looking up at him. He was anticipating their first encounter.

After all the kids were buckled in and settled down for the trip, there still was no Jessica. Right behind me he thought to himself, so he waited and growing impatient he waited until he saw her come thru the front door scampering around like a squirrel loading up nuts for the winter. She reached for the door and dropped her makeup she reached down to get it while muttering loudly " I am coming I know I know I am coming " as aggravated as Kim was at having to wait it was all washed away by seeing her in that vulnerable moment. He knew where Little Miss Cassie Frass (as he called her) got her charm, she looked so innocent and naïve at that moment he wished he could freeze frame time.

She finally made it in the truck. "I am sorry I was really trying to hurry" she apologized over and over.

"It is OK" Kim tried to reassure her, but she continued to ramble about what all she had to do, and she was trying to get out and she knew he was getting "antsy" she was sorry. He just kept telling her it was ok he wasn't mad. Finally he looked at her grabbed her chin and gently turned her head to look eye to eye with her at the red light and said " I know you are sorry and I am not mad but if you don't quit apologizing I am gonna have to make you ride in the back of the truck." The two of them leaned closer to one another to kiss and Dylan yelled out "Cowboy the light is green" another missed opportunity so they each just looked to one another and smiled as if to say there will be a better time and place.

At this point each of them knew there was something between them and they were already getting too close to deny it but neither of them wanted to overreact and scare the other one away or to be rejected by another love gone bad.

It was not far into the trip the kids all fell fast asleep in the back seat and Kim and Jessica carried on a casual conversation taking special care to not bring up relationships or anything that might resemble past love.

Jessica looked to Kim and said "I really want to thank you for letting the kids come out. I know they will just love being out there with all the animals."

"Well I am the one who should be thanking you. You have done so much for us already and you don't even hardly know us."

"I know I don't really know ya'll, but I feel like I know enough to say that you are all good people and wouldn't hurt a fly without a reason. I really would like to get to know you better. If I can." She went out of her comfort zone and said something she was trying to avoid again. After her comment she sat there for a few seconds in anticipation awaiting a response hopefully a good one, but anything would do, the silence was deadly, and her heart was going to explode.

He looked straight ahead and pondered on his response. He did not want to say something that would sound to mushy or something that would make him look like a ladies man. He finally responded to her after a few brief seconds which, seemed like hours "I think I want to get to know you a little better too or at the very least have a chance to get to know you"

After hearing the first syllable from his lips she was able to breathe again. She was not exactly sure what level of getting to know one another he was willing to go to or how fast. Her brain was swimming as fast as her heartbeat and all she could think of to say was" I think that would be nice"

At this point in time she would have said yes to a proposal, but she was quite content with his response. Shortly after her reply he began to speak with a soft and somber voice to her, telling her he had never been really good at relationships and that he thought he had just never met the right woman. He compared his relationships to having a food craving but not knowing what he was craving. He said "you look in a refrigerator, that is full, and you see all this stuff, but you don't want any of it. Then you see something you like but it really isn't what you want and you take a bite anyway and the craving is still there so you do it again and no matter what you eat, you still have the craving.

She would reply with the similar responses and how she had always ended up with guys who were nice at first then turned to jerks later on.

Kim assured her that he is the same regardless of who is around, and he is too old to change

Jessica leaned in towards him on the console between them and told him "Please don't think I am crazy I have never been this way before but for some reason I feel like I am supposed to be here with you. I don't know if it is just right here and right now or if it is for eternity? I just know it feels right to be doing this with you. I hope that does not scare you off but there it is I have wanted to say that to you since the moment we met but I was afraid to. I hope it does not scare you if it does, I am sorry but don't think for one second I will do any of this for anyone else."

"Wow that is kind of crazy "he said in a nice way "but I do know that I have been interested in you as well, but it is different than with the other women. I am not in a hurry with you. I want to slow it down and enjoy things with you. Normally I am always in a hurry to get something done or rushed to get somewhere. With you I don't mind waiting as much. Maybe you are what I have been craving all this time?"

She was touched deeply by his response and not long after that they arrived at the ranch. Each of them again feeling emotionally naked they stopped in the front yard neither of them talking. Kim reached for her hand and kissed it lightly and again she looked him in the eyes, and he told her "lets don't go to fast let's just enjoy each other's company and we will see what happens." Kim did not want to go down the same path as all the others after Stacy he really wanted to be a friend and not a sex puppet.

She said "I think that is the smartest thing either one of us has said" then she leaned in and gave him a hug. Neither of the two wanted to be just friends but they were OK with it as long as they were together.

They both unloaded all the bags from the truck and let the kids sleep so they could focus on all the excitement of the kids when they awoke at the ranch.

Chapter 9

SPRING BREAK BEGINS

$\mathcal{D}$ylan was the first one to get out and he was astonished by how big the place was his first question was "when do we get to ride the horses?"

Cassie was the last one out and she asked, "where is the pool?"

"Well we don't have a pool, but we have a pond you can swim in" Kim replied.

"I thought we were on vacation."

"Well we are" Jessica quickly answered.

"When we go with Nana and Papa on vacation, we always have a pool"

"Well this is not one of those vacations" her mom quickly responded, "now come inside and I will show you the house."

The 2 girls went inside, and Kim asked Dylan to give him a hand in the barn. They made their way toward the barn and Cowboy asked him "Well what do you think so far you gonna be able to hang around out here for a week or so? I got lots of work you could do for me."

Dylan said "I like it. It is a nice spread" as he spit and kicked some dirt with his boots, Cowboy looked at him wondering what in the heck he was doing. Dylan finished with "as far as the work? It depends on what it pays."

Cowboy said "Well you little punk! You are not gonna help me around here unless I pay you?" He grabbed him in a head lock and rubbed his head

"No, I will help you I just saw that on a show once and it sounded like something cool to say."

Cowboy laughed at him and then kicked him lightly in the butt as he took off running to the barn hollering at him "Come on you little sissy don't let this old man beat you to the barn" They both scurried to the barn and Cowboy opened the door. When Dylan saw the inside of the barn his eyes got big. He looked like a pirate that had just opened a chest full of gold. "Whoa" he said "this is cool"

"You think so? Do you know what any of this is? Or what it does?"

"Well those are horses, and these are saddles."

"That is a start I will explain it as we go. You are gonna help me feed the horse. That can be your job while you are here if you want."

"Heck ya I want to feed the horses."

"Ok now you gotta listen to me cuz some of these critters are not as nice as the others. Let's get us a couple blocks of hay "as he pulls some flakes off a square bale of hay stacked in the corner. Dylan follows right behind him mocking his every move. They walk to the first stall and Cowboy asked him "have you ever seen a horse before?"

Dylan said "yes but I never fed one before"

"Where did you see one?"

"On the street in downtown a policeman was riding it and he let me pet him."

"Well you are gonna do more than just pet them around here. You are gonna be riding one."

"Really" he yelled out with excitement? "I get to ride a horse?"

"You sure do but not until you learn how to take care of them. Now this one here is Strawberry she is my best momma horse she loves attention. Now take that hay and put it in her feeder on the fence."

Dylan tried to tip toe to the top of the feeder to put the hay where Cowboy pointed. Cowboy made his way to the next stall watching Dylan wrestle around and try to get the hay in. Cowboy had a rule that he never helped anyone unless they asked so he just watched and admired the boy's tenacity. It took Dylan a little bit but finally he held the hay in one arm up close to his head and climbed the fence to the stall with the other, one rung at a time when he reached to the top he lofted the hay towards the feeder and much to Cowboys surprise he made most of it in. Cowboy laughed at the determination of the young boy but did not want him to get a big head.

"Ok now go to the barrel over there and grab one scoop of feed out it and dump it in the bottom of that same feeder."

Dylan ran to the barrel and did as he was told. When he was done, he asked Cowboy "Why do you feed them hay and this stuff?"

"Well they are big critters. You don't like to eat the same thing all the time, do you?"

"No"

"That is why we feed them both"

"OH OK"

Cowboy reminisced the past when Brat was that big and all the fun, he had with him teaching him how to do things. He also remembered all the jokes and pranks they played on him. Cowboy realized he missed having someone little, looking up to him both physically and as a role model. It brought back a sense of pride he had not felt in a while and did not even realize he missed until he could see the sense of accomplishment in Dylan's eyes

They continued to feed all the horses in the barn. Cowboy showed him all the horses and explained to him which horse belonged to who and what horses he could pet and play with and what horse's not to mess with.

After they finished feeding the horses Dylan looked at him and said, "all the other guys have a horse which one is mine?"

"Well I tell you what. You help me out around here and make a good hand for me and I will make sure you have a horse."

"My own horse? Cool!!!"

"Hey but you have to work for it I am not gonna just give you a horse. That means get up early and get to work no layin' in bed or video games"

"I can do that"

"OK well I am gonna hold you to that come on let's go inside and see what your mean old mother is up too."

They walked across the drive and through the yard to the 2-story house. Dylan ran inside and started talking really loud and fast to his mother about the barn feeding the horses and that Cowboy was going to give him a horse.

Cowboy said "now wait a minute I did not say I was giving you a horse? What was the deal?"

"Oh, yea I am going to work for the horse I have to feed, get up early, no TV or video games and I have to work! So, get me up early!"

Jessica laughed at his excitement and said "Well OK I will do that. Why don't you go outside and play but don't go too far dinner will be done in a little bit?"

Dylan ran back outside the screen door slammed behind him and the pitter patter of his feet could be heard across the floor until he jumped off the porch

Then came the look from Jessica to Kim. "Why did you tell him you were gonna give him a horse?"

"I am not giving him one he is going to work for it. Were you not listening to him?"

"Still what am I gonna do with a horse in the city?"

"Well he can leave him here that way you have a reason to come back after all the dust settles"

"You are a conniving old man aren't you"

"Unless you don't think you want to come back."

She extended her arms toward him and fell gently to his chest, then wrapped her arms around him. "You are too good"

"No, I am just me. He is a good boy and if he works which I am sure he will then he deserves a horse."

She pulled back a little to look at him but not to break the embrace and said softly whispered "where have you been?"

He continued to hold her and not let her go as he leaned down gently kissed her on top of her head. "I have been here all my life."

Her eyes glimmered with joy and they just held one another to seize the moment. After a few seconds she pulled back away and caressed his chest with one hand and patted him lightly then said" I better get back to the kitchen and you need to go make sure my boy is not getting into something he is not supposed to"

He stood up tall and said" There aint nothing around here he can break that we can't fix."

The 2 of them parted ways Cowboy went back to his work outside and she returned to the house chores and tending to the baby. She made her way inside to see Cassie playing with the little girl on the floor. Cassie loved playing with her babies in her room and to have a real baby to play with she was in heaven. Jessy watched them for a second and then she intervened to check the baby's diaper. "I guess we need to get you some dry pants on, so you don't get a rash." Cassie immediately asked if she could do it, so Jessica allowed her to change the girl while she supervised and much to her surprise, she did a very good job. When she finished, she took the wet one to the trash and sat down by her mom and LG "look mom she wants me"

"Well I guess she does. I think that is the first time she has done that. Let's put her on her back and see if she will do it again"

They rolled her over on her back and sure enough she flipped back on to her belly. "Well I guess she is pretty smart and has that figured out." Jessica said.

Cassie was giggling and said "let's see if she can walk now"

"I think we should let her learn that on her own we don't want to rush her" her mom replied.

It was nice to be out there with Dylan outside and Cassie entertained by the baby. Jessica felt like she was on vacation no kids fighting or running through the house she was in heaven. She asked Cassie to baby sit for her while she went to take a bath and relax but, if she needed her to come get her.

Cassie was tickled pink to have the responsibility of watching what had now became her baby. So, her mother milled around the house and found some candles and went to the bathroom to relax in the tub she left the door cracked so she could hear but no one could see in. With lighted candles and her bath wash used to make bubbles she lay in the big cast iron, claw footed tub and drifted away to her perfect world. She sat there for a few minutes and she heard the door open and footsteps walking through the house.

Cowboy asked Cassie where her mother was, and Jessica heard him, so she said, "I am in here." He made his way to the door of the bathroom and pushed it the rest of the way open much to her surprise. You could see she was startled and embarrassed so she sank in the tub hoping the bubbles would cover her body and threw a wash cloth at Kim "What are you doing" Stammering and shielding his eyes Kim stuttered " I – I – well you said you were in here"

"I did not say come in here"

Kim peeked between his fingers toward her "Well you can see where I got confused. "As he was sneaking a peek her direction." You do know that door has a lock on it. Most people use it unless you wanted me to come in and you are just acting" as he took his hand from his face he saw her sitting in the tub and the bubble covered her female anatomy but he could still see a little cleavage and he smiled real big she was embarrassed and a somewhat elated.

So, she threw towel at him and smiled back with a playful voice she told him "get out, old pervert" as she smiled. "Remember we are taking it slow."

He turned and walked out shutting the door behind him and talking through the door. "That was mean Jessy, and this is how you shut the door. Now hurry up so we can go."

She talked back through the door as he heard her stand up in the tub "where are we going?"

"Don't worry about it and don't catch my house on fire with them dam candles. I would hate to have to carry you out of my house naked if it caught on fire. I guess it is OK I done seen you naked now the new has worn off already" as he laughed.

"You did not I was under the bubbles"

"Well can I come in and see you now?" snickering

She had already put her shorts and shirt on but that was it and he did not know she had already gotten dressed.

She said "oh what the heck you have already seen me so sure come on in as she flung open the door knowing he was right there. He turned his head not to look and she pranced right by him in boxers and a tee shirt.

"You like what you see?"

He opened his eyes and said "I sure do"

She sexily turned her wet head to him with no makeup and very little on she, smiled and said "I think you really like it. Now, where are we going anyway?"

"To find Brat and Cross on the 4-wheeler."

"I better not I have to help Cassie watch her baby and make dinner for you boys why don't you take Dylan"

"Oh, yea the baby I almost forgot about her. Well alright but you are gonna miss out on all the fun."

She turned away and strolled into the kitchen. He turned around and walked thru the door.

Cowboy yelled out for Dylan. He came running around the corner of the house. Cowboy asked him if he wanted to go find Cross and Brat with him. He gladly accepted the offer

They made their way to the shed behind the house to get the 4-wheeler.

Dylan could not wait to see the 4-wheeler. Cowboy got on and fired it off and looked at Dylan. "Hop on" then he tore out of the shed with a cloud of dust Jessica standing on the front porch saw the two leave and thought to herself dear lord I hope he is careful. She could see them going thru the field by the barn Dylan bouncing off the seat with a death grip on Cowboys shirt and she could hear Cowboy yell out "Hold on" and Dylan just laughing and giggling. They road up the hilltop, where I had taken Jessica a few night ago. To look for me and Bratton. After a little harassment going up the hill from Cowboy, Dylan looked over the property speechless. Cowboy looked to him and said "aint that something?"

Dylan just nodded and looked across the horizon with bewilderment. Cowboy spotted the two of us in the distance and instructed Dylan to mount up so they could help them out before dinner.

They road for about 5 minutes and came across the two of us mending the fence on what was called the south 40 because, it was the 40-acre field furthest south and admittedly by Cowboy because it sounded kind of cool. When Cowboy rode up with Dylan on the back the Me and Bratt started what they called dogging on him.

"Glad you could make it during the last 10 minutes of work. We would not want you to overdo it old man.

Cowboy got off the 4-wheeler Dylan followed closely. Cowboy introduced Dylan to Bratton and started to introduce him to me when Dylan interrupted him and said "I know who he is" as he grabbed Cowboy's pant leg and pulled him close in a shy way. "He is Wyatt Earp I have seen him on TV" Cowboy and Bratton snickered a little while managing to agree with the young boy. I looked really serious at the boy and said, "son no one has called me that in years and you don't need to be calling me that either I go by Cross now." Then I turned to Cowboy and said "what did you tell him for? Now I gotta move everyone is gonna know I live here thanks a lot."

"Ah come on now Cross he won't say nothing I am sure. He works for us now" I looked at the boy and said "promise you won't say anything"

Dylan looked at him with fearful eyes "ye ye yes sir I I I prrromise I work for you my lips are sealed" he eased behind Cowboy scared to death and waited for me to quit staring him down with a scowl on my face.

I waited a second and said "alright I guess but not a word to any one you understand? We got a deal?" as I extended my hand to the boy for a handshake. Dylan reached toward me and put his hand in mine. Dylan's fingers could not even grip the old callused hand but when he shook my hand I fell to my knees and hollered out in pain "OUCH easy there muscles I am old don't squeeze so hard" The young boy giggled at the joke and I snatched him off the ground and ran to the 4 wheeler " come on let's get some supper they can clean up"

Cowboy had a good feeling about this before he had gotten home the kids had already brought back some good memories to him and he could tell that little boy was gonna do the same for Cross.

Cowboy and Brat Loaded up the tools and followed the cloud for red dust, left by Dylan and me, back to the house.

When Dylan came back with me, Jessica and Cassie were on the porch looking at a magazine, waiting on us to return. Jessica Asked Dylan "Who is this? That is not who I sent you off with."

Dylan smiled and said "You know who this is. This is Wy "and I cleared my throat

Dylan realizing, he was not to let anyone know my real identity and covered it up by saying "Why we went out on the 4-wheeler to find Mr. Cross and Cowboy's son Bratton."

I smiled and nodded my head in approval. Dylan looked at me, smiled and nodded back, as if they were reading one another's minds telepathically.

"Come on here Muscles let's get washed up and fix some dinner"

Jessica looked up from the magazine and said "I think you two are gonna be trouble but no need to cook I already made dinner. We were just waiting for you boys to quit playing around and get up here so we could eat."

"Well I am glad you cooked it has got to be better than Cowboy's cookin'"

We walked up the steps and into the house. Not long after we went inside the other 2 drove up in the farm truck (a truck Cowboy's dad had bought years ago and it never left the farm after he got it home) "Hey Jess I see you made it back in one piece." Bratton yelled out.

"Hello Brat, how was your day?

"It was long but good who is that pretty girl you got there with you?" he asked as he made his way to the porch.

"This is my little girl Cassie"

"Well she sure is pretty you know I don't have a girlfriend right now you think maybe she would be my girlfriend?"

Cassie grabbed her mom's shirt sleeve and pulled her down close to whisper in her hear because she was embarrassed "OMG mom he is just as cute as you said"

Bratton could hear everything she said, and he acted like he was embarrassed by her comment and shyly walked into the house.

Jessica said "Well hello stranger" to Kim as he approached the porch "did you work up an appetite? In your 5 minutes of work" as she smiled his direction and arose from the swing to meet him at the door "I will go warm everything up I hope you like it"

"I am sure I will as long as it isn't dog food" he said with a smirk

"Well I guess you will have to find out for yourself."

Chapter 10

DINNER RULES

The boys all washed up and made their way to the kitchen. The table was made and as they entered Jessica asked everyone to have a seat. Kim noticed there were only 4 chairs and 6 plates. Jessica quickly remarked "the kids can eat on the porch I am sure they won't mind."

Kim would not hear of it he went through the house and managed to round up something for the kids to sit on. He found an old chair his mother used to put her makeup on from upstairs and another from the desk they paid bills from. He returned to the kitchen carrying the 2 chairs and immediately said "I guess I need to go and get some chairs and a table so we will all sit and eat together."

Jessica said, "you don't have to do that we will manage without them."

"Nope in my house we all eat together like it or not. Mad, sad or happy we sit and eat and no TV. Those are the rules. We will run to town and see what we can find."

"you sure are getting real good at getting out of work these last few days" I piped off "I may go find me a lady friend to go shop with tomorrow."

Kim jumped right back and asked me if I need the keys to his truck to go pick her up in a joking tone.

I muttered "we get more done without you any way" under my breath without even looking up.

We bantered back and forth a bit and added a playful mood to the table. Everyone ate and talked and laughed about the event and then Dylan and I began planning our day out while Kim, Jessica, and Bratton all aggravated Cassie about having a crush on Bratton.

When dinner was finished Jessica got the kids ready for bed. The men began clearing the table and cleaning up in the kitchen aggravating one another like bunch of middle school boys. Jessica returned to the Kitchen with a sassy tone telling everyone to settle down the kids were going to sleep so we retired to the front porch like we did almost every night. Bratt sat on the hand rail away from the cigar smoke, I would sit in the old rocking chair because they called me the old man and it just fit me, while Kim sat alone on the swing like he normally did smoking a cigar and drinking a beer. That is until Jessica made her way out. He immediately snuffed the cigar out and began complaining about it tasting cheap to cover his actions in front of us. She smiled in appreciation for him putting it out and sat beside him. Me and Bratt had started noticing the 2 of them were already getting close and were not really trying to hide it anymore like the past weekend. She cuddled up to him on the swing pulling her feet up beside her and resting her head on his shoulder "Burr it is chilly out her" she said.

Kim got up and grabbed an Indian blanket from the couch and handed it to her to cover up with.

She said "you did not have to do that I would have been fine"

"I need to go check on the barn" as he moseyed down the porch toward the barn.

"Did I do something wrong? "Jess asked

"No, you didn't he checks the barn every night me and Bratt don't do a good enough job cuz he checks it every night."

"Oh, I thought I did something"

"No that is just him not to say you haven't done anything cuz he sure is acting different"

"Why do you say that? He has been fun to be around. The kids love him"

"That is what we are talking about. He has been in a good mood since you've been around"

"I can't tell you when the last time he was in this good a mood for this long. But don't tell him that we don't want to jinx it." I told her with a jovial smile.

Bratt was quick to tell her "We like having you around so just keep doing whatever it is you are doing. Unless we can trade you for him, you need to hang around as long as you can. Maybe you can buckle him in the car again" he said with a wink

I spit beer all over the porch and she screamed out "Bratton Lee you know I was not doing that" as she smiled with embarrassment "I was helping him move the seat back in that stupid car."

"I don't need to know. You just keep moving his seat back or whatever it is you've been doing" Laughing as he said it.

"I cannot believe you said that you are awful" as they all laughed about it.

I could not believe Bratton had said that, but I knew there was nothing to stop what he was thinking from come out of his mouth. They often said he had diarrhea of the mouth

Kim returned shortly after they calmed down and said, "what was all the noise about?"

We all just shook their heads and said "nothing Bratton was being retarded"

Kim did not question what he did because he knew the boy was not right in the head and always did goofy stuff just to make people laugh. He said, "I am going to retire ya'll have a good night" and went inside I followed his lead and made my way to the bunk house. Bratt and Jess sat on the porch talking she inquired about Kim and his past but Bratt was not much help then she started asking about Susan and wanted to know if he had talked to her about the baby

Bratt just shook his head "I have been thinking about that a lot I just don't know what to say. Do I just blurt it out or him haw around? What do you say?"

"Well you could start by saying hello to her and asking how she has been or how things are going in Odessa."

"It is hard for me to just talk to her on the phone. She and I were real close and well before she left, I guess you know what happened. I am really surprised when dad found out that day, he did not flip his lid. She is like family, like a daughter to him and my best friend and I don't want all that to change but we can't reverse what happened"

"No, you can't all you can do is work around it and either embrace it or get past it. Do you regret being with her?"

"No not at all she was my best friend. She is what I want in a woman to settle down with. I don't want to be old and single I want to have someone to come home to but, as you know I don't have a very good role model for that."

"Oh, now sure you do you just have not seen that side yet. He just has not met the right woman"

"I hope he does. He needs to wind down and take it easy for a while."

"Maybe he will I know he has mentioned it to me. Maybe this baby is just what you 2 need to bring back what is important that you have been overlooking. Have you been thinking about you and Susan much lately?"

"Every day since she moved but more so now. I can't help but think I screwed up her life and if I did, I don't know what I would do because aside from Dad and Cross she is the only one who really knows me."

"Why don't you call her? See what she is doing. Then go see her in Odessa or meet her ½ way and you will be able to tell when you see her or at least have a better idea of whether or not it was her."

"Yea I could do that I am not that good on the phone I would rather see her in person. It has been a while since I have seen her. I may do that. Thanks Jess, I appreciate the help. It is hard to listen to advice on stuff like this around here, about sensitive stuff like this. This would've been a good time for a mom to be around."

"Anytime you need to talk I am here whether you have to call me, or I am here I will help you."

"Well I better get to bed I got school tomorrow Thanks again it is nice having you here and I was just teasing you earlier"

"I know you were I am sure it looked really funny from your point of view it is OK, but I will return the favor now get to bed."

Bratt made his way to his bed and she sat on the porch for a minute or two thinking about everything going on with the baby. Her mind kept going back to these men sure need a woman around here to help them out. She never pictured herself has a housewife or stay at home mom before because she never was given a chance with all the dead beats she had dated.

The one she actually married, she always had to work. The longer she was on that property the more she liked the idea. Having the heart to heart talk with Bratt made her want that even more. Again, her brain was getting way too far ahead of her life she was pushing for something that might not even be an option. She coaxed herself back to the real world and went in the house. Kim lay on the couch asleep snoring lightly. She went to the room to change and get ready for bed and came back into the living room to get Kim off the couch so he would not wake up stiff in the morning. "Kim" she whispered several time in his hear as she lightly shook him by his shoulder. He opened his eyes ever so lightly and muttered something she did not understand. She whispered "you need to get off the couch, so you are not stiff tomorrow"

He then mumbled "you sleep in my bed and I will sleep here I will be fine"

"I will sleep on the couch you go ahead to bed"

"No go ahead"

"OK we will both go to the bed like at my house we are both adults it will be fine"

She finally convinced him to get up and she walked him to the bedroom and sat him down on the bed. He was still in a daze, so she pulled his boots off and said, "I am going to brush my teeth you get your clothes off and finish getting ready for bed."

That got him out of his haze because he perked up "I like the way that sounds"

"You stop that and get in bed"

"I like being told what to do" he said with a smile

"Stop it" as she walked out snickering

She came back to the room and he was in bed almost back to sleep she crawled under the blankets and lay there a second. He moved his arm under her head and pulled her toward him "I slept better with you laying on me the other night". She did not fight him because she slept great as well. It was nice for the 2 of them to have someone by their side at night with no pressure but the tension continued to build between them and everyone on the property could see it.

Chapter 11

TOO SOON TO LET GO

The week went by too fast to keep track. Bratton had decided to take a road trip to Odessa to talk with Susan like Jessica had suggested. He told his dad what he had planned and headed west for the weekend. He called Susan to tell her he was coming out and made up a lie about meeting with a college that weekend. Her family insisted that he stay at the house with them while he was down. Bratton left shortly after school. He took just enough time to go home grab his bag and a little surprise he had picked up for Susan during the week. He had learned from his dad to never go see a woman empty handed. He figured he would grab a bouquet of flowers when he got there for her mother so she would not feel left out. The whole trip Bratton could not decide if he was more excited or nervous about seeing her again and if her father knew what had happened. If her dad knew he would have already come back. Her father was described by most people in town as a corn fed rough neck he was not a small man, definitely not a man you wanted to cross but, a good man who would give the shirt off his back to a friend. Bratton's mind raced and he thought back to the short call he and Susan had, he dissected every word of it in his head to see if he missed a hint or something that was said to let him know she was the mother. Nothing was said she acted fine but he was still unsure of what to say when he saw her and if she was not the mother, he did not know if he should tell her or what she would think if he did tell her.

Thinking about the whole situation made the 4-hour trip go by like a trip to town. He made it to their house around 7:30 that night. He wandered his way up the winding sidewalk with his bag over his shoulder. The walk to the front door seemed to take longer than the drive to Odessa. Just before he made it to the steps of the house, the door flung open and Susan ran and jumped on him and held on. The two fell to the ground and tussled about like kids in a pile of fallen leaves. When she finally gave up trying to pin him to the ground, he lay beside her on the front lawn and the two of them gazed up to the heavens. The night was clear, and the stars were almost close enough to grab. Susan looked to Bratton and said "God I have missed you"

Bratton lay silent for a second and told her he missed her being around too.

Susan told him she missed him more than peaches and he told her he missed her more than the rain in the dead of summer. They bantered back and forth like they always did to see who could come up with the lamest line. Susan told him she would give all the oil in the world to be next door to him again; her tone was much more serious. Bratton lightly said if he could catch a falling star, he would throw it back in the heavens to have her back home with him. The conversation was taking a turn to the serious side. They lay there of several minutes in silence. Susan rolled over on her side with her head resting on his shoulder and said "I really miss looking up at the stars from old baldy with you. I just miss you."

"I miss you too" he added

Her mom came to the door and loudly cleared her throat and told the two of them to get inside and get ready for dinner.

"Come on Brat I'll show you to your room"

Bratton stood to his feet, "That would be good I was getting a little teary eyed with all your sappy talk."

"Me too "she claimed sarcastically

They made their way through a maze of a house and outside to the pool house. "Where are you taking me? Do I have to sleep in the barn?"

"Well you know my dad. He is not going to let you sleep in my room anymore"

Bratton stopped dead in his tracks and startled by what she had said "No not that God no he does not know. No one knows about that but you and me, right?"

He hesitated for a moment," Well"

"OMG you told your dad?"

"No No hell no he would kill me and then drag me behind the truck all the way to your dad so he could kill me no he doesn't know"

"Well who knows? Did you tell Case?"

"No not Case either"

"Then who??

"Well it was Jessica?" Before he could finish explaining she interrupted "Who the hell is that and why tell her stuff like that...."

"Hold on hold on wait just a minute let me explain"

"Oh, you are going to explain go ahead" as she crossed her arms and patted her foot impatiently "Explain"

"Well it is complicated"

"Is she your girlfriend? Who is she? Is she pregnant?"

When she said that, he looked at her funny. "You got a girl pregnant? You are really something I cannot believe I saved myself for you. You are pig I hate you?"

"No wait just a minute I did not get her pregnant and she is not my girlfriend she is kind of dads girlfriend but not really. I promise I will explain it all after dinner let's just go to the room so we can get back and eat."

"You swear to me you are not dating this girl?"

"I promise and you did not get anyone knocked up?"

"Let's go and I can explain it later" as he started walking away trying to find a way out of this conversation without lying to her. He never was good at telling lies to her he had tried, and he would end up laughing or smiling and telling her the truth.

"Bratton Wayne Lee you got someone knocked up?"

"No, she is not knocked up I told you she is kind of with dad"

"OK but you better tell me everything after dinner."

Bratton set his bags inside the door of the pool house and the 2 of them made their way to the dining room. When they got in the house they zig zagged their way throughout the house he noticed the pictures that adorned the walls were mainly of him and Susan growing up through the years at picnics, bar-b-ques, and other social events they had attended together over the years. He never realized that growing up how much time they had spent together. Aside from social events they were together every day of every summer. She had always been there for him and he was always there for her. Now he was second guessing telling her the truth about the baby.

They all sat down to eat and caught up on the local gossip. Then the conversation turned to the ranch and how things were going around the house. Susan's mom asked how Cowboy was and Susan was quick to chime in "oh he has a girlfriend"

"Oh really" he has "A girlfriend? Just one?"

"Yes, her name is Jessica, she and Bratton are real close." And looked at him with an I need answers look

"Well it is a little more complicated than that but he has settled down somewhat in the past month or so and Jessica has been over there quite a bit this month so who knows???"

He maneuvered around the rest of the question and diverted the conversation to other topics like where Susan's dad was and how they liked living in Odessa. Both the ladies said Odessa was OK, but they would prefer to be back in their hometown. They sat for an hour or so at dinner and then Mom got up and started cleaning the table off. Susan got up and helped her; then told her mother that she and Bratton were going to run around town. Her mother gave her approval and told them to be back before midnight. They agreed and they made their way out the front door to head out for the night. They no sooner got to the car when Susan said "Ok let's hear it I want to know what is going on"

Bratton began to tell the story about finding the baby on the porch and how they took her to the hospital. Susan just sat and stared in disbelief of the whole situation. Then he got to the part of how Jessica had come out to help with the baby and Kim talked her in to staying a little longer and even invited her kids to come out and stay. Susan did not know what sounded more like a lie the part about the baby or the part about Cowboy latching on to some strange woman he had just met.

As Bratton finished the story, he told her he had come to Odessa to see her and make sure it was not her. He tried to explain that he knew she would never do something like that, but he really hoped that if the baby was his that she was the mother. He continued that he was not with anyone other than her for about a 2-month period after she left. They say the baby was conceived during that time so, he was feeling better about the child not belonging to him.

When the story came to an end and he finished talking Susan sat in silence not knowing what to say, feeling a little betrayed, Shocked and empathetic to the situation. "What are you going to do?"

"Well knowing that it is not yours really makes me feel better about the whole deal cuz I don't think I am the father now at least I hope I am not"

"How do you know I am not the mother? And if I was or am what will you do about it?"

Bratton turned toward her and looked her square in the eyes" Susan we both know it is not you. If it was this would be so much easier."

"How do you know it is not me?"

"Look at you!! There is no way a body like yours spit out a baby less than 6 months ago."

She smiled showing her dimples on her cheek and blushing ever so lightly. "What do you mean it would make it easier if it was mine?"

"I don't know it is just you….. Well you know you are you, and I know everything about you. I can live with you but someone else?? I don't know I just know everything comes easy, when I do it with you."

"Well what are you going to do? What if it is yours?"

"I am almost certain she is not mine because I have not been with anyone since you left."

"Now I know you are lying Bratton Lee. I know you better than that."

"No, I am serious I haven't I swear it."

"Why? I know how you are you can't go 7 months without. Remember I am or at least was your best friend."

"You still are but after you left, I just could not find anyone that I even liked to hang around. There were a few dates here and there and I just ended up comparing them to you and they never added up."

"AHH!! You are so sweet. What are you telling me that you think of me as your girlfriend? Well if you believe it or not you are still the only guy I have been with and I don't have plans of being with anyone else. I really have missed you. With you being so far away I wake up every morning and think I am forgetting something. I don't have you beating down my door rushing me to get to school or dropping me off just before I go to bed at the house. It is really kind of lonely here without you."

"I know what you mean I feel the same way. Have you thought about college anymore?"

"Yea I thought about it, but I am not real sure where I am going. I think I want to be a teacher or a nurse but not real sure."

"I guess I am going to Tarleton if they give me an offer worth taking or maybe TCU somewhere close in case Dad or Cross need me, I won't be far."

"Wow!! What has gotten into you? You have always said you were going to get away from all that. Why all the changes?"

"I am not sure I think LG has something to do with it. I have seen a different side of dad lately and being there has actually gotten a lot better with her, Jessica and the kids being there. I think it has been good for all of us."

"Wait a minute you said Jessica's kids... She has kids and they live there?"

"Yea! She has a boy who is 8 and a little girl who is 6 they are good kids. Cross has taken a liking to her boy Dylan and Cassie she thinks I hung the moon. Dad, he aint drinking as much and he has been smiling a lot here lately. I kind of like seeing the old man that way. They are just there for spring break not living there. At least not yet."

"Well sounds like I may have to meet this girl and your newfound family. To think just a few weeks ago that place was 3 bachelors and livestock. Now it is 3 men a girl and 3 kids. I hope ya'll cleaned the house. Where do they all sleep?"

"You will love this. We cleaned out the whole upstairs and got a new mattress for the bed. All of Oma and pops stuff got boxed up and moved to the shed finally."

"You are kidding me. Your dad let you do that finally?"

"I am not done. He told us to do it. You remember how the shrubs looked when Oma was a round?"

"Yes, and her garden was always so pretty."

"Well Jessica cleaned out the shrubs and trimmed them out. Then she planted the garden, and everything is growing. It looks like it did back then."

"Wow. She must be a keeper. Well you think your dad will finally settle down?"

"I am not sure this is uncharted territory for us, but it looks like he might actually like this one."

"I need to come home and see what is going on to see if I approve of this girl. We are on spring Break next week I will see if I can come out."

"That would be great we are going to need some help getting everything ready for the Historical Site Dedication. You think your dad will let you?"

"I am sure they will."

"If they let you, I could take you back with me and then when they come to the Bar-b-que they can take you back if you want."

"I guess we can ask. It is getting late we should head back so you can make it to your meeting tomorrow."

"Oh, yea about that. I don't really have a meeting tomorrow I kind of lied about that to come see you."

"I know that, but mom and dad don't."

"Well I am not going to lie to them. I feel bad. Do you think we should tell your mom about LG?"

"What is LG?"

"That is what we call her. It stands for little Girl. She is cute as a button. You will love her."

"I think we might tell mom about her, but we will leave out the part about her possibly being yours and just say she was left on your steps."

"Ok but you will have to do the talking. Mom knows when I am not telling the truth."

The two of them made their way back to the house and by that time her dad had made it home. "I see JT has made it home, how is he?"

"My dad James Talon is fine. Don't you dare call him JT especially when he worked this late."

"I won't. I only say that when we are jacking around with one another."

"You better not! Come on let's get inside and see what they say." She leaped from the small car and trotted to the door as Bratton rolled out of the match box car and slowly got up off his knees. "Come on slow poke. Are you sore from me kicking your butt earlier? You are out of shape."

"No, I am just sore from the long drive out here. I am coming go ahead and go in I am right behind you"

She opened the door and went in leaving the door open as she entered, she went to the kitchen to get a drink and her dad was eating in the living room watching TV. "What did you do with Bratt" he hollered out to her

"He is coming he had trouble getting out of my match box car as he calls it. Plus, I beat him up when he got here just so he would remember who is boss."

"She did no such thing I let her win just like I always do."

James turned his head toward the door" Hey Brat. How the hell are ya son?" As he stood to his feet, he placed his plate on the end table and extended his right hand towards Bratton who was walking toward him. Bratton stuck his hand out and the two grasped hands and James pulled him to him and gave Bratton a one arm hug. "It is good to see you. How is your dad?"

"He is good trying to get the place cleaned up for the big party next weekend"

"Oh, that is right. Next weekend I gotta make sure and get someone to cover my area so I make it out there. We have all been looking forward to getting back over there and seeing home again?

"Well you sure have a nice home here"

"Yea it is nice, but it is not really home. We will get back out there eventually but for now this will do."

"Well if you are going to rough it. This is the way to do it. It really is pretty. I appreciate you letting me stay here."

"You don't even have to ask. You are family to us."

"Glad to hear that, we all think of ya'll as family also."

James shook his head in approval and looked up the stairwell and hollered out "Stephanie the kids are back come on down here and we will play some cards."

"I will be right down I am almost done cleaning up here."

"While she is cleaning up, I will run take a shower. You boys don't break nothing down here unsupervised" Susan said as she skipped her way down the hall to her room.

James sat back down to finish his supper. "You need a drink or anything there is the kitchen just help yourself. This place aint any different than the other one."

"Thanks, I think I will get me a drink". As he walks toward the kitchen. "How is work going? Obviously, they are keeping you busy."

"It is killing me we run from sunup and sundown and can't find any good help. You know after you graduate if you don't go to school, I can get you on here. It is tough but it pays good."

"I will keep that in mind, but I am still planning on going to school somewhere close to home."

"Well I would rather you go to school, so you don't have to break your back like your daddy and me your whole life."

Bratton made his way into the living room and sat on the sofa. The 2 of them stared at the TV for a few minutes as James flipped through the channels to find something worth watching. Before Bratton said, "looks like there aint much on the tube."

"No nothing on the dam thing. I pay 100 dollars a month to get nothing worth watching crazy aint it. Why don't we go outside and sit by the pool?"

"Sounds good to me I'd rather be outside any way. I am not used to all this A/C"

"Ya'll still don't have A/C, I guess. I don't know how you do it"

"If you never had it you never miss it. It really aint all that bad, the trees shade the house and at night we just leave the windows open."

"I remember those days, but I sure like my A/C"

They strolled to the back yard and sat at the table by the pool. James leaned over and turned on the pool lights and the waterfall from the hot tub to the pool. "Ha-ha how you like that?" He replied

"That is nice. I like it."

"Well what is on your mind? You sure are awful quite."

"I have been meaning to talk to you about something. So, I will just come out and say it. Would you be opposed to me and Susan Dating?"

Her dad chuckled lightly and said, "son what have ya'll been doing the last 18 years?"

"No, I mean really dating?"

"I don't have a problem with it, and I am sure I won't have a problem with you but, I am going to tell you just like I would anyone else. That is my little girl and if you hurt her in any way, I will hurt you. If they find you, you will be laid up in a hospital with plenty of time to think of what you done wrong."

"Yes sir. I understand but you know I would never hurt her. And I guess the real question I wanted to ask is could I have her hand in marriage?"

"Whoa now wait a minute son. Do you know what you are asking me?"

"Yes, sir I do."

"You two are awfully young. Are you sure you want that?"

"Yes, I know all that but ya'll have been gone for 8 months and I still have not stopped thinking about her. She and I have always been together, and it just is not right without her with me. I am not saying we get married right away. I don't even know how I will ask her. I am not even sure she will say yes but I do know I love her"

"Well I am sure she will say yes but I don't want this to be a big mistake. I know you two are inseparable but, you need to think about what you are saying. Bratton you are the closest thing I have to a son and she is my only girl and I know your daddy and Cross feel the same about her. I would love nothing more than to have you for a son in law but, think about everyone else before you jump into getting married. What if it doesn't work? What if she says no? It will put a strain on more than the 2 of you. You have my blessing, but I really wish you would think long and hard on it before you go and propose to her."

"Yes, sir I will. Please don't tell anyone about this no one not even dad knows about this and I would like to keep it between you and I until I pop the question if I do but, I will think long and hard on it first."

"Sounds good let get some cards and play, so I can kick your but again like old time."

"Easy their JT. We all know I let you win cuz you was all down and out about moving and I did not want to put any strain on your old heart."

"OHH is that right" as he stood to his feet towering across the table towards Bratton.

"Sit down there big fellow, you don't want to get hurt," standing to his feet.

Then James lunged toward him like he was going to dump the table on him. Bratton grasped the table and they tugged it around laughing at one another and taking verbal shots back and forth. James went to pull the table from Bratton about the same time Bratton let go of it. James stumbled back several steps and almost went into the pool before falling on the table and bending the legs under. Bratton saw him getting up and while laughing at him he said "I guess that table is not rated to hold an elephant"

"Come here you scrawny little punk" running towards him.

For an older man as big as he was, he sure could move around pretty good. By the time the girls had finished taking a shower, finished their chores and they realized the men were outside wrestling on the ground like a couple elementary school kids. Immediately after walking outside Susan saw the table legs bent and mangled from her dad falling on them "I could have sworn I told you to not to tear anything up."

Her dad quick wittedly replied "You said inside, and this is outside" as he held Bratton in a head lock.

Bratton gasping for air add his confirmation "you did say try not to break anything in here while I am gone"".

James released the death grip on Bratton and patted him on the back "yep the old man still has it. Don't cross me boy I will rip you a part" as he stood to his feet extending his hand to help him up. It was not unusual for the 2 to wrestle around or rough house. Bratton was truly like a son to their family and James loved to have him around to do guy stuff with. "Sorry you girls had to see me humiliate him again. I am just trying to teach him a few things so maybe he can at least beat up a girl one day. Hopefully"

Bratton grabbed the helping hand and rose to his feet "yep maybe one day I will beat up a girl" he laughed and pointed to Susan "it just maybe you"

Susan's mom Stephanie standing with cards in her hand and a drink in the other told the men you had better get this cleaned up." I guess we will be playing cards in the house since the table is BROKEN"

"It aint broken Momma it is fine" as James turned the table back over and attempted to bend the legs back around to resemble table legs again. "See it is fine" as he leaned on the table it rocked to one side almost collapsing again. He quickly grabbed a flat rock from the water fall and crammed it under the shorter leg. "Like new," smiling trying to convince her.

"Like new my butt" Stephanie joked "like new is what you will be going and buying me in the morning. How do you like them apples?"

Knowing it was not an option James conceded and just replied "ok I will get you a new one tomorrow."

"No, I will go buy it you can pick it up"

"Wait a minute why can't I buy it?"

"Because you will buy the cheapest thing you can find, and I want something nice. Your little wrestling/testosterone display is gonna cost you"

"Well I think Bratton should have to foot ½ the bill he started it."

"WHAT?? I did no such thing mom he started it you know I would never do that. Besides it was the GREAT WHITE BUFFALO who fell on it not me."

"OHH that was good Brat I gotta hand it to you. I will get you for that" and it started again. But Mom quickly settled them down and made them be civil so they could play cards. She even went as far as making them play on the same team.

Chapter 12

PARENTAL MANIPULATION

During the game the girls continually accused the men of cheating and they were blatant about the mischief but he girls had been doing there fair share as well and the boys knew better than to bring up any accusations because the women would deny any wrong doings . During the game Susan brought up the subject of going to the Bar b Que. Bratton quickly admitted that there was still much work needing to be performed around the place and more especially the house, trying to make it her parents' idea to send Susan to help out. Mom was the first to mention that she and Susan could go down this week, with her being on spring break, to help out. Until she recalled a meeting she had to attend in the middle of the week. Susan respond rapidly "I could go help out and just ride back with Bratton. Then when ya'll come I can ride home with you"

"Well I don't have an issue with that since you are out of school this week"

James sat back and listened to the whole thing develop. After the conversation he and Bratton had earlier he had a funny feeling this had been pre-planned. James grumbled lightly about the situation stating" I am not sure I like that idea"

"Daddy please? It will be fine"

"Well you staying there when you were younger was different now you are both growing up it worries me a bit" as he stared down Bratton.

"Sir you have nothing to worry about. I will be at school and you know my dad he doesn't let me in the house until after dark and I am dog tired. Plus, he will be there the whole time. I give you my word no funny business"

"I still don't know let me think about this I am not real crazy about it."

"Daddy it is just Brat. We are like brother and sister we are family."

"Yea you are, and I don't want no inbred kids"

"James Talon" mom hollered out "you watch your mouth".

"I guess it is OK with me so long as you two are in different rooms and I am gonna call Kim to make sure you ain't left alone. So, it is up to your mother."

"It will be fine" mom replied

Susan jumped up from the table and wrapped her arms around her Dad " Thank you Daddy" a phrase that she knew he could not say no to "I promise no funny business with my brother" she proclaimed laughing as she made her way into the house to pack.

"You better not mess with her or we will be having a funeral at the Bar-B-Que."

"Yes, sir you have my word nothing will happen."

"I trust you"

"Come on let's get in bed"

James went into the house and Bratton made his way to the pool house to settle in for the night. He jumped in the shower and was getting ready for bed when he heard knocking at the door. He threw on a pair of shorts and an under shirt to see who it was. Susan stood in the doorway with a huge smile. "We make a pretty good team. We did not even have to ask. I am so excited." As she tried to make her way in the pool house Bratton stood in the doorway to blocker her from coming in. Susan looked at him puzzled "what are you doing? I am cold let me in"

"Oh no you are not coming in here we can sit outside and talk but not in here. I don't need your dad burring me in your back yard somewhere."

"You are such a baby. Grab me a blanket so I won't be cold. I am not ready to go to sleep yet and I am already packed."

They sat by the pool side and talked for a few hours about the old times, what was going on around town and the ranch. In the morning Bratton got up with the sun like he does every morning and made his way into the house. Mom was cooking breakfast and JT was drinking a cup of coffee before he headed out the door to work. "How did you sleep?" mom asked

"Oh, I slept great that is a nice house out there."

James leaned over from the coffee pot and kissed Stephanie "I will see you when I get in"

"Ok honey. I love you and BE CAREFUL!"

"Bratton you better be careful on the way home and remember what I said."

"Yes, sir I will, and we will see you next week."

Stephanie walked him to the door and kissed him one more time goodbye as he walked out. The she returned to the kitchen and continued to make breakfast. She and Bratton sat and drank coffee, ate and talked for a while until Susan arose from her slumber and made her way down. Still in her night clothes, a pair of cotton shorts and a white cotton tank top. She still looked amazing to Bratton.

"How nice of you to join us this morning." Her mom sarcastically announced her presence

"Um" she groaned as she stretched her arms up in the air with her hands clasped together and her shirt rising up showing her mid drift. "What is for Breakfast? I am starving". It caught Bratton's eye and he was in a stare for a brief second and shook it off. He always knew she was beautiful but "Wow she is hot" he thought to himself.

"I made omelets and I am sure yours is cold"

"I don't care I am hungry ", she proclaimed. She sat at the table and mom placed the plate in front of her and she bowed her head about 2 inches from the plate and began cutting and scraping the food from it like a bum who had not eaten for several days.

"Susan Talon you eat right. You know better than that". She lifted her head with part of her food hanging from her mouth and looked at Bratton across the table then began to laugh.

"You are not right in the head. That is gross" Bratton said as he turned away from her. She then opened her mouth and showed her food to him just to aggravate him. She knew he could not stand bad table manners and she knew he would get mad, but she thought it was funny. Even though Bratton did not like what she was doing he still laughed at her and told her to quit. Knowing she was doing it on purpose he knew the more he made it a big deal the more she would do it and it would only get worse.

"Hurry up and eat so we can get out of here"

"Bratton what time do you have to go meet with the scout?" Mom inquired.

"I don't think I am gonna go to that"

"Why not I thought that is why you came down?"

"Well it was but the more I think about it the more I don't want to go."

"Go where, to college?"

"No, I am going to college, but I think I am going somewhere a little closer to home incase dad needs me I won't be far away."

"Well that is sweet, but you better be going somewhere"

"I am I promise."

"I did not raise you two to be dummies you both need to go to school."

The 2 of them replied simultaneously "Yes mother" as if she were bothering them. And then proceeded to laugh about it

When Susan finished eating, they all went separate ways to get their things together and to clean up the house. Bratton finished packing and loaded the truck. By the time he made back into the house Susan's bag was already by the front door and he knew she wanted him to take it to the truck so she would not have to. He carried his bag and wheeled hers along behind him. He lofted his bag into the bed of the truck and turned to throw hers in, but the bag did not budge. "What the hell does she have in this thing?" It looked more like a crate than a suite case and weighed more than a block of lead. He wheeled it around to the back of the truck, opened the tail gate and heaved the bag into the back. "My gosh that thing is heavy" he muddled to himself. Bratton then went back into the house and sat on the couch watching TV, awaiting Susan's egress from her room. He only had to wait about 15 minutes before she hopped down the stairs and cheerfully exclaimed " I am all ready to go" Carrying a duffle bag in one hand, her purse on her shoulder and her cell phone in the other hand.

"Wow I have to admit I figured you would take a lot more time than that to get ready. I am impressed."

"I can do my make up in the truck lets go"

"Bye mom" she hollered through the house "we will see you next weekend."

"Hold on I am coming." As she scampered threw the house. "You are not leaving without a hug." She gave each of the kids a hug and made them promise to be extra careful and to call has soon as they got to the house. Each of them agreed and they went about their way.

Chapter 13

HOME SWEET HOME

The trip home went by in a flash. The 2 teens laughed and joked harassing one another the entire trip. When they made it to the gate at the entrance of the property Susan rolled down her window and stuck her head out "smells like home" then she pulled herself out the window to rest her backside on the window seal of the truck as Bratton continued to drive slowly towards the house. "It is so pretty this time of year. I miss this place so much"

They pulled in the drive close to the house and no one looked to be around. Bratton grabbed the bags from the truck and sluggishly pulled Susan's up the steps. As he entered the door, he saw Jessica coming from what had become the baby's room. "Hey Brat, I did not expect you home so soon. How did it go with Susan?"

Bratton did not reply he just turned and looked out the door in Susan's direction. As she twirled in circles with her arms open wide as if she were trying to hug the air. She really looked like she was crazy in the head at that point, acting all goofy smelling the flowers and chasing a butterfly.

Jessica watched for a brief moment and hesitantly asked "Is she the mother?"

"No, she is not."

"OK I was worried about it for a second. Is she drunk?"

"No, she is just acting goofy right now. She is going to help out getting things ready for next weekend."

"Oh, I see does your father know she is staying here? I did not know, or I would have fixed up a place for her to stay."

"It is OK. Dad won't care and she knows how it is she spent most her life at this house." Bratton made his way in the house and sat the bags on the floor by the door. He went into the kitchen to fix a glass of tea and heard the door open. When Susan made it in the door the first person, she saw was Jessica. Who was straightening things up around the living room?

"Oh, I am sorry I did not mean to barge in I should have knocked I did not think anyone else was here."

"It is fine you know more about this place than I do. I am just here to help out. Come on in. I am Jessica."

"I figured that. I am Susan. I have heard a lot about you. Bratton thinks you are the sweetest lady."

"Oh well that is good to hear. I have heard much about you as well."

"Oh, where is the baby can I see her?"

"Sure! I just put her in the crib so I could clean up let's go get her." The 2 ladies went to the room with the baby.

Bratton hollered out "You 2 have fun I am going to find Dad and Cross."

"Your dad went to town and Cross is in the field below old baldy"

"OK" as he let the screen door slam behind him.

Bratton knew the 2 of them would hit it off and figured if he left, they would get acquainted on their own. So, he made his way to the field where Cross was to help out.

While playing with LG Susan inquired "Bratton said you had kids also. Are they still here?"

"Yes. Well not here obviously but Cassie went with Cowboy to town to get feed and whatever she wants cuz he cannot tell her no when she asks, and Dylan is about 2 steps behind Cross doing any and everything he does. The boys all call him Muscles and I call him shadow because he follows Cross everywhere, they all have him believing that Cross is Wyatt Earp."

"Oh boy I know that trick. They did that to me when I moved out her. I was about 4 I guess, and they told me Pap paw Lee was Jesse James and that is why he never left the property. I believed them for a long time."

The girls stayed up by the house and played with the baby until it was time for her nap. Then the 2 of them made their way around the house Jessica telling her about what all she had done and Susan telling her about what all had happened in the past and reminisced about growing up around there. Jessica realized just how close Bratton and she were, by the stories that Susan had told. She began to wonder if they were ever apart. So, she thought she would ask. "Were you to ever away from each other?"

"From the time I moved here Bratton and his Grandmother came over our first night to stay in the house to let us know if we needed any help at all they would be more than happy to give it and she brought a cobbler. Oh my gosh my Daddy loved her cobbler. She had to make him one at least every Holiday and Birthday.

"She sounds like such a sweet lady I wish I could have met her"

"Oh, she was the best. She would buy us anything we wanted and spoil us rotten. I cried for a month strait when she passed away. But if we really wanted something Bratton would have me go to Pap Paw and ask. He was a sucker. To this day I still have never heard the word NO come out of his mouth."

"I see now where Cowboy gets that."

"Oh, he is a sucker too. Don't let him fool you. I know him better than any other woman now other than maybe my mother, but I have spent the most time around him and she says he is just a teddy bear. He acts all tough and mean but he is the sweetest guy in the world and so is Cross. Back to me and Bratton since that day we have not spent more than 24 hours apart until I moved to Odessa, I hate it too. The town is OK, but I don't like being away from my guys. I feel like it is my time to take care of them and I know they are here all alone. They have to have a woman around, or the place will fall apart."

"Trust me I know. It was not filthy in here but needed to be really cleaned. I thought when I met them that it was going to be a wreck, but they surprised me. It was not that bad, just needed some dusting and the upstairs especially."

"Well no one has been up there for years. I am really surprised that he went up and cleaned it out. I am glad but surprised."

"Susan? I want you to know that I am not here to take over or to try and move in"

"Oh, I know"

"No, I want to make sure you know that I am here because I really enjoy being around them and also the baby. Who am I kidding the baby is just an excuse? I will be honest with you. I think I am falling for Cowboy. He is so sweet and honoree and grumpy. I just love everything about him. Please don't say anything." It was nice to have another female around to vent her emotions.

"Oh, girl that is so sweet. He is a wild one, but it looks like you may be taming him. He has never even had a woman on the property that I know of and to clean up the upstairs. I don't think he would do that for me. You still have a lot of work to do before you tame that old dog."

"I don't want to tame him I like the way he is. I just don't want him with another woman."

"Well see I have been training Bratton since day one, so I don't have to break him I am just being patient."

"Susan you are bad. But I like the way you think. So, you think you and Bratt will end up together?"

"O yes he don't have a choice but yea I knew the day he walked in the door. He knows too."

"I think your right he knows too we have talked about you several times and he misses you a lot."

"Well he said he has not been with anyone since I left. I know he told you about that night. I hope you don't think I am a slut but that was the first time and the only time so far."

"No, I don't think that. Now days to make to your 18th birthday is a real chore from what I hear."

"How was it your first time?"

"It was awful. I was not ready, and I was 16 he was 18 and he really pressured me to do it. It was terrible" she smiled. "It actually took me a while to get over that"

"It was wonderful for me. Bratton never pressured me. That night was perfect, and I loved every minute. I have to admit he tried stopping and not going all the way, but I talked him into it, and I am glad. I love him so much and it hurts to be away from him. I do not regret it at all."

"That is so sweet. I think you and I are going get along just fine."

"I was a little worried coming up here, but I think you fit in here pretty good. I will give you my approval" as she acted like she was stamping her on the back.

"Well thank you very much that means a lot coming from you."

The 2 of them laughed and talked the rest of the afternoon as they cleaned, rearranged the furniture, cooked, rearranged the furniture, and again rearranged the furniture. With Susan there Jessica felt like she had more freedom to do as she pleased so the 2 of them just made their selves at home and moved things around as they were cleaning to make the house more like a home. They had dinner ready a little before dark and Jessica was worried it would get cold. "Normally they are hear by now"

"Why don't you just call them up?"

"I guess I could try but do you think they can hear me that far away?"

"Sure"

Jessica cleared her throat and began to holler "Dylan,Br...."

"No silly use the triangle like this." Susan grabbed up a metal rod off the porch rail and rang the triangle". They will be here in about 10 minute."

"I thought that was just a decoration."

"Not much of this stuff around here is for decoration. It all has a purpose if you don't know ask I will help you out."

"Well thank you Susan"

"Anytime you just call me on the phone and I will take care of you."

"I really have enjoyed having you here today it has been fun. How long are you staying?"

"I am staying for the week unless I can talk Daddy and Cowboy into letting me stay here until I finish school."

"That would be nice."

"Probably not going to happen but it is worth a shot. Maybe I can say I am gonna help you with the baby and that will convince them."

"It may work but if you are here they won't need me anymore."

"Sure they will. I will be at school for half a day. Besides you have a job in town you will have to go back too."

"You are right it is just; I really like it out here it is so peaceful and quiet. The boys are all so nice and polite."

"Ohh!! I see. You have the fever. Don't worry everyone gets it. They all come out here and think this is nice until they realize they are constantly working trying to make ends meet. All it takes is one bad season and you are bankrupt trust me I know. That happened to Cross. Then his wife got sick. Before that he had the second largest ranch in the county. It just takes one little bobble in the system to lose it all."

"I know it is a lot of work that is what I like about it, there is always something that needs done but, I don't have to worry about the kids out here and it just seems like where I belong. Maybe you are right maybe it will wear off. We will see."

"How is Cowboy handling you being here?"

"Kim oh he is great. I enjoy sitting on the swing and talking with him in the evenings drinking coffee. I cuddle up by him and sometimes we talk other times we just sit. That is one of my favorite things to do."

"Oh yes him and his cigar on the front porch"

"No, he won't smoke them around me usually. Just coffee and us."

"He won't smoke them around you?? Wow that is a first. I always gripe at him over those damn things and he just puffs a ring of smoke up in the air and laughs saying yep but they sure are good."

Chapter 14

THE BOYS ARE BACK

Cowboy and Cass arrived back from going to town in the truck and the others followed behind on the four wheelers. Cowboys got out of the truck and said "There is my little Susy Q. God it is good to see you. How have you been?" As he hugged her lifting her off the ground and spinning her around.

Then I came up "There is my little girl. You are all growed up now. What happened?"

As she kissed me on the cheek. And replied, "I had to grow up so I could take care of all you grumpy old men."

Everyone grabbed groceries from the truck and made their way in the house. Cassie was carrying a stuffed bear about half her size; a Barbie doll and a small toy make up box.

"What is all this Cass?" Her mother asked.

"Just some stuff."

"How did you get it?"

"She must have stolen it." Kim quickly insisted.

"Well if that is the case then she will have to take it all back."

"Well she got it for helping me out today. That is how I paid her."

"Kim you do not need to buy her stuff. She has plenty"

"I wanted to. So, I did. Where is muscles? I got him something to'

"He came running from the bathroom. What did I get?"

"Well that depends. Do you have anything shinny like a penny or anything? A marble?"

"No, I don't."

I knew what Kim was giving him, so he tapped him on the shoulder and handed him a dime and said, "you owe me."

So, Dylan handed over the dime and Cowboy gave him a brand-new pocketknife. "Now this aint no cheap knife. This is a real Case pocketknife just like my first knife and Bratton's first knife. It is not a toy but a tool you can use all through life, but you have to be careful with it."

Bratton reached in his pocket and said "Look I still carry mine. It is just about wore out."

They all put the supplies away and sat to eat dinner. Each of them telling embarrassing stories about the other to Jessica and tattle telling on one another of things that had happened long ago. They finished supper and settled all the kids in for bed then retired to the front porch.

"I sure will be glad when all this historical crap is over with." Cowboy said as he eased into the swing on the porch.

"Boy you can say that again, but we are getting some things done that we have been putting off for a while now. "I replied.

"I guess I will head out in the morning and pick up the new tractor in Abilene. You want to come with me" as he looked toward Jessica for an answer.

"Oh, me you want to know if I want to go. I would love to, but we would have to take the baby".

"How long will we be gone?" Susan immediately offered to watch the baby and Cassie. Dylan always went with Cross.

"Well I guess what time are we leaving?"

"I figure we will head out around daybreak and we should be back before lunch."

"That should be fine." Then she looked to Susan and began to tell her everything about the baby. "She will probably wake up around 7 or so I usually just change her and give her a bottle and she will go back to sleep. Then she will wake up around 9 and I try to feed her a little cereal. It is in the pantry but not too much I don't want her to get a belly ache."

Susan stopped her. "Jessica she will be fine she is not the first baby I have watched I am sure I can handle it. Don't worry about her enjoy your quite time away."

"I know you will take care of her. We will be back early enough. I am just a mother hen and worry too much. If I am getting up that early, then I better get the kitchen cleaned up and take care of a few things before I go to bed." She got up from the swing and walked through the door.

Susan arose to her feet and followed her. "I will give you a hand and you can show me where everything is for the little one"

The men unloaded the feed from the bed of the truck and hooked up the goose neck trailer so everything would be ready for in the morning. I retired to his bunk house and Kim and Bratton went inside to retire for the night as well. Bratton walked through the door and announced he was going to bed as he passed the kitchen. Kim walked into the kitchen and said he was tired too. Susan left the kitchen to follow Bratton asking him to show her where she was sleeping. And where everything was for her bed. It was really just an excuse to be alone with him before she went to bed.

Kim stood up from the table and made his way to the coffee pot by the sink. He poured himself a cup and asked if Jessica would like one as well. She declined his offer because it was getting late. He leaned against the counter while she was washing the last of the dishes. "Hand me that towel I will help you finish up so we can get to bed." She gladly handed him the towel and she washed while he dried and put the dishes away.

These were the time she was the most attracted to him. She liked him when he was grumpy and trying to be tough and he was cute when he would cut up with her and everyone else but, the times his softer side came out is when he impressed her the most. She knew that he did not just do it around her because she had seen it with other people he did not even know. Holding the door for them, helping them carry things to the car or load up something heavy at the store. It was just how he was, and she knew he had been that way all his life because Bratton and Cross acted the same way. She had never known a man to be like that before and it never really crossed her mind that he would be so kind but that he did these things without even knowing he was doing them. It was just a way of life to them. When the dishes were done. She leaned her head on his shoulder." I am so tired."

"Well you should be you have not stopped since you got here. You have been working your tail off. I really appreciate everything you are doing around here to help out. You have no idea how big a help you are to us, as he put his arms around her and rubbed her back."

"Thank you." She said in a quiet voice muffled by her head buried in his shirt.

"No Thank you."

"I mean thank you for letting me come out here. It has been a vacation to me, and you all are so nice to all of us I really appreciate it."

"You deserve it you work hard, and I am glad you enjoy being out here."

"You are a good man Kim Lee. I hope you know that."

Kim just sat in silence for a second to absorb what she had said. He had never had a woman say something like that to him. He would trade a million of the meaningless I love you's from the women of his past for that one "You are a good man" it was heartfelt, and he knew it was. It was not the same lie he had heard before and she was not out for his money. He truly felt better just being around her. The silence was broken when Susan walked back into the kitchen to see Cowboy holding her." Oh, I am sorry"

"Why" Kim asked?

"I was just getting a glass of water before bed." As Jessica turned around. Kim kept his arm around her.

"Well get you some water you are fine little missy. It sure is good to see you. I felt like I lost part of my family when ya'll moved off."

"Me too. Mom and dad feel the same they cannot wait to get out of that town."

"Are they gonna come next week?"

"Yes, they are."

"Well it is good to have you here. I am sure Jessy likes not being the only woman in the house too."

"I am really glad you are here now they can pick on you and give me a break" she said with a smile as she turned toward Kim and rubbed his chest, lightly hugging him."

Susan knew then and there this was not just a one-night stand for Cowboy. In all the years she had known him she had never seen him do anything remotely affectionate to a woman around her. Normally he would have pulled away and give any other girl a dirty look. Then they would be gone but not this time.

"Well I am going to bed I have to watch a baby in the morning" she gleamed with excitement.

"Good night sweetheart."

"Good night Susan."

"Good night ya'll"

Kim and Jessy finished up the kitchen and shut down all the lights, then made their way to the living room.

"Well good night. I will see you in the morning."

"What do you mean? Where are you sleeping?"

"I recon I will sleep out here on the couch."

"You will not! You will get in bed with me we are both adults and I will not sleep in there while you are in here on the couch folded up like a lawn chair. You get in there and get to bed. We have been down this road before. Besides I am not sure I can sleep on those pillows. I need you to hold me, so I don't get scared."

Kim just smiled and said "yes ma'am" with his deep southern drawl.

Jessica smiled and told him "Now that is better you stubborn old man"

Then she swatted him on the butt and smiled. She was really embarrassed, she did not know what had come over her, she just did it. It was like she had no control over her hand and then she wacked him on the butt. He turned and looked at her and smiled from ear to ear. "You better be careful I am just a man and I can only control so much."

"You get in there. That will come soon enough. We are waiting remember that is what you said, and we have to be up early."

"Well can I at least get a good night kiss?"

"Yes, you may but that is it. He leaned down toward her and kissed her gently on the lips. For a man, with such a rugged exterior, callused hands, and his lips were so soft and tender. It just made her melt.

"Good night Jess"

"Good night" she replied with a soft sigh as she crawled in bed beside him and laid her head on his chest still trying to catch her breath from the brief touch of their lips.

Chapter 15

GETTING FIRED UP

The next morning Jess and Cowboy got up before the rest of the house and grabbed a cup of coffee for the drive to pick up the new tractor a few hours away. The trip there was uneventful they talked a little and Jessica would doze in and out from time to time and only waking up when her head would fall against the window. Each time she would awake she would apologize for nodding off then follow up with the question "Was I snoring?" Cowboy would lightly reply with a no and tell her to lay down on the console and get comfortable so she would not get a sore neck. When they arrived in Abilene Kim told her she could stay in the truck and sleep if she wanted to but, she wanted to get out and stretch her legs.

They walk into the building and all the employees greeted Kim by name. He would take the time to shake each one of their hands and talk to them briefly. It was like following a politician running for office. He had away to make everyone feel like they were special, and he treated each of them as he was a true friend to them. He also introduced her to each of them and each of the employees were so polite she was seeing a trend among the people that surrounded Kim and his family were all similar to them.

Cowboy walked thru the back door leading to the shop area and hollered out "Curly were you at?"

"Back here" a deep voice cried out from the back bay of the shop

"You got my stuff ready to go?" Kim yelled again as he weaved his way thru the equipment in the other bays.

"I am just finishing up the last of it. All I got left is to put the quick connects on the hydraulic line and you can get this peace of shit out of here." Curly replied as he looked up and saw Cowboy and Jessy approach "Oh!! Excuse me ma'am I did not know you were here. I apologize for my language." As he wiped the grease from his hand and extended it towards Jessie "Names Curly"

Jessica stood toe to toe with a man who was really rough looking to say the least. He was about 6 foot 4 around 350 lbs. with long greasy hair and a beard that hung down to his belly. He looked as if he had eaten half of the ZZ Top band. She just stood in silence not sure how to react to the monster of a man.

Cowboy said "This is one of my new helpers Jessica"

"Helper huh??" in disbelief "she is a little too pretty to be a helper. "I say she is an angel if she can stand to ride around with you." Laughing as he shook Cowboys hand.

"Well thank you Curly it is nice to meet you too. And don't worry about the language I have heard worse"

"How you doing you old cuss" Cowboy asked

"Doing better now. Things are finally picking up with spring and all we are finally getting busy as you can see in the shop, we got more than we can handle."

"Well as long as mine is the finished the rest of these can wait" Cowboy joked.

They lingered in the back while Curly finished the hydraulic lines on the tractor. Kim would hand him a wrench and help out. Kim could not stand around if someone was working, he had to help out regardless, if they needed it or not. Curly tightened the last fitting and threw his hands in the air" done"

"It took you long enough," Kim razzed him

"I'd a been done sooner if you would have kept him out of the way," Curly told Jessy. "He apparently can't read cuz there is a sign right there that says all customers stay up front." As he pointed to the sign.

"You would still be trying to put this thing together a month from now if it weren't for me helping you out. Now let's get this loaded up so I can get out of here I got stuff to do."

Curly crawled into the cab of the tractor and fired it off. He backed it out of the shop and close to a disk plow where Kim was standing. Kim directed him back slowly to the plow and hooked up the lines and the plow to the tractor. Curly lifted the plow off the ground and drove to the tail end of Kim's trailer. They loaded the tractor and boomed it to the trailer. Kim thanked curly for getting it done so fast. Kim and Jessy said their goodbyes to everyone and headed back to the ranch.

They stopped off at a little Café not far from the shop to grab a bite to eat. Jessica told Kim "Curly sure isn't anything like he looks."

"Well what did you expect?"

"I don't know but he sure is nice. I just never would have picked you two to be friends."

"Why is that?"

"He just doesn't look like your kind of people"

"So, you made an assumption based on his looks? He is a great guy and I would trust him with my life. You are prejudice that is what it is. You don't like rednecks"

"Kim that is not true now be quite"

"Does that embarrass you? I am sorry I will be quite about your imperfections."

By this time, she had already figured out that if she got embarrassed then he would just keep aggravating her, so she just closed her mouth and decided not to talk to him anymore. She was refusing to talk to him even after he apologized he continued to try and get her to talk and laugh and she just sat there with her lips sealed tightly together only breaking the seal for moments at a time to let out the pressure built up from holding in a laugh. Their lunch came and she finally had to break her silence to get him to pass her the salt. They talked over dinner and she mostly listened to his philosophy about people and not judging them until you have actually talked with them. She had not found anyone he just did not like but she knew she did not want to be that person because even though he was nice she could see that he was not a person that anyone wanted to be on his bad side. They finished up eating and got back on the road. Again, Jessica was having trouble holding her eyes open and was nodding off from time to time she would wake up and smile pretty at him and apologize from time to time, saying that she was not a very good co-pilot.

After they turned off the highway to the county road, they saw a cloud of smoke in the distance. Kim's mood changed as soon as he saw the smoke, he became very somber and had a serious look on his face. "This ain't good!" he said quietly to himself.

"What is wrong?"

"That fire up there aint good. It is too dry for a fire right now. I hope it is not bad."

As they got closer to the smoke it went from Black to grey smoke. Kim got really worried. "Now it is in the grass that black smoke is usually a house or trash, but the grey smoke means it has hit the grass and will take off like well like a wildfire." Kim changed his path and now instead of heading to the house he was chasing the fire. Jessica was worried not knowing anything about grass fires other than what she had seen on TV. She envisioned a forest fire like the ones in California each year burning houses and people being evacuated. As they approached the fire Cowboy pulled over and began unhooking the chains on the new tractor and plow, he had just picked up. Jessica got out of the truck and walked to the back to help him, not sure what she could do she asked. He said, "I got it you need to get in the truck this smoke will get to you if you are not used to it."

Not sure what to do again she asked him what he was gonna do. "I am gonna try to save some of these houses."

By this time the fire had spread to the brush and was taking on to the trees. You could see the fire for miles around and hear the sirens from fire trucks coming in the distance. She looked ahead of the vehicle towards a small group of houses to see people scurrying about with water hoses and wet towels trying to keep the flames from all the houses and barns. The hay bales would flame up and then smoke each time a layer of hay would fall from the round bales to the ground a flame would shoot to the sky.

With all the commotion going on she ran to assist with keeping the fire off the houses. Shortly after she had made to the house, she saw cowboy back the tractor off the trailer and head toward the flame he dropped the plow into the dirt and made several laps around the houses and barns. Grabbing the burning bales and moving them a safe distance away from everything so they could burn out without catching anything else on fire. He then made his way into the brush and cleared a path which was later used by the fire department to access the back-hay fields that were surround by burning trees. He made several laps in and around the property and headed for the next property. As he crossed into the next property, he drove through a pond to cool the tractor down before continuing on his heroic expedition.

After plowing a few laps around the next field Jessica's phone rang and it was Kim. He was running low on Diesel, so he asked her to buy some from one of the farmers at the house and have them meet him on the road. She located the diesel and none of them would hear of him paying for it they just jumped in the truck to meet him so he would not have to stop for a long time.

The fire was out around the houses where they stopped to unload the tractor and Kim was nowhere in sight. Jessica made her way back to the truck and stood there processing what all was going on. She never realized that this was a brand-new tractor that had never even made it to the ranch, that was now in the middle of a field running over trees, logs, brush, and all of it on fire. He never even thought once he just re-acted like it was his family's house on fire. A couple of the local ladies brought Jessica a glass of tea and some wet rags to clean up with. Her face and clothes cover with soot, sweat and hay she was a sight to see. Her parents would never believe that she was in public looking like this. The ladies asked her to come and sit with them at a table under a shade tree in the front of the houses each of them thanking her for what they had done. Jessica tried to play it down as if she had not done anything special but knew her makeup and clothing showed otherwise.

One of the ladies asked where they were from and told her I am glad you loaded that tractor up and got here so fast we would not have a house if it had not been for ya'll.

Jessica said, "The tractor was already loaded we were taking it to the ranch about 30 more miles away when we saw the smoke, we thought you could use some help and turned your direction."

"Well your husband is a great man for doing that. The tractor looks brand new I don't know if my husband would do that with our old tractor."

Jessica grinned and said, "You could say it is like new we picked it up from the dealer this morning and we were heading home."

"Oh, my goodness you are kidding me I feel so bad he is tearing it up, but we are so glad he came. You are a lucky woman to have him"

"Well I don't really have him we are not married we are kind of dating or friends something like that. We have only known each other a few weeks."

"Well you better get your claws in him now he is a keeper."

"I am OK with the way it is now. He is a great man and we get along really good. I am not gonna rush anything I think we are both pretty happy for now."

The ladies sat out and talked for a few hours and one of them had their oldest daughter make some sandwiches and bring them out. Jessica called Kim to see if he needed something to eat or a drink but one of the guys who had brought the diesel out had given him some peanut butter and cracker with a water cooler that had water and beer in it. He was in the cab of the tractor with Cowboy and they were knocking down brush and still working the fire. "He sure is a better navigator than you. He has been awake the whole time telling me where to go and keeping me out of the ditches." He laughed about it. She could hear a squawking radio in the background that the fire Department had given him to help direct him to spots they could not reach. He told her if she needed to get back, she could take the truck and he would drive the tractor, but she decided just to wait on him.

"I talked to Susan and the baby is fine she was working on supper and for us not to get in a hurry." The ladies listened to the conversation and inquired about her baby.

She said "oh it is not my baby. I have 2 children the baby is not one of them."

"Oh, so he has a baby"

"Well not really, maybe, we are not sure."

Each of the ladies looked at her with an "oh I see" look

"It is complicated" Jessica said with frustration

"Well we won't bring it up again."

By this time, it had begun to get dark and the men had a generator hooked up to the house, so the electricity was working. The ladies went in to begin making dinner. "Now ya'll are staying for dinner so just sit down. Do you need a drink? Or something else? Just make yourself at home."

"I would like to use your restroom if you don't mind"

"Second door on the left."

She went to the restroom and made her way back to the porch. Janet the owner of the house offered to get her some close so she could shower and clean up. She respectfully declined "I am fine. I don't want him to think I did not pull my own weight while he was working. Matter of fact if you would do me a favor and take a picture of me so I have proof that I got dirty I will use it every time he starts in on me about being a city girl" The other ladies laughed at her remark because they all knew exactly what she was doing. She was going to rub it in that she got dirty and he was all nice and clean.

Kim returned with Janet's husband, Bill, in the cab of the tractor. Apparently, they did not have to rough of a time because the two of them jumped down from the tractor with a beer in their hand and cutting up. Bill made his way toward Janet, leaned over and kissed her on the head. Then he inquired about what all they had lost to the fire. Kim leaned down to kiss Jessy on the head and paused, "Good lord woman what have you been doing?"

"Some of us have been workin', not just riding around in a tractor all day with A/C and beer."

"Well I am soo sorry you got dirty. Bless your little heart. Would you like a beer?" Sarcastically

"I would love a beer go get me one since you have so much energy."

The other ladies looked her way and laughed lightly. He had played right into her web and she was gonna lay it on thick. She had never drunk a beer in front of Kim, so he was surprised she asked for one. He went to get it, just out of spite, and he was gonna dog on her until it was gone. She really did not care for the taste of beer but when he handed her that open Miller Lite can and she took a drink it was cold as ice and was the best thing she had ever tasted at that point in time. She took 2 quick slugs from the aluminum can and said "Ahhh that is good I hope you have more where this came from because I am thirsty after all that hard work."

Kim looked on in amazement at her and said, "I am sure we can get more on the way home."

"Oh, we are staying for dinner so you may have to run to the store."

Bill quickly replied "I am sure we got plenty if not we will get some. You two just sit and relax you have done enough for us"

Kim changed the subject quickly trying to stay away from the mushy conversation about how much they appreciate it and someone offering money or trying to give them something for the work they did. So, he started in on Jessica about finishing her beer.

"I am going to get another beer. Are you done yet?"

"Yes, I would like another one since you are headed that way." She knew she did not need one but the first one was good, and she was determined to not let him show her up. So, she was gonna match him beer for beer.

Janet and Bill's daughter Melissa came out and asked where everyone would be eating, because dinner was done. Janet made her way up to the house to help bring the food out and to get plates for everyone. Jessica followed shortly behind her to assist with bringing the food out. They sat and ate dinner and drank a few more beers until it began getting late. Kim had to load the tractor and told everyone they had to head out before it was too late. They said their goodbyes to their new friends and made sure to extend an invitation to the big bar-b-que at the property the following week. As he eased the tractor on the trailer Bill made his way over to help boom it down. Kim rushed to get done and in the truck before Bill could come talk to him. Jessica sensing his urgency to get away she had already made her way to the truck and was waiting for him to get in so they could go to the house. Kim finished up and looked across the truck to tell Bill he appreciated the help and headed for the driver's seat. Bill ducked under the gooseneck and scampered to the driver's side of the truck catching him just before he sat down.

"Cowboy we really can't tell you thank you enough if you had not come along when you did, we very well could have lost our house and everything we own. I know it isn't much, but Janet and I want you and Jess to have this" as he stuck his hand out with a hand full of money in it.

"Oh, I can't take that. You know I would have done for anyone. Enough of that talk ya'll need to go replace what did get hit by the fire and the fence I run over." As he laughed lightly.

"We really want you to have it."

"You got 3 girls spend it on them that is what I would do with it." As he took the money from him and placed in the top pocket of Bill's overalls "Now we gotta get out of here so we can unload this tractor before it gets too dark outside."

Bill said, "alright I'll let you go but this aint over."

"Ya'll have a good night we will see you next week."

Bill made his way around the truck to Jessica and she lowered her window." It was nice to meet you Jessy here take this and get you some new clothes."

Jessica looked at him with an, are you serious? I am not taking that from you look and he said "Well it was worth a try. Ya'll be careful and we will see you next week"

"You have our number if you get lost. We are looking forward to seeing all of you again" As she rolled the window up and waved bye to everyone. They started down the road.

"Boy I thought that was going to be a lot harder to get away from than it was." Kim said.

"I know I thought we would be there for a month refusing things from them. They are nice people I hope they come to our house"

"Our house!!!"

"Your house whatever"

"So, are you moving in on me? Do we have a date set? Our house that sure is a little sudden. I thought we were taking it slow."

"You know what I mean you are an ass Kim Lee"

"I am not saying, I am just saying."

"What does that mean? That does not even make since Kim"

"Hell, I don't know I am just trying to get out of this pickle, I'm in here without too many bruises on my ego. What makes you think I want to be hooked up with a dirty girl like you? Good lord you need a bath."

"I know I do. I need a beer."

He reached in the back and popped open a cooler. "Bill give me a few for the road. I thought you did not like beer."

"I like it, but I have to be in the mood for it. I am already feeling pretty good now but its sure tasted good tonight for some reason." As she reached in the cooler with a mischievous look in her eyes. 'Too bad you don't want a dirty girl like me cuz beer make me feel a little frisky."

Kim looked at her and smiled "you are still gonna need a bath."

"Why do I smell?" she raised the center console and slid close to him and place her hand on his upper thigh and started kissing his ear.

"Now you better stop that you are gonna cause me to wreck"

"You better quit rejecting me or I may get a complex."

"I really am driving. Keep it up and I won't be driving anymore"

"Ok" with pouty lips "I will leave you alone. That was really nice of you to stop and help them with a brand-new tractor. I don't think anyone else would have done that."

"I know if it were me, I would want someone to stop and help so I try to do it when I can. That way if something happens and I need help maybe someone will stop and lend a hand."

"You were crazy on that tractor running over everything insight and driving thru the pond. Did you do that to cool off the tractor?"

"OH Hell" laughing and smiling ear to ear "no that is not why but if anyone ask that is why"

"Why did you do it then"

"I come out of the briars on that fence line and the smoke was so thick I could not see; I felt the front end go down and all I saw was a wall of water. I thought what the hell just happened. I did not know how deep it was, so I figured I had a better chance of making it across if I hit the gas, so I grabbed another gear and went for it. I sure was glad O'bill got up in there with me. He knew the landscape so that did not happen again."

"Are you serious?"

"I swear it I had no clue. It scared the crap out of me I thought the tractor was done for when I hit that pond, but it worked out."

"How funny you looked like a super star or a big green stallion coming from a cloud of smoke. You hit the water and the wave went all the way across and put out the fire in the trees in front of you and then it came back and washed out the fire in the briars behind you. We all figured you knew what you were doing. Everyone looked at me like wow this guy is amazing he really knows what he is doing."

"Well we will just keep the part about it scaring the piss out of me and not having a clue to ourselves and let everyone think I am a super star."

"Your secret is safe with me" she smiled and lay her head on his shoulder. "I won't say a word. I still think you were a superhero. That was the kindest thing I have ever seen anyone do for a stranger."

"Well we are not strangers we just had never met before today, besides the good Lord sent me down that road for a reason. I really had nothing to do with it."

"Oh, now we are getting religious?"

"Not religious I just believe everything happens for a reason and I know the Good Lord has a reason for everything. I am just here for his entertainment."

"Well he certainly was entertained today. You were great. I was proud of you."

"Well enough of that talk I did what any red-blooded American would have or should have done in the same situation. I am not a super, hero, or an angel just a normal guy. So, don't put me on no pedestal. I am just a guy like the rest of the people in the world. I have done good and I have done bad just like everyone else"

She could see he was not comfortable when someone was giving him praise for a job well done so she dropped the subject and just squeezed his arm tight. "You are going to make it hard to go back to my house"

"According to you we are going back there right now you having second thoughts now?"

"Nope I like it out here. I may just move in and kick you out. I am sure Cross, and Bratton will have my back if you don't like it"

"So, the three of you are starting a mutiny"

She laughed "If we have to, we will".

"I don't think that will be necessary so far, so good I kind of like havin' ya'll around. We will just play it by ear for now"

"Yea play it by ear, don't get your hopes up so you don't get let down that is my philosophy too. I don't want to think that way anymore though. It hasn't gotten me anywhere so far"

They pulled up to the house and both got out and walked to the house. Jessica went in and headed straight for the shower not saying a word to anyone. Kim came in and asked me and Bratton to give him a hand with the tractor. Kim told them the all about the fire and what all had happened. Boasting about Jessica and telling them that she had saved the house and barn. The two of us just went with the flow and even throwing in a few good words for her saying she may be a keeper and I knew she was a hard work and not too bad to look at. Little things to get Cowboys wheels a churning. I told him "I don't know what she sees in you when she could have a looker like me" Kim never said a word which was unusual, but he knew everything they were saying was right. We got the tractor off the trailer. I looked at it and told Cowboy" this is the dirtiest new tractor I have ever seen what you paid for this thing?"

"I know it looks rough, but it has been put through the test and I sure did like it. It never batted an eye and I did some stuff with it."

"Like driving it through a pond at 90 miles an hour" Jessica hollered from the porch wearing a button up shirt of Cowboys and a pair of boxers like shorts with a beer in hand

"Wow" I looked up "she is gonna let you have a beer. You must have done a real good job out there."

"That beer is not for me she has been drinking since we sat down to eat. She is sowing her oats tonight so ya'll might watch out" as he spoke louder almost hollering "the cougar has her claws out"

"I heard that Kim."

"You were supposed to Jess"

Me and Bratt looked at each other and could see really easy that it was going to be an early night for everyone on the ranch with all the grade school flirting. Susan heard the talking on the porch and came outside to sit by Jess on the swing. "Sounds like you too had fun."

"In some crazy way, fighting a fire and getting dirty and yucky was somewhat liberating for me. It was a rush at first and then it was just what had to be done." She rambled on about what all Kim had done and the new friends they had made. She had never been involved in anything like it before. It made her feel good and between the adrenaline rush and the buzz from the beer she was not ready for bed. Susan had not known Jess for long, but she could tell they had a few drinks and apparently, they had grown much closer during the catastrophic event. She also had come to the conclusion that it would be an early night for everyone else on the ranch.

Jessica made small talk asking about the kids and the baby with Susan until the men had finished unloading the tractor. The guys came up on the porch and I was not wanting to interfere with the courtship going on so, I

132

immediately retired for the night. Beating Bratton and Susan to the punch they did not want to make it obvious, so they stayed for a few minutes mostly listening to the two of them brag on the other about being hero or heroine that day. Jessica lay on his shoulder with her feet up in the swing beside her and sipping on a beer that she was sharing with Kim. Susan went in the house to finish cleaning up the kitchen. Jessica offered to help but she declined stating that she probably needed to relax after the day she had. Bratton gladly stepped up and offered his assistance. While in the house they could hear giggling and whispers from Kim's deep voice that carried through the house even though he was trying to be quiet. Bratton and Susan both would look to each other and just laugh lightly whispering to one another about how blatant the two were being and in disbelief that Cowboy was acting this way with people around. Bratton stuck his head out the screen door and said, "we are going to call it a night do ya'll need anything before we hit the sack?"

"No, we are good but, ya'll better be hitting different sacks"

"Kim Lee!!" Susan squealed out "We are not like that"

"You better not be either"

Jessica looked up at Susan and Bratton with big eyes and an open mouth like OOPS!!! He doesn't know does he?? Jessica did not say a word but tilted her head to the side and squeezed her lips tight as to say no and please don't tell him.

"We aren't" the two storied simultaneously

When everyone was off to bed and only the two adults acting like teenagers remained it was peaceful, and a giggle would break the silence. Kim and Jessy both decided to hit the hay after a long day. Kim opened the door for Jessy gently patting her on the butt as she passed through the door telling her "come on dirty girl let's get to bed."

She smiled and told him "I am only a woman you better be careful doing that."

Kim went in the bedroom to get some clothes to change into after he showered, and Jessica followed him into the room and falling backwards on the bed. "I know I should be tired. My body feels tired, but my mind is racing, and I know I can't sleep"

"You will be asleep before I get out of the shower."

"You are probably right but, right now I am not tired".

"Well I am getting in the shower"

Kim went in the shower and Jess stayed on the bed recollecting the day's events. When Kim returned from the shower, he was surprised to see Jessica still on the bed with his button up shirt on and she had removed the shorts. Thinking she was asleep he made his way to his side of the bed and admired her beauty for a brief moment before getting in bed. When he laid his head down on the pillow she rolled over and kissed him she was not going to let this moment go to waste. Stunned at her aggressive move he lay still, in shock. "Do you like clean dirty girls?" as she smiled.

"not usually but I have a feeling I am gonna like this one tonight" they kissed and embraced playfully taunting one another and tussling in the sheets exploring each other's bodies. She questioned him about all his scars and after he would tell her the stories of bulls horns, Doctors knives, and hoof prints she would kiss the scar, say " oh baby " in a sweet seductive voice " I am sorry" and ask about another one. When she had finished, he asked her about a scar above her eye that could only be seen if you were close enough to kiss her.

"That one happened in daycare a boy threw a rock and hit her in the eye"

He kissed it and said "I am sorry. That Stupid Boy" then he asked if she had any more and she pointed to her knee.

"What happened here?"

"I cut it learning how to shave".

He leaned down and kissed it "I am sorry. Stupid razor" and looked at her with a smile. "Anymore?" she did not reply but pointed to her bottom lip." What happened here? I don't see a scar".

"Nothing I just wanted you to kiss me"

He fulfilled her request and kissed her passionately and continued to kiss her. That night the taking it slow and waiting all went out the window. The 2 of them could no longer hold back the sexual cravings and tension that had been building over the past several days. The next morning Cowboy woke up to Jessica holding a cup of coffee in her hand for him. She was wearing his shirt again. "You are going to have to quit wearing that shirt" he told her "you look a lot better in it than I do. And it looks better on the floor than on you."

She smiled as he sat up in bed taking the coffee from her hand. She lay down in the bed, wrapped her arms around him and placed her head on his chest squeezing him tight. "I liked the shirt better on the floor too."

He smiled at her and put his arm around her rubbing her back. "I think I can get used to this."

"I think I already am"

Chapter 16

GOOD TIME SECRETS

They lay in the bed while he sipped slowly on his coffee. Jessica got up, put some shorts on and went back into the kitchen to start breakfast for everyone. Cowboy took his time getting out of bed and making his way to the kitchen in his boxers and a white tee shirt. He sat at the table and talked to Jessica while she was cooking and waiting on him hand and foot. One by one the rest of the house came to the kitchen. Cassie came in and sat at the table still sleepy eyed and in a daze. Her mother asked if she wanted some juice and she nodded her head while rubbing her eyes. Jessica poured the cup of juice and she got up to get it from her. Then she latched on to her mother's leg as if she was shy and hiding from a stranger. Cowboy asked her if she wanted to sit with him while momma finished cooking and she nervously nodded and made a few steps toward him. He gently picked her up and sat her on his knee. She took a sip of juice and placed it on the table in front of her and Cowboy, then put her head on his shoulder and snuggled up to him like she was going back to sleep. Cowboy turned to butter every time she would hug up to him. He was a sucker for little girls. Jessica got a little emotional seeing the 2 of them sitting at the table. Cowboy talking to her in a real quiet and deep voice and her nodding her head in agreement with the day's agenda he had planned for her. Jessica looked and smiled at him Cowboy asked her why she was looking at him like that and she just said, "oh no reason I am just happy to be here and I am pretty sure little miss spoiled rotten is too."

"Ahh she aint spoiled. Are you Cassie girl? Cassie shook her head with a definitive NO!

Bratton and I came in the kitchen dressed for work and ready to eat. When we saw Cowboy sitting in his boxers and tee shirt at the table, we were surprised he was always the first up and ready to go waiting on everyone else. I whispered to Bratton "This isn't good"

"Yea! He has it bad."

Neither of us acknowledged his attire. We just went about our business and fixed some coffee and sat at the table waiting on the meal to be served. Susan with the baby and Dylan sat at the table. Susan was wearing her sleeping shorts and a white tee shirt much like Cowboy.

She looked to him and said "I guess we have the same designer for our clothes"

"I guess so" Cowboy replied

"Well you aren't going to get much work done dressed like that. Are you sick or something?" Susan had a good idea of what had happened that night because, she could hear the 2 down the hall from her throughout the night. So, she was trying to get him to fess up about him and Jessica being mischievous.

"Nope just got a late start today. What is your excuse?"

"I don't like work or mornings. Did you have a late night? Was it a bad dream? I heard something coming from your bedroom, last night. Are you Ok?"

Jessica turned red faced and was embarrassed. Me and Bratton almost spit coffee across the table. Cassie said, "I heard it too."

Susan eating up the fact that Cowboy and Jessica were both embarrassed and speechless she agged it on "What do you think it was?"

"It sounded like a monster in the house"

"Oh, really that is what I heard too. It was like a lion" Cassie shook her head "yes or like a cheetah? No, it was a Cougar" Cassie still shaking her head yes. "Cowboy did you have a cougar in your room last night?"

Without hesitation Cowboy said in a proud and satisfied voice "yes I did" with the cat out of the bag he decided to just go with the flow." I wrestled with that thing all night you want to see the claw marks on my back?"

"OK that is enough you too" Jessica proclaimed

Cassie wanted to know if he killed it and Cowboy just could not help himself, "Nope I think she went back in her cage."

"And she will stay there if all of you don't stop talking about it"

"Your mom is the one who let her out."

"Momma? Can you let the cougar out so I can see it?"

"No, I don't think so. There is no cougar in the bedroom. They are just aggravating you. Me and Cowboy were"

"NO NO NO I don't want to hear this" Bratton stopped her "we don't need to know what ya'll were doing let's just eat and get to work please."

"Well we can eat but we are not working today. We are taking the day off." Cowboy muttered as he sipped his coffee and stared at the morning newspaper.

"Really you are taking a day off and the weather is good? What is wrong with you? You must be sick"

"I figure we could all head for the lake and just have fun for a change"

Susan said "you won't hear any argument from me"

The kids hollered out" yea!! We get to go to the lake."

Jessica was startled and replied "we have a lot of work to do"

"I know but everyone has been working hard and I have been working all my life. It is about time to enjoy life for a change. If everything gets done it does and if it don't It don't. We won't know half the people who come out anyway."

"Dad you are scaring me. But if you say we are going I am on my way"

I just said "ya'll have fun"

"Nope we are all going together you are going. If anyone needs a break from here it is, you. You don't ever get away from this place."

"No arguing everyone get your swim trunks and towels. Brat you fold up the baby bed and Cross will you grab that canopy thing we use when we cook out by the pond."

"I will but I aint taking no swim shorts." I grumbled

"Fair enough."

"Susan will you help Jess load up a cooler with hot dogs and the fixin's and make sure we get some matches?"

"I will go back to bed let me know when ya'll are done"

Everyone laughed. "I don't think so mister Lee this is your idea you will help too."

"I am just funnin' I will get LG and load her up"

Everyone dispersed to perform their specified task. Kim and Jess went into the bedroom to get ready. She cornered him and backed him up to the bed. "You keep surprising me. If you don't stop it is going to ruin your bad reputation." As she tiptoed to kiss him, she leaned in and the 2 of them fell to the bed as she kissed him.

"I don't know what it is about you, but you make me want to be better. I just want to be with you."

"Oh, I hate you"

"What"!!!"

"I hate you. You are so amazing and say the right things, do the right things and I hate you for that"

"OK I won't be like that anymore."

"No, I want you to be like that, but I just am not ready to feel this way. I was not planning on you being the man of my dreams. I figured you for a player not a chivalrous knight"

"A chivalrous knight? Is that good? I don't know but, why do you keep trying to figure me out or try to guess what I am going to do next? Why don't you just go with the flow and be with me. That is why I want to go to the lake I just want to be with you. I know yesterday was nothing special to you but to me it was I got to spend the day with you. Talking, laughing, cutting up and I even got to watch you sleep. That was a good day for me. I know it got a little crazy in the middle with the fire but, the entire time I was in that tractor I was worried how you were and if you were uncomfortable around people you never met and when I got back and saw you talking and having fun with them I was awe struck. You amaze me."

"OK we have to stop because I will end up crying and we will not get out of the bed. I know I sound crazy, but I have never in my life felt this free and happy before and I want to find something wrong with it. I know I am crazy."

"Everyone is crazy you just have to find someone who is crazy like you. Come on and let's get ready and we can finish this on the porch swing tonight when we get back if you want." He kissed her on the lips and rolled her over to hover above her body, resting on his elbows. "Just so you know I don't put on a show for anyone I am who I am, and I want to do this for me as much as ya'll." With a gentle peck on her cheek he stood up and pulled her to her feet hugging her tightly she reciprocated the gesture by squeezing him tightly and then patting him on the butt.

"Let me go or we will end up back in bed and we don't want to embarrass your son."

"UMMM!! Sounds fun but I already made a promise"

He turned his back to her and made his way to the door as Jessica began to undress. He walked to the door he could see her reflection in the mirror as his shirt, she was wearing, fell to the floor and she stood wearing only a pair of panties. He was paralyzed by her beauty. He knew she was beautiful but seeing her there she was amazing. He looked in the mirror at her for a few seconds as she bent over to get into her bag for her swimsuit. He was not thinking of her in a sexual way but like someone would looking at a work of art. He stood in astonishment. Jessica stood up and saw him looking at her. In a quiet voice she said, "Kim get out of here."

"I I I am sorry I was just I mean I didn't see I wasn't looking at you I was just."

"Staring at me?"

"You look incredible. I better go"

Kim went out to the barn and aired up a few old inner tubes for the kids to play on and loaded them in the truck. He went back into the house to get the baby and all of her things. Jess took the baby and put a small sun dress on her and a hat. Kim put her in the car seat after playing with her for a bit and started the truck. Kim began honking the horn and hollering out the window of the truck "ya'll c'mon we are gonna run out of day light". Bratton load the cooler. Muscles got in the truck with him, Susan and Cross while Jessie and Cassie loaded up with Kim and the baby.

Bratton hollered out the window to his old man "you lead the way this is your expedition" so Kim put the truck in drive and made his way down the long drive to the road. He would intentionally let the rear tires of his dually drop off the side of the drive to stir up dust and throw pebbles at Bratton's truck because he was following to close, and he would laugh each time he did it. Jessy requested that they stop at the store to pick up a few things they needed before going to the lake and Kim told her they did not have time that they were already late.

"Late for what?" she asked.

"For going to the lake"

"Did you have to make a reservation to go to this lake?"

"I guess you could say that. Now just sit back it won't be long. We can get that stuff at the marina. If they aint got it, we can send Bratt or Cross to get it down the road."

"What is the big deal? Why are you in such a good mood? You are up to no good Kim Lee."

"Oh, just hush and enjoy the ride."

They drove through town and down the windy lake road. Then he went over a narrow 2 lane road across the dam and pulled into the marina. He parked the truck under some trees and told them we are here.

"WHAT? NO sand, no Beach. How are we supposed to swim here?"

"I didn't say anything about swimming I said we were going to the lake." As he walked into the Marina. "Hey Joe"

"Well howdy Kim. I was beginning to wonder if you were gonna show up or not."

"I would have been on time. I was ready but I had to wait on all them slow people out there."

"I know you better than that. You don't get in no hurry for anything Kim. Who do you have there with you? Is this the infamous Jessy I have been hearing about all around town?"

"Yes!! Sir that is the woman right there in the flesh. The woman who tamed the west. She is a living legend." Jessy just looked dumb founded that he had heard about her. She was curious to know what he had heard.

"It's a small-town ma'am don't be offended" as Joe stuck his hand out. "My name is Joe Shaffer I believe you met my brother in law Curly the other day. He was right about you. You are way to pretty and sweet for an old badger like Kim."

"Well I am trying to soften him up a little at a time. I am not sure it is working."

"Well if you get tired of trying with him, I am just a big old teddy bear." As he winked and smiled at her jokingly

"I am sure Nora would just love that."

"Hell, as pretty as she is, she wouldn't blame me a bit" as he laughed. "Now come on out here I got it in the water" as he walked out the back door. He motioned for Jessy and the others to follow along. They walked down the rickety pier past several boats and stopped

"There she is what do you think?"

"That is nice."

"Yep I like these here you can fish, ski, or just lounge around on them. I looked at the grill to mount on the front, but they were ridiculously priced, so I built you one and installed it for a lot less."

"Shoot this one is perfect" as he made his way on to the deck of the boat.

"Dad what is this?"

"Son it is a boat"

"I know but whose boat?"

"Ours"

"When did you buy it and where did you get the money?"

"None of your business and I ordered it when I ordered the tractor."

"Yep he has lost it" I whispered to Bratton

"Good Lord we deserve to have fun every now and again. Cross you used to fish in tournaments all the time. You are always talking about how much you enjoyed fishing. Bratton you are always going to the lake with your friends during the summer now you got a boat. I figure with the kids here and Jessy they would like to go out on it too. Now how crazy am I?"

"OK whatever you say." Bratton replied. "I still don't know where you got it."

"To be honest with you all three of us own it. I would skim a little off the top of all our winnings and put my share back every time we won a ropin' and I paid cash for it, if you must know. I will gladly pay you for your share of the boat if you want."

"I don't care how he paid for it" Susan said as she took off her tee shirt and got aboard and shimmed off the blue jean shorts to reveal her 2-piece swim suite and her tan fit body." I am ready to go."

Bratton just smiled "That does it for me. I like it already" as he sat beside her, pulling his shirt off and then putting his arm around her.

"Cross are you in?"

"Hell, yes I am in I can't buck the system so I might as well join in."

"Good deal cause I never have driven a boat before, so you are the DD till we get her down"

"Fair enough. Everybody get aboard and we will take her around to load her up by the boat ramp."

Everyone boarded the boat. "Wait a minute the kids all need life jackets," Jessy exclaimed

"Where is mine Cowboy?" Asked Cassie

"Your what?" Jessy inquired

"My pink Hanna Montana life jacket we bought"

"Your what? You don't have a life jacket"

"U huh. We got it the other day at the store and brought it out here. We got Bubba one too."

"Kim Lee I am going to kill you"

"What?" he replied as he pulled out the too life jackets from under the seat of the boat and smiling from ear to ear. He handed Cassie her Swimsuit/life jacket and pulled another blue jacket / shirt out for Muscles. "Here try that on."

"Cool. Thanks Cowboy"

"I got you one too Jess try this one on" as he tossed an orange, generic, over the head cheap life preserver at her

"Thanks now when my hair turns green from the water, I will look like a big fat pumpkin instead of a dead whale floating."

"Awe come on now I's just funnin' about. Don't go getting all pissy. You know you aint gonna look like no whale out there. You will look more like a barracuda." As he started singing the Pat Benatar song "Barra Barra barracuda"

"You are crazy"

"Did you hit your head?" Everyone was thinking he had gone nuts.

"Come on Cross fire it up and let's get this show on the road." I started the motor and eased the boat around through the boat slips to the wooden dock by the boat ramp. He tied it off and everyone jumped out and began unloading the trucks into the boat. Bratton and Susan went in to grab a bag of ice and were talking about Cowboy as they opened the door. "He has gone crazy." Bratton would say

"No, he is just having fun. I like it when he acts goofy like that. I have not seen him like this since we were little."

"I know it scares me"

Joe heard the conversation. "I asked him why he was buying a boat and he said just thought we would have a little fun every now and again. I never seen him like this before either. But it seems to be pretty happy. Just be glad he is not blowing money at a casino or drinking it away. I have seen that too many times. Let him have some fun, he deserves it. Hell, all three of you boys need to do some playing. I told him if he didn't like the boat, I would buy it from him so there is no risk involved."

"I guess ya'll are right. All he ever does is work. It will get Cross out more too." They grab the ice and went back out to the boat.

Everyone loaded up and Cross grabbed the wheel "where to boss"

"Just go we will know when we get there. What do ya'll wanna do?" as they began their journey across the water. The baby loved the boat when the water would splash up the mist would hit her in the face and she would take a deep breath and giggle so Cross would weave through the water to make it hit her on purpose and everyone watched her as she would giggle.

They made their way to an island in the middle of the lake with a sandy beach. Cross ran the boat up into the shallow water until it came to a complete stop then he stretched a rope out and tied it to a tree to keep the boat from floating off. Jess began to make sandwiches for everyone, and the kids bailed out with the tubes Kim had filled with air for them to play on. Everyone seemed to be enjoying themselves. After they all had eaten. Susan, Bratton, and Cross took Cassie and Dylan out to pull them on the tube. Kim and Jess stayed on the beach with LG playing with her in the shallow water. It did not take long for her to get tired so Jess sat with her in a tube for a few minutes until she fell asleep from the rocking side to side and Kim set up her play pin so she would have a place to sleep and covered it with a small sheet to keep the sun off of her.

With the baby asleep and the kids gone the two of them lounged on the beach with their feet on the water. The 2 of them sipping slowly on a beer and talking about everything they had done in the past few weeks like it had all happened years ago. The kids would come by screaming on the tube having the time of their life. Cassie would ride with Susan and Dylan and Bratt would ride together.

Jessica was having the time of her life just watching the kids and relaxing with Kim beside her on the beach. Everything seemed so surreal it was like a dream or a fairytale. Cross brought the kids back to shore Susan and Bratt took over the baby watch while Kim and Jess went on the boat.

While in the shallow water Susan and Bratton lay back like they were sunbathing. Susan floated up to him and slowly made her way to kiss him and tell him how much she had missed him. "Your dad sure seems to be happy"

"I know it's weird"

"Well it took some heat off the two of us. I never told dad why I was going to Odessa, but I know he knows. He just aint said nothing."

"They are so cute together"

"She is pretty cool to be around, and she works her ass off. All she had to do was watch little bit there and help out with her, but she insists on working around the house and cooking. I think she is just glad to be out of the city. She fits in good around here so far. I like her."

"What do you think your dad will say when you talk to him about me staying here to finish school?"

"I am sure he will be fine. I figure your dad has already talked to him and I know that Jess knows but I don't think she has said anything."

"How does she know?"

"We were talking one night on the porch and she asked if I knew who the Momma might be and I thought back and the only one it could have been was you and I knew you would not do something like leave a baby but it got me to thinking about you and there was no one else to talk to, you are the only one I ever talk with about serious stuff like this so I came and got you."

"Nice cover up you smooth talker" she alleged as she stood up and pulled the baby from her floating boat. "Come on let's feed the baby she is probably hungry".

Bratton strolled out of the water and spread a blanket out on the sand of the shore, while Susan pulled a baby bottle from the cooler. They sat on the blanket while the baby nursed the bottle rapidly. "I guess she was hungry." The two of them lay back on their sides facing one another with the baby between them. "You know you are pretty good at this baby stuff as they locked hands above the baby's head." She did not reply she just smiled and looked out toward the water.

145

The others returned in the boat after a trip around the lake. They made sandwiches and had their lunch that was packed in the cooler. They stayed at the lake until just before dark. On the trip back to the house all the kids fell asleep in the back seat. After making it back to the house and unloading all the supplies everyone was exhausted, they all went straight to bed.

The next morning the men woke up early to start the day as they always have, trying to make as little noise as possible and not to wake the kids and others in the house. Bratton made his way off to school while Cross and Cowboy went out to feed and mend fence. After hearing the front door creek open and close lightly Jessica woke up in Cowboy's bed again. Sleepy eyed and groggy she rolled over on her back to stare at the ceiling. She stretched here limbs as far as she could, sprawling out in the big bed working her arms and legs as if she were making a snow angel and smiled with satisfaction. She was happier than she had ever been and had not even thought about her work or even her house in the city.

After rolling out of bed she grabbed one of Cowboy's old tattered button up shirts and put it on as a robe. She cuffed the sleeves, then pulled the collar up to her face and to take in the aroma of his cologne still lingering on the fabric. She inhaled and held her breathe as if she was a hippie smoking marijuana and slowly twirled around. She exhaled in disappointment because he was not there when she woke up but quickly regained her bearings and went to the kitchen for a cup of coffee which was left still warm on the stove by the thoughtful men who had just left. The coffee tasted so good from the old-style coffee pot which was left on the burner to percolate for her. It was not some fancy brand or made in a bistro, but it just smelled better and tasted better than any other coffee she had prior to coming out here. "it is just coffee she told herself" but the coffee, the comfy shirt, and his cologne it was all part of what was slowly becoming her morning ritual and it all just seemed so right. She had no worries and was not rushed to do anything but somehow it all got done. Why had she not met him before all the jerks she had dated in the past? She did not know but she was thankful to God that she had met him.

She finished her first cup of coffee and was making a second when Susan made her way in the kitchen rubbing the sleep from her eyes and wearing Bratton's button-down shirt just like Jessica was doing.

"Oh I see we have the same clothing designer" Jessica said with a smile

"I guess we do. Every time I see Bratton, he makes me give his shirt back, so I always steal another one before I leave, and I have a bottle of his cologne at home so after I wash it, I spray it. It just makes me warm and cozy on the inside. Is that silly?"

"Not at all!! Why do you think I am wearing Cowboy's shirt? I feel like I am being silly walking around like a teenage girl. No offense but I am a lot older than you."

"You didn't offend me I think it is cute to see two old people flirting with one another" as she laughed.

"HA! Ha! Very funny. I know it is silly but I just love being here. I feel like I belong here for some reason and I am not the type to act this way. I never pictured myself out of the city until I met this crazy bunch."

"You fit in good out here and the boys all love you and the city really isn't all it is cracked up to be. I live in Odessa and it is a far cry from a big town, and I don't like it. I can only imagine what it is like in a big city."

"You are not missing anything trust me the people are rude, and everyone is always in a hurry. You try crossing the street and people speed up and try to hit you. It really is awful, and the kids act better and enjoy it out here. Dylan has not picked up his game boy one time since we have been here and normally, he is on that stupid thing 24/7 I hate that game. He thinks Cross hung the moon. I am so grateful that they all take him under their wing and Cassie to she loves Cowboy mainly cuz he spoils her rotten but still she loves him. Normally they would not even talk to people unless they have been around them a few times, but they act like they have known them all their lives."

"Well get use to Cowboy because he loves to spoil little girls all she has to do is bat those pretty little eyes and say PLEEEASSE and he is done for. That is just the way he is. It is nice out here, but you do have your problems they still have drugs in the school although not as bad as in town. The main thing is to graduate high school without being pregnant or getting someone pregnant, but it is a better way of life for a family out here."

"Wow the time is flying by I am not gonna want to go back home and leave all this. I wish there was a way I could move out here"

"Why are you leaving? Cowboy is not going to make you leave. If he did not want, you here he would not have rearranged everything so you could stay."

"I know but the kids have school and I have work and the house it just would not work."

"Move the kids out here. They will love it."

"But I don't want them to feel like I am forcing myself on them or trying to weasel my way into their lives. The kids are a lot and I am I mean I don't think he is ready for that; I just don't want to mess this up. I really care for him, well all of you."

"I understand but if you want to move out here and not live with them then I can check to see what houses dad has available for rent in town. You would be close by and not living here."

The baby started bouncing around in her crib and talking to herself, so Jess got up from her chair to go check on her as she walked away, she turned back to Susan

"I am not sure let me think about it. I guess we better get dressed and get the kids up and moving. I am sure the baby is starving right now since she didn't wake up all night."

"OK just let me know. You go get the baby and I will make her a bottle and feed her so you can get dressed. I am sure she will Zonk out after eating."

Jess went to the room and pulled LG from the crib the baby girl was smiling and laughing as Jess changed her diaper. Jess was tickling her and making funny faces as she brought her into the kitchen with Susan.

"Hey there little piggy what are you doing this morning?" Susan asked in her baby voice as Jess relinquished the little one to her. "Are you hungry little girl? I bet you are" as she brought the bottle into hands reach, she snatched it away and went to town sucking it down. Stopping every few seconds only to let the air displace the milk she had rapidly ingested from the bottle. "Wow!! You were hungry. You chugged that thing down in record time" as Susan held the empty bottle up to see that nothing remained. She placed the baby on her shoulder and began rubbing her back unlit she let out a loud belch. "O my I bet that felt good" as she pulled her away to see if she had spit up her and just as she expected LG was out like a light again. Susan tip toed across the creaking hard wood floor trying

148

not to wake her until she made it back to the crib and gently kissed her on the cheek before laying her back down to bed and covering her up.

Jess heard the loud burp and came from the shower drying her hair with towel to check on the two of them standing in the doorway of the room she whispered, "did she go back to sleep?"

Softly whispering back "yea she did. She is soo cute I just love the way she smells, and she is so warm and cuddly."

"Well you can play with her no need to rush anything" Jessica told her has they exited the room and gently closed the door.

"I am not going to get in a hurry. I have college to finish before I even think about kids."

"I am glad to hear that. What are your plans for today?"

"I don't know I thought we might go get some decorations in town."

"That works for me I need to order some side dishes at the store and get a few things also"

Chapter 17

NAME THAT BABY

The two ladies worked as a team getting the kids up and dressed and loaded in the car. They drove into town and looked through the local store for decorations and stopped at the grocery store to order the side dishes for next weekend event. Neither Jess nor Susan could find the decorations they liked so, they decided to go the city and shop there.

While they were in town Jess stopped by the hospital to see Shirley and let her take a look at the baby so they would know she was being taken care of and to show Susan where she worked. Susan met Shirley and the Doctor friend who had been trying to get a date with Jess for several months. Shirley ate lunch with them and told her she was crazy for going out there like she did, but she could see that she was more relaxed and happier than she had been in years. While they were there Jessica talked Shirley into coming out and doing a home evaluation earlier than originally planned so she would for sure be there when they came out because she did not know how well Cowboy and the others would do under that kind of pressure. The day passed by quickly and they managed to get all the tablecloths and other decorations like plates and cups for the celebration. The 2 of them had been together all day and still had not run out of things to talk about. They connected like long lost sisters. On their way back Cowboy had called to check on them because he was worried, they were not in town or at the house and there was no note. She was flattered that he was concerned but took the time to razz him for stalking her and being to controlling but he spun the concern to Susan and LG and the other kids telling her she had his 3 girls and his top working hand with her and that he was not worried about her. The girls made it back around 6 that afternoon and Cowboy had already made dinner and set the table.

Jessica came in with the baby in her arms carrying the diaper bag and few more sacks. Susan and the 2 kids came in with their arms loaded with more boxes and bags. Jessica looked in the kitchen and saw the dinner table set with food on in it. "Now this is first class service dinner is ready and I had a handsome man make it for me. You can't beat that. What is this going to cost me?"

"By the looks of things about what all that junk you bought cost me, but we can work that out later tonight.... Ya'll come eat before it gets colder"

Jess set the baby in her chair and kissed Cowboy on the cheek, asking if he had missed her and began making plates for everyone. Cowboy instructed her to sit down he would take care of making the plates. Dinner was good as usual with fun conversation and harassment being served like a dish in the middle of the table. Jess and Susan told them about their day and gong to the hospital.

Then Jessica informed them that Shirley would be out on Thursday to do their home evaluation. Cowboy was not too sure how to react to the news so asked what all that stuff meant and what they were going to do when they came out. Jessica just reassured him everything would be fine, and she would handle it for him. After dinner was over and the table was cleared everyone went off to their little quite places. Susan and Bratton to the pecan tree between the barn and the house that had a porch swing hung in it. Cross and Dylan went out to the barn to tinker with stuff, Cass lay on the floor watching TV and playing with LG and Jessica curled up next to Cowboy on the front porch swing drinking coffee while he smoked a nasty cigar and drank a beer. She knew something was wrong with him because he had not been drinking or smoking around her the past few days and tonight, he was. She asked him what was bothering him several different ways and he just replied that he had a lot on his mind. So, she just lay in silence with her head now in his lap looking up at him. He broke the silence by asking if they were gonna try and take the baby away from them. Jess assured him that would not happen.

"Well how are they going to feel with you going back to work and not being here?"

"It will be fine Kim don't get worked up about this. This is just a formality they have to come out by law, but Shirley is not out to take LG away from you. She is one of my oldest friends and she knows I would not be here if you were not good to that baby or me."

"I just don't like stuff like this"

"I know that is why I made sure I would be here when they came out so you or ya'll don't have to do it alone." She could see the worry in his eyes and the stress building on his shoulders. Such a strong and commanding man was almost scared to death to have them come out and all she could do was try to comfort him and let him know she would be there to handle the situation.

"Kim I am sorry if I overstepped my boundaries, I just thought you would like to get it out of the way while I was still here every day other than to wait."

"You didn't do anything wrong I appreciate you taking care of it I just have heard a lot of stuff about these kinds of people and I really don't think the lady even likes me."

"You will be fine, and she likes you she is just doing her job and looking out for me. Don't worry about it" she said while pulling him down toward her and lifting her head from his lap she gave him a kiss. "You do your job and I will do mine OK I will make sure nothing bad happens." Then she wrapped her arms around his neck and squeezed him tight holding him for a few seconds before breaking the tension with "that cigar has got to go."

"I know I will put it out."

"No it is fine I will just lay down here and the smoke won't bother me" she placed her head back in his lap with a grin because just him offering to put it out made her feel like they were taking steps towards a relationship "but you better be brushing those teeth real good before you get in bed and kiss me tonight"

"You sure are getting demanding maybe you are a little too comfortable now."

"I am and I like it. I like it just like this. You, me the kids, Susan and Cross if it is like this even a 10th of the time out here I would still be the luckiest girl alive. It is going to be hard to leave next week."

"Why do you have to leave?"

"The kids have school; I have work, and the house."

"So that can all be fixed. You can stay here and work for me. Moving his hand down to her breast and winking at her"

"Then I would just be a prostitute"

"No not like that I was just funnin' with you. You could stay here and help out with the baby and around the house. You and the kids move them to school here and they can help out to. We got plenty of room"

"Don't you think that is a little too fast?"

"At our age we don't got a lot of time."

"I know it is a nice thought but a little to fairy tail'ish to me. I would love to be here with you but let's give it some time and see how we do before we jump into that situation let's not rush a good thing."

"I guess you are right. I just don't know if I am going to like being away from ya'll. It has gone by fast, but it seems like I have known you all my life. I think I know how Bratton feels when Susan is around now."

"Ahh…That was sweet. I have known you all my life, I just never knew where to find you. Let's not talk about this now we still have a few more days let's just enjoy them together."

That night and the next day flew by and Thursday was there before anyone knew what hit them. The day started off like any other day. The men were up at dawn and the girls shortly after they had left would start their day. By time noon had come around and the guys had come back to the house Jessica and Susan had the house clean, lunch ready and all the other chores done. Jessica had received a call from Shirley telling her they were on their way from Fort Worth to the house. Jessica figured it would take them about an hour and a half to make to the turn off from the hi-way and she would meet them there so they could follow her to the house. She told Kim she was going to meet them, and that Susan would stay and watch the kids until she got back. Kim unsure what to do paced around the house and tinkered with little thing to occupy his mind not sure what was to come of this meeting. After waiting 45 min to an hour they came down the drive. Kim had some sun tea making on the front porch. He met Jessica at the car and the 2 of them greeted Shirley and her entourage as they got out of the vehicle. Shirley had another man and woman with her to help get the evaluation done in a timely manner. Kim introduced himself to the new guest and invited them inside. They followed him across the walkway under the big pecan tree with the homemade swing hanging from it and up on the porch. Kim grabbed the sun tea as he crossed the threshold of the door. "Ya'll make yourselves at home. Would anyone like some iced tea or something else to drink?"

"No, we are fine" they all replied in unison

"Well I would like a drink" he muttered as he stammered into the kitchen with Jessica in tow

"I heard that Kim" as she patted him on the back "just breath it will be over soon it is really no big deal"

"If you say so"

The 2 of them went back into the living room together. Kim sat in his recliner and Jessica sat on the arm of his chair.

"This is a really beautiful place you have here Kim" Shirley said in amazement.

"Well thank you it has been in our family for over a hundred years now and we kind of like it. It aint much but it is all we need."

"They are having a big celebration this weekend for them because after your family has owned a piece of property for more than 100 years it becomes a historical marker for the state. The governor will be here, and a few other local politicians are coming" Jessica added.

"The governor?" The other gentleman, Paul inquired "That sounds like a big deal"

"No not really his family and mine have known each other for many years and I am sure he feels obligated. We used to run around together in the summer when we were growing up. He would come up here or I would go down there. When we made it to high school that all kind of stopped. It will be good to see Rick again."

"You mean to tell me you know Rick Perry the governor?" Jessica questioned him

"Well yea why you think he is coming out?"

"You never said you knew him, just that he was coming."

"Well you never asked me either. We can discuss that later let's get this business out of the way so these nice people can get home at a descent hour. What do we need to do?"

"Well for starters you need to get all these dead animals off your wall they are scaring me" Shirley joked but Kim was not sure how to take it.

"OK, I guess. They are dead they aint hurting nothing."

"I know I am just giving you a hard time. You need to relax. I have already talked to Jessica and you are fine we just need to take a few pictures and look around to see if anything might put the baby at risk. If there is something which I am sure there isn't then you fix it, we are good. No big deal"

"Well that makes me feel better. How long do you think this will take?"

"Maybe an hour or so"

"Well do you need me?"

"Actually, I thought you and I might talk while they do the rest of the stuff. If that is Ok with you."

"Sure, you bet you want to walk and talk, and I can show you around, while we talk?"

"That would be great."

Cowboy thought he would butter her up while she was there, and it would make things go easier. Cowboy and Shirley took off for their walk about and Jessica went with Paul and Jana to show them the house. Shirley and Cowboy walked out to the barn and looked at the horses and a few calves that were in the stall. Shirley was doing most of the talking asking questions about how things were going and how he felt about the baby being there and then she asked what the plans were after Jessica left and went back to work. She needed to know for her work, but she was also being just a little bit nosey.

Kim looked at the ground and raked some hay around with his boot. "Well I tell you as for the baby? She will be fine I raised my boy out here and he turned out pretty good we will make it work. If I have to hire a nanny or something I will but to be really honest with you and from a selfish standpoint I would just prefer her to stay. It works real good with her here and we all get along. None of us mince words, we say what is on our mind and that is it."

"That is pretty selfish. She has a life of her own and you expect her to uproot her family because it works better with her here? Look from a personal standpoint I think she probably would drop everything and move out here if you wanted her too, but would that be fair to all of them?"

"Well them kids love it out here. We would treat them just like family and I think she is happy out here too. I know it is crazy. I know it is selfish. I also know that she is a great woman and means a great deal to me."

"How does that saying go about the milk and the cow? You can't have you cake and eat it too. You know what I am getting at?"

"I know you are right, and I am not going to pressure her into doing anything like that but, if she wants to, I certainly will not try to talk her out of it. You seem like you are a pretty good friend to her, and I appreciate you taking the time to talk with me. Most people don't have the nerve to talk with someone face to face like this they would prefer to talk behind their back, and I can respect you for not doing that to me."

"She is a very close friend and I certainly see what she sees in you. I have to admit you are much different than I envisioned you. I figured you to be like a trailer park redneck and just putting on a show, but you are real and honest, and I like that in a person. I know Jessica definitely likes that about all of you out here."

"Well we both have stereo types but at least our first impressions are not set in stone and we take the time to talk to someone before we pass judgment. Enough of this talk for now are you interested in taking a ride and seeing the rest of the place?"

"I am not sure how long will it take and what do you mean by ride?"

"Well I was thinking the truck but if you want, we can take the horses or the 4-wheeler it won't take but about 30 min or so to take a quick trip."

"The truck sounds safe I am not one for adventure, but we will need to be getting back soon so we can't stay gone long."

"It is a deal come 'on and hop in"

Cowboy started the truck and they were on their way across the pastures and through the thickets bouncing around but not going to fast so he wouldn't worry Shirley. He made his way over to the fishing pond and back around to the back 40. Shirley loved the secluded pond in the middle of the property and struck up conversation of her grandma taking her fishing back in the Louisiana swamps where she was born. Cowboy saved the best for last and began making his way through the trees to old baldy.

"Normally I would take you up her right at sundown but we are running out of time so I will just have to tell you about it when we get up there." He topped the hill and passed through the trees immediately after that she saw the world open up to her.

"WoW!!! "She stated in amazement "this is gorgeous. You can see forever from here."

"Yes, ma'am you can. We kind of like it up here. This is like our sanctuary for us up here. We all come up here to clear our minds. My mom and dad taught me that when I was real little. Mom said if you had problems or questions about life that you could get the answer sitting here on this big rock looking over Gods creation. She told me that you could hear God better up here because you were closer to him and there was nothing to interfere with his voice."

"I am speechless I would not know how to tell anyone how beautiful this is. I may start coming out here to figure my problem. My goodness I could sit here for hours"

"At sundown a lot of the time you can see little rainbows in the field and then all the animals start scurrying around to either bed down for the night or start hunting. There is no telling what you will see from here it is always something different."

"Have you shown Jessica this? I am sure you have but what did she say?"

"Actually, she has been here, but Cross brought her up here one afternoon just before dark. I think she liked it."

"How could you not like it?"

They sat on that rock for 45 minutes talking and Kim showing her different things in the panoramic view that he had discovered over the years and explain the history of the property to her in an abbreviated form. She soaked all the information up and asked several questions about the old days on the farm and even inquired about his great grandparents. Then she asked the question without realizing what she was asking or what the answer might be

"Did you have slaves out here working?"

"Slaves? Well I guess you could have called them that, but they never thought of them that way. They considered all of them family. Technically yes, they were slaves, but my grandpa never once kept them here against their will. And grandma taught them all how to read. The little ones at least when they were freed most of them stayed here and worked and nothing changed. I remember when I was little there were still a few left out here and it never dawned on me until I got older that they had all stayed because they were always treated like family. They ate with us showered in the house and had the right to go work at another place if they wanted. We even paid for a few of them to go up north after the war, but they returned shortly after leaving."

"I am sorry I probably should not have asked that it was out of line."

'It is quite alright if you had offended me, I would have told you. I am not ashamed of my family's past. Owning a slave is different than having one work with you. and they did not own them."

"That is nice to hear I just didn't think before I asked but I am glad to hear that they treated them so well."

"Maybe someday you can come back out here and I can show you some old pictures and tell you more about the ones I knew."

"That sounds like something I would enjoy." She sheepishly replied. Listening to his story made her reminisce of the stories her family told her when she was young about the slaves she could tell she was becoming emotional and did not like anyone to see her in that vulnerable state of mind so she quickly routed the conversation another direction.

"Look at you. You old charmer I see what you are doing trying to soften me up."

"No, I was just being honest with you"

"I know what you are doing, and it is working. I can't help but like you. You old scraggly cowboy, you are a charmer I gotta hand it to you but we have to get back before I end up marrying you and we would both be up the creek with Miss Jessy."

"Well alright if you say so but I am serious you come out any time and we can sit and talk about what I know if you want."

She opened the door to the truck and hopped up in the seat. "I may take you up on that offer when I get some time."

The two of them meandered back to the house at a slower pace and cut up with one another the entire trip back. When they stopped the truck, you could hear the 2 laughing and cutting up. Jessica was on the porch with the other 2 CPS members. They all convened in the living room to do a recap of the audit. The audit went very well overall, there were a few things that needed to be replaced or corrected but aside from that the biggest problem Shirley had was with the deer heads and dead animals.

"You are gonna have to do something with these things you got on the wall."

"Come on now they are not hurting anybody they are for decoration"

"Well you need a new decorator for your house then cuz these things scare me to death. That little one is probably already scarred for life." She joked.

"I guess I could move them to another room or something, if I have to but I don't see the point. She will have one on the wall before too long"

"It better be a long time before that happens."

"I am sure it will be. Is that all you got to complain about? I figured you would nitpick everything as grouchy as you are" he said to Shirley as he through his long arm around her and pulled her to his side. "You aint so tough"

"Actually, there is another issue you need to fix."

"What is that sweetheart"

"Her name, you can't call her LG. She needs a real name."

"I agree" Jessica blurted out as the rest of them nodded in agreement with the two ladies.

"Now that is an old family name" Cowboy started

"I don't care it is awful" Jessica reminded him of how he came up with the name.

"How are you going to explain that when she grows up?"

"Ok. Ok. Don't send the lynch mob after me we will find a new name for her. What do we need to do for a birth certificate?"

"You get the name and we will get you a birth certificate." Shirley remarked sharply with a smile.

"Yes, ma'am we will get right on that. I should have it by the end of the week We will run a search make sure there are no babies missing that match her and as long as no one files an inquiry we will have to do adoption paper work and she will be all yours."

Shirley and the others made their way to the car outside with Jessica and Cowboy trailing behind them. Cowboy thanked each one of them and gave them an open invitation to come back anytime. He made his way to the Drivers side of the car and opened the door for Shirley and gave her a hug. "I really enjoyed talking with you I hope you get a chance to come back and visit."

"I had a good time and I will see what I can do about getting back out here. I really like your place and I am sorry I miss judged you at first, but I am glad we had time to talk."

"NO problem ya'll be careful on the way out" as he slowly walked to the porch. Jess said her goodbyes and stood by the driveway waving as the pulled away. Then she walked up to the porch and wrapped her arms around Kim placing her head against his chest. "You are such a player"

"What do you mean?"

"I seen you over there hamming it up with Shirley and you were just loving it weren't you"

"NO, I wasn't" smiling from ear to ear and trying not to laugh" I was just being me." As he chuckled, she slapped him lightly on the stomach

"You are awful but thank you for taking the time to get to know her she really is sweet."

"I know she is great to cut up with when you get to know her. That wasn't so bad, I guess. Thank you for helping me out with all this I would have been a mumbling idiot if you had not been here"

"You are welcome, but I would not have done it if I didn't care. So, what are you thinking for her name?"

"I am thinking Jayla"

"No, I was thinking Maddy, or Emma, I don't know"

"I tell you what we will do. Tonight, after dinner we will all come up with a name and set her in the floor and whoever she goes to we will use their name."

"That sounds like a good idea. You are so smart".

They went back to their daily routines and dinner came and passed. Everyone gathered on the front porch that evening to join in the activity for the night. Cowboy explained the rules of the game to everyone and why they were doing it. So, they started with the youngest and each one of them gave out a name.

Cassie "Barbie"

Everyone sighed. "We all know the rules' Cowboy reminded them.

Dylan "Jenifer"

Susan "Madison Ann we could call her Maddy Ann"

"That is cute" Jessica muttered lightly nodding her head

Bratton "Kylie"

Jessica "Jayla Marie" Everyone ooed and awed as if to mock her

Cowboy "Emily Rose"

All their eyes lit up "I like that' Jessica commented

"If it were me, I would name her Elizabeth after my wife because she is the prettiest thing I have seen since she passed." I said.

Everyone got quite and shook their heads as if it were a great idea. Cowboy grabbed up the baby and said, "alright LG that is the last time you hear that name." He placed her in her walker in the middle of the porch and turned her loose. She sat still and looked at everyone around her. The adults began to make funny faces and sounds to entice her to come their way and she would start towards one person and then turn to another. Everyone was sure to keep her from Cassie because none of them wanted to call her Barbie. After a few minutes she made her way to Bratton and then turned to her side and reached out for Jessica. "Well that settles it her name is now Jayla Marie"

"I think I want to change it I like Cross' name better Elizabeth. We can call her Libby for short. Libby Tate Lee. Tate after your mother's maiden name Cowboy. How does that sound?"

They all agreed it was the perfect name Cross grabbed her up and held her in his hands with his arms stretched out to the ceiling. Talking to the baby "Are you gonna be able to live up to that big of a name baby girl? I bet you will as he pulled her back to him and hugged her tight." The old man's whiskers tickled her face and she began to giggle. "You love your uncle Cross don't you Libby girl?"

"Uncle??" Bratton coughed out "you mean great grandpa is more like it"

"You watch your mouth" I replied "I aint no grandpa I am her great uncle then. Who cares she still loves me?"

"Ok we will compromise great uncle Cross."

Jess knew she had made his day by seeing him play with Libby. He would hold her and talk to her, but he never really played with her until they named her and now all the sudden no one else was good enough to hold her but him. His eyes were gleaming with joy and pride he was smiling and talking to everyone.

They sat on the porch for an hour or so before Jessica and Susan went in the house to put the other 2 children to bed and clean up the kitchen. Me, Cowboy, and Bratton all stayed on the porch talking and I was still latched on too little Libby. I would place her in her walker from time to time, but she would make her way back to me shortly after and hold her hands up smiling at me. I was a sucker and picked her up every time. It was apparent that the little girl was related to Cowboy and Bratton because she already knew how to get what she wanted, and she knew how to soften an old man's heart.

Chapter 18

THE BIG SHINDIG

After Cleaning the kitchen and getting the other little ones in bed Susan and Jess came back out to the porch with the others. Susan retrieved Libby by giving her a bottle she had just made and took her off to lay her down for the night. Shortly after that I retired to my quarters leaving Jessica, Susan, Bratton, and Cowboy on the porch. The 4 of them talk and discussed plans for the upcoming event. The girls lined the men out on what they needed done on each day. Kim was to ensure the yard was mowed on Friday and Bratton was to go and pick up the tables. The trailer needed to be set up in front of the barn so it could be used as a stage and the girls could decorate it. Jessica described the structure she needed to be built and Susan explained the backdrop for the stage. The two women had taken over the celebration and never even asked any of the men what they wanted. The guys were fine with them hijacking their celebration but felt a little left out. Cowboy made the remark "looks like you girls have it all figured out. Do I get any say in this at all?"

"You had your chance and you decided to have bar-b-que so that is all the say you get other than yes ma'am!! We don't have time for you guys to him haw around to make decisions we have to be ready this weekend so be ready to work." Susan sassily replied

"Yes ma'am!!" Bratton exclaimed quickly "We are on it"

"I guess I have no choice but to say Yes ma'am too. You just tell me what to do next and I will do one thing at a time." Kim explained to Jessica "Whatever you want you come see me I will be your pack mule." As he walked by her toward the door of the house dragging his hand lightly across the small of her back as if to tell come on let's go without verbally saying it.

"I am tired, and we are going to be busy we better get to bed" as Jessica followed quickly behind her man. The other two followed closely behind them and retired for the night as well. The next 2 days went by like Christmas for a parent with no money. Saturday came around and everyone was up early and moving. It looked like a fire ant mound someone had stepped on. Trucks coming and going, people scampering about. Jessica's Mother and father showed up early to help out and Susan's Mom and Dad drove up shortly after. Susan had called earlier to have them pick up the meat from the smoke house and bring it to the ranch. By lunch time everything was pretty well done the tables were set up the food was warming on the smoker and the stage was decorated and set for the band. Susan and Jessica had decorated everything in red, White and blue much like a Fourth of July celebration. The invitation said the party started at 3 but people began showing up at 1:30. Kim had called a couple of Deputy Sheriffs that he had gone to school with to help keep reporters out that might try to sneak in, other than the ones from the local paper he had already talked with. He did not want his old buddy Rick to have to deal with them today. Rick was scheduled to be flown in by helicopter around 3 and Cross had roped an area off in the field behind the house for them to land in and a few of the State troopers assigned to him had shown up earlier in the day to get familiar with the place and to guide them in when he arrived. Jeromy Marlin a friend of Bratton's had a band and was performing before and after the dedication. He began playing right at 3 and stopped briefly for the County Commissioner to introduce Rick Perry who gave the speech for the dedication. After the speech Gov. Perry called Kim to the stage to receive the plague he had made for the event. Kim motioned for me, and Bratton to come up with him to receive the award. He gave a simple little speech thanking the Governor, Commissioner, and everyone who had come out. Then he made a special thank You to Jessica and Susan for everything they had done to get the place ready and giving them the credit for the whole event. The Jeromy and The Back-Road Drifters, his band, fired up the music again and the party kicked off. Kim and The Governor took a walk around the property and reminisced before he had to get back to Austin. Gov. Perry was like a kid again out there. He remembered how simple everything was when they were little and wished it could go back to those days. Cowboy assured him that he was glad it was him who was running the state and not himself. He could not deal with the headache and gave him an open invite to come back any time he needed to clear his head and get away. Prior to leaving he shook everyone's hand and kissed all the babies. He got to me and gave him a hug. He told me "It is hard working people like you that made me want to run for Governor. You taught me a lot growing up and I owe you for that."

I was taken off guard by the comment he did not even think he would have remembered me from so long ago and told him he was welcome and that he was doing a good job and it made me proud to be part of his past. Shortly after that he boarded the helicopter and flew out.

Everyone sat around drinking, eating and dancing for hours. The party did not start winding down until about 11:00pm and it was not until 1:00am before the last person left aside from Jerry, Gayle, James and Stephanie who all had decide to stay the night. JT and Stephanie brought their travel trailer. Gayle and jerry would be staying in the living quarters of the horse trailer the boys had bought for out of town rodeos and camping trips. Jess had already put the little ones to bed around 10 and her, Susan, Gayle and Stephanie would check on them from time to time. The ladies had been picking up things throughout the night, so the place was pretty clean. The men collapsed the tables and chairs and loaded them on the truck. Kim said everything else could wait until the next day so they could all sit and talk. They sat outside cutting up and drinking beer. Kim, JT and I were feeling pretty good. Jess thought Bratton might have been drinking to even though she never saw him drinking but wasn't going to say anything because they were all having a good time and her dad was feeling no pain either. They were too funny to stop they all laughed, razzed one another and tested their testosterone with stupid little games they came up with to see who was tougher. One game in particular was a game they played with a rat trap, Jess had never seen a rat trap before, it was a mouse trap but 4 times the size and much more powerful. They would take a penny and set it on the trigger of the trap with it cocked. If you set one on there without triggering the trap the next guy had to set his penny on top of yours. If the trap went off, you had to take a drink for each penny on the trap and yours as well. She knew it had to be painful when you got hit but none of them would admit it, even her father who was acting like a teenager with the rest of the men. She had never seen her dad act like this before and knew she was gonna have trouble getting him to go home after the bonding time with all the guys. Even though the game was stupid she knew her dad needed something like this to keep him going. The game carried on until 3:30 am and they finally wound down and called it a night. Jess and Kim got Jerry and Gayle settled into the trailer and Bratton and Susan helped hook up her mom and dad's trailer. It was about 4:00am before Jess and Kim got to bed, they were both exhausted and fell fast asleep.

Chapter 19

TOO SOON TO LEAVE

*T*he next morning Kim heard Libby crying around 8 o'clock. He got up and changed her and made her a bottle. He sat in the kitchen playing with her and fed her before she fell back to sleep. He returned to the kitchen and began making breakfast. Bratton woke up next and came in to help. Before Breakfast was done all the men were in the kitchen helping out and drinking coffee. The women on the other hand were all still asleep. Stephanie was the first lady to arrive in the kitchen about 30 minutes after the food was done. In disbelief that all the men had been up for an hour and had breakfast made she sat in JT's lap and enjoyed a cup of coffee and intriguing conversation before Jess stumbled into the kitchen wearing her normal morning attire except with a pair of boxers on under the shirt. Still sleepy and not thinking everyone else was already awake she was a little embarrassed and surprised, walking out of Cowboys room with his shirt on in front of her parents and new found friends, but she needed coffee so she pretended like it was no big deal and made her way to the stove to poor a cup of morning pick me up. After pouring the coffee she nuzzled up to Cowboy who quickly draped his arm across her shoulders and told her good morning beautiful. She finished her coffee and went to check on Libby. Cowboy quickly stopped her and told her she was fine, and he had already fed and changed her this morning. She then decided to take a shower and get dressed. JT who always liked to stir the pot blurted out "no need to change I like that look." As he winked at Cowboy and gave him the two thumbs up. Stephanie was quick to hit him and put him in his place as he laughed about the whole thing asking her "what did I do" Cowboy smiled and Jessica rebutted "I think I will change so you don't get in anymore trouble."

Stephanie got on to him "James see what you did you up set her"

"I was just kidding her. You think I should go tell her that while she is in the shower?"

"I think you should shut your mouth before you really get in trouble."

Cowboy defused the situation "you did not embarrass or offend that one in there she is tough as nails and don't scare easy. She has been out here for 2 weeks now and aint left yet she is used to it from all of us"

"Well she sure seems to be a sweetheart" Steph commented

"You know I approve of her "JT chirped

"She is good to have around" Bratton added

"Well I guess there is no point in taking a vote on whether to keep her around. It don't matter she has to go back to work tomorrow anyway.'

Her dad sitting in silence listening to the conversation could see the disappointment in Cowboys eyes and hear the frustration in his voice.

"What are ya'll gonna do with the baby?" Jerry asked

"Oh Libby? She will be fine we will figure that out."

The conversation became very somber and the rest of the people found things to do like get the kids up and ready. Wake up Susan. So, they all departed the kitchen and dispersed throughout the house or the property. Cowboy was left in the kitchen by himself for a brief moment and started to clean up when Gayle wandered into the dining area "Good morning Cowboy how are you?"

"I'm fine how did you sleep?"

"I slept great the night air was cool and the bed was comfortable."

"I am glad to hear that. There're some biscuits in the oven and bacon on the stove if you are hungry. I am gonna go get dressed." As he walked to his bedroom.

He was in the bedroom when Jess came out of the shower wrapped in a towel and drying her hair with another one. He was on the bed with no shirt on, his pants pulled up but not buttoned and pulling his boots on. She stood in front of him looking down at him and he did not acknowledge her. She inched closer and closer to him and he still said nothing and did not look up. So, she reached for his head with both hands to hug him she pulled him to her at that same time her towel fell to the floor. That managed to get his attention his face against her bare midriff and her standing there naked. Then she quickly grabbed it back up and covered herself up quickly. Shocked at what has just happened but not really embarrassed she sat on the bed beside him and laughed. "I can't believe that just happened"

"That is one way to get my attention"

"It was an accident"

"I don't care I liked it. You should do that more often"

"Maybe I will"

"Who are you kidding you are going home tonight."

"Oh my gosh I do have to go home tonight. I forgot all about that. I have a lot of work to do."

"Well you better get to it"

"What is wrong with you? Are you just tired?"

"Yea that is it I am just tired"

"Cowboy don't be like this what is wrong."

"Nothing"

"Let's cut through the chase we are too old and don't have time for this. I will ask you 100 times if I have to, but it will be much easier if you just come out with it."

"It is just we have been so busy; this week went by too fast. We were just getting to know one another before this week, and we got so busy that we didn't really get a chance to enjoy the week and now it is time for you to go. There just ain't enough time and I know it isn't fair to you to ask you to stay but being selfish I wish you would"

"I would love to stay here, and it will be hard to go but maybe being a part, we can decide whether or not this is what we really want. You may find someone else as soon as I leave and decide you never really needed me. I hope that doesn't happen but if it does then we were not meant to be together. Me and the kids will be back on the weekends to check on ya'll. It will only be 5 days."

"Well I aint looking for no one else. I guess you are right this will be a way of slowing things down like we talked about, but it still isn't what I

169

wanted. I guess I just thought you would stay here but I know that is not an option right now."

"I wish it were. I cannot afford to miss work and the kids need to finish school. I also need to pre-warn you that Susan is wanting to move back here so she can graduate from her hometown. Don't tell her I told you but her and Bratton have already talked about it and they are planning on talk to you and her dad about it today before they leave. She can help with Libby after she gets out of school and this will give her time to adjust to being here again with all you boys if ya'll decide to let her stay."

"She knows she can stay here, and I am sure JT won't have an issue with her staying here. As for Libby I aint worried about her she will be fine. I am glad she came along or I would have never met up with you."

"Ahh!! You are so sweet I love to hear you say sweet things like that to me. She raised herself from the bed to kiss him on the cheek and squeeze him tightly "come on let's get dressed before I lose this towel on purpose and we are locked in here for hours. She stood up from the bed and started walking back to the bathroom. He watched her float across the floor and as she crossed the doorway, she grabbed the door. Just before she closed the door, she let her towel fall to the ground and closed the door real fast and locked it just to tease him.

"That was all kinds of wrong Jessie. A beautiful woman like you should not tease the beast like that. I am going to clean up. Hurry up and get your stuff done so we can spend a little bit of time together." He left the room as she hollered out "I will be done in about 30 minutes."

While they were in the room Susan had already gotten all the kid's things together and packed their bags for them. Not to rush them out but she didn't want Jessica to have to do it she wanted her to be able to enjoy her last few hours on the ranch and not be rushed.

Jess finished getting dressed and came out to see everything packed and ready to go. Her mother had helped Susan out with feeding the kids and making sure they were dressed. All Jessica had to do was pack her clothes and she was done. She began putting all her clothes in the bag and remembered what Susan had told her she did with Bratton's shirts. So, she took one of Cowboy's shirts squirted it with his cologne and placed it in her bag with her other clothes. She went outside to be with the others and help pick up what remained from the party last night/ this morning. Her mother pulled her to the side and talked to her in for a few minutes and Cowboy could see the two having a discussion about something but was not sure what it was about. He could see that Jessica and her mother were very animated with their conversation using their hands and moving their heads, but it did not appear they were arguing. Cowboy was curious if he had done something to upset her mother or what was going on. When the conversation was over Jess walked over to him. He wasted no time "Is everything OK?"

"Y'yea?? Why?"

"Well it looked like you and mom there were having a heated discussion over there and I wanted to make sure I didn't do something wrong to upset her."

"No, she is just crazy and so are you"

"Why what did I do?"

"Nothing you are just being you and everybody just loves to be around you" she sassed off to him

"Hold on. What is going on you sound pissed right now."

"No, I am not pissed just aggravated. Everybody wants to be around you and do things for you including me and I can't be around you because of everything I have going on."

"Why don't you tell me what she said, and we can go from there."

"O!! alright! She wanted me to let you know if you need help with Libby, her and Dad would be more than happy to stay around and help out. If you need them to but they did not want to be a burden on you. They are retired and don't have to work so they can do that and not have to worry I can't, but I want to." Her eyes tearing up and she leaned into him placing her head on his chest with her arms crossed

He put his arms around her and rocked her side to side "Look if you don't want them to stay here that is fine I will tell them no but really they are welcome to come out her any time they want that is if they don't mind that old horse trailer out there. When it comes to you and them kids, I already told you, ya'll don't have to leave you can stay here as long as you want. Your parents don't have to work to come out here."

"I know but mom is right dad loves this kind of work and she doesn't mind being out here. She thinks it will do him some good to be outside working and in the fresh air. It will keep him young she said. And I know she is right, and I know you will let them, and you will take care of them, but I am just jealous is all it is." She wiped the tears from her eyes and looked up at him. Her cheeks were red and swollen from being upset.

He reached up and lightly grabbed her by the chin to make her look into his eyes when he said "Well don't be jealous of them. I like you better than all of them."

"Yea. You like the fringe benefits is what you like." She joked with a halfhearted smile

"Well that don't hurt but that's not all I like about you." He lightly kissed her on the forehead. "Tell them to hang out as long as they want, we can always use the extra hands during hay season if your dad wants to work. Or should I tell them?"

"You tell them. I am just frustrated I am trying to be strong about leaving but I don't want to go, and I know I have to be a responsible adult and do what is right for the kids".

"I tell you what. Let's try this until the end of school and when the kids get out if you feel the same way ya'll come live out here. Don't worry about the money we are not hurting. Bratton is going off to college and I will need the extra hand if your dad likes it, they can hang around and we can build them a shack off by the barn if we need to."

"I hate it that you have all the answer and that you are so nice. I am not going to know how to act going back home. You are too nice this has got to be a dream when I wake up at home I will not even want to get out of bed."

"Come on don't go getting all sappy just yet we got a few hours left here so let's enjoy them. I will go and ask your dad if he wants to help out"

Walking towards the trailer they knocked on the door. Kim asked Jerry if he would like to help him out around the place through the hay season.

Jerry was quick to reply, "only if you really need help, I don't need no charity."

"No Charity at all it is long hot work, on a tractor most times and under the tractor all the other times. Bratton will be going off to school and I honestly need the help, or I would not have asked you. If Gayle wants to hang out and watch Libby while we are out, then I will pay her to be a nanny but she aint doing it for free. Now those are the terms you will have to stay in the trailer for the first few weeks, but we can make other arrangements later on. Take it or leave it that is my offer." Cowboy had a way of making people think they were doing him a favor by working for him, but he genuinely needed the help.

Jerry looked to Gayle "What do you think momma?"

She shrugged her shoulders and then nodded in agreement because they had already discussed it after Jerry had heard the discontent in his voice from their conversation earlier. It was all his idea, but he made Gayle think it was her idea.

"Looks like we got a deal: as he extended his hand toward Cowboy's. Cowboy dusted his right hand off on the thigh of his blue jeans and grabbed Jerry's hand firmly to shake it "welcome aboard."

"Sounds good I need to be working and not laying around. We will run home get our stuff and be back tomorrow unless you need me before then."

"No that will be fine"

While their conversation was taking place Bratton, JT and I had picked up everything and Steph and Susan had gotten all the trash and decorations picked up and were involved in their own conversation about Susan. When Jessica and Kim headed their direction, he could hear JT emphatically saying "let me discuss it with Cowboy…. no more talking we will discuss it and let you know" Cowboy entered the conversation

"What is going on over here?"

"These kids are plotting against us"

"What now?"

JT put his arm on Cowboy's shoulder come on let's talk." Walking Cowboy toward the barn.

"What is the deal" Cowboy asked

"Well it is like this Susan wants to stay here and finish out school in her hometown. Now I don't have an issue with that but when Brat came to see us the other weekend, we had a little heart to heart, and he is wanting to ask Susan to marry him. I don't get no problem with that I love him to death but they aint getting engaged until after they get out of school and I don't want no grandkids on the way. You know where I am coming from don't you"

"I sure do" Cowboy remarked "we can settle this as he hollered out for Bratton to come over there.

"Bratton hustled to the barn and stood between the two men towering over him and I came up from behind him to see what the problem was.

"Yes sir?" not sure what was going on or what had been said.

"JT just told me about you and Susan and her wanting to live here. None of us have any problems with her being out here. Our problem is with you and if you so much as lay one finger on that girl inappropriately we will bury you out by the big live oak. Keep in mind I did not say kill you just burry you because we would want you to have time to think about what you did. Do we understand each other? They all stood with their arms crossed and took a step in towards him so close he could hear the three of them breathe.

"Yes, Sir I give you my word"

"I love you boy you are like a son to me but that is my little girl and I am serious about this."

"I understand no funny stuff. Hay season is fixing to kick off and I wouldn't have time anyway."

"I will see to that" I added my 2 cents worth.

JT grabbed him with one arm around the neck and pulled him into a choke hold. "you know I love you but don't cross me"

The 4 men walked back to the girls and JT said "come on Momma load up so we can get back to the house. Susan you better be back next weekend to get your clothes."

Her mom pulled her to the side to tell her she would withdraw her from school on Monday and send her record and that she would call the principal here to get her in school. Also, she wanted to tell her she loved her. They hugged and the 2 of them made their way down the long drive. I took Jerry around the property so he would be familiar with everything. Susan and Gayle went inside, and Susan showed her were everything was for the baby. Bratton took Dylan and Cassie off on the 4-wheeler one last time. Jessica and Kim got in the old truck and went for a ride up on old baldy where they could enjoy a couple hours together before she had to leave. Sitting on the old rock they called the alter they talked about the whirl wind of events they had been through since they first met. Thinking back that just a few short weeks prior there were only 3 lonely cowboys on the ranch and now there were 4 more people living there in such a short time. Both of them wishing there were 3 more to add to that number. She lay on his shoulder like she had been doing every night for the last 2 weeks and neither of them said a word, but their hearts spoke to one another's. The time had come for her to go so she stood up and told him they needed to get back before it was too late. He stood up and held her tight to his chest and leaned down to kiss her. It was a kiss to remember, a loving kiss and embrace something for her to come back to and look back on while she was a way.

Chapter 20

GOODE OLD WISDOM

The trip back to the house was silent and lonely. Everyone was packed the cars loaded everyone was anticipating their return. They all hugged and kissed one more time to say goodbye and they left. Their taillights faded down the long drive and drama free goodbyes are what Kim likes but not this one. Not this way. He did not like this at all and it was apparent to the ones left behind at the house. Bratton and Susan quickly made a getaway so not to have to listen to him gripe and complain. I stood on the porch waiting on Cowboy to come back up. Cowboy sat on the swing and I was in my rocking chair whittling on a piece of wood. We had sat in silence for some time and when I leaned back in the chair looked out toward the road "man what a month this has been. I am sure glad that is over with so we can get back to work"

"Yep it sure was crazy around here maybe thing will be somewhat normal without all the distractions."

"Maybe."

"Everybody was getting a little lazy with all the extracurricular activities going on."

"Yep"

"I am glad they are all gone."

"Yep"

I knew once he started the conversation Cowboy would continue on and try to reason with himself to make it easier on him, but he knew he did not want to see her drive off. Even if she was only an hour or so away, he still did not like it.

"Those are some good kids, but we got work to do and they would just be in the way"

"Yep"

"Well Dylan probably would have been able to help out around the barn and stuff, but I don't know if it would have been worth it."

"Yep"

"Cass she never even really came around during the day except to run to town with me so no real loss there"

"Yep"

"Jess was good to have around but we can do all the things she was doing"

"We have for years"

"We can handle raisin' a kid out here we raised Bratton"

"Yep but he was a boy we don't know a lot about girls"

"Well I figure Susan will be around"

"You don't reckon she will run off to College with Brat?"

"You are probably right"

"You reckon she will come back"

"I am sure they will for holidays and stuff, but I know Brat has wanted to get away from here and see the world. I am sure one day they will, but it will be a few years"

"I wasn't talking about them boss"

"Who are you talking about?"

'You know damn well who I am talking about"

"I'm sure they will come back a time or two, but I figure the drive will get old and they will skip a weekend or 2 here and there and then just eventually stop coming around."

"Sounds like you got this all figured out."

"Well it is true. This kind of stuff never works out. Women don't like to be on the road or have a long-distance relationship."

"I am guessing you know more about this stuff than I do so I will just have to trust you."

"Well that is what happened with Stacy she just could not stand me being gone all weekend at the rodeo and only see me one or 2 days a week. So, she went on the road with me and she didn't like that either"

"You don't think having a baby on the road was hard on her?"

"I am sure it was, but I was helping out. She just was too much into the Hollywood seen for all that kind of life. She found out that having a Cowboy wasn't like on TV it was hard work".

"Yep. Them girls, like that, don't know what to do with guys like us. I am sure there is one out there that does but where are you gonna find one of those?"

"I am assuming you are gonna tell me at the hospital"

"You tell me. It seemed to be working out fine and now you got one foot in the grave and she aint been gone more than an hour." I paused briefly waiting for a response. "Look I don't know a lot about chasing women. I married my high school sweetheart and aint been with any other woman. Now I don't normally get involved in your personal life but, it sure looked to me that you two were doing pretty good together. She is a good girl and thinks the world of you. So, you have to spend a few days apart. It will probably do you some good so you can see what really matters here. All these years I have watched you and your boy, who seems to have figured it out already, run around and worry about right here right now and getting by on sex and lust to feel the void of having someone to come home to and argue with you and fight about stupid stuff just so you can make up. I am sure it was fun running around putting notches on the bed post but that has to get old and at some point you have to realize that special woman is right in front of you and you have to step out of your shell and chase her for a change. I know what it is like to be married and I will tell you I'd rather be tied down than running around because from what I see it just makes you old and bitter the longer you do it."

"I guess you are right. I just don't know what to do. I haven't been in no relationship for so long I don't know how to."

"I don't either, but you might start by going into town and taking her out to dinner or lunch. You could send her some flowers or even take her some flowers. Boss you do what you want but I aint gonna let you mope around this place like you did when the last one run off. I don't know what happened I don't care but don't let this one slip away." I got up from the rocking chair and stretched my arms out to the ceiling. I staggered to the steps on the porch and put my hands on the rail leaning out toward the driveway. "I hope that helps" and walked toward the bunk house.

Cowboy sat there for a few minutes and pondered on the conversation which was a very unusual one to have with me. He knew to listen when I was speaking because we never really talked much but what I had to say was always worth hearing and I have always given him good advice in the past.

He finally stepped off the porch and got in the old truck driving across the property checking the fence or so he wanted it to appear and made his way to his destination atop of old baldy were he sat and watched the sun go down as he had so many times before when he was deliberating where his life was leading him. He had come to the conclusion that it was not just the relationship with Jessica bothering him but the transformation he was making in his personal life. He had a conviction weighing on his heart to change his ways for quite some time and meeting her had magnified it. His heart had never felt so heavy and the stress from fighting within himself felt like he was having a heart attack. Their family had never been much on church. They would go on special holidays and a few times during the colder months. Normally they were too busy working to make it the other times, but they did believe in God and the rock alter they had on top that hill was their church. Cowboy was lost and asked the Good Lord to tell him what to do. He knew what to do with Jessica and he knew Cross was right, but he was scared to go out on that limb and be rejected. That is the only thing that he was afraid of was the rejection.

Chapter 21

BABY TALK

The sun went down and Cowboy drove back to the house. Susan had made dinner and the crew ate and went to bed for an early night. His bed was cold and lonely he would toss and turn occasionally holler out to the living room to Bratton and Susan to settle down, who were laughing and joking in there. The next morning after he and little Libby ate breakfast and checked on the livestock, he went into to town to take back the tables and chairs they had rented. They stopped by the florist to see what they had for Jessica. He wanted to send something to thank her but nothing to extravagant. They fumbled through the shop for a little while before Debbie a lady he had graduated with asked if she could help him. "Well I am looking to send something to a friend, but I don't really want to send flowers."

"Where are you sending it?"

"She is in Fort Worth"

"Well we have a book over here with a whole bunch of stuff you might like. Now what is the occasion?"

"I just wanted to thank her for helping me out"

"OK and no flowers. How about candy? Stuffed animal? Or a fruit basket?"

"Ahh. No fruit what do you have in the way of candy."

She thumbed through the catalog. "Here they are" she turned the book to him so he could see it.

He looked through the pages and asked Libby her opinion.

"She is cute how old is she?"

"This old thing she is 6 months of spoiled rotten"

"She is not spoiled she is a doll what is her name?"

"Libby"

"That is a perfect name for her" as she came from behind the counter and took the baby from his arms so he could look through the book with ease. He found a little basket with chocolates and medium size Teddy bear with it. "So, what do you think there Tater you reckon Miss Jessica will like this?" The baby leaned into the book he held close to her and patted it with her free hand, smiling and cooing. Debbie traded Libby for the book and went to place the order. "What is the address?"

"Um I am not sure. Send it to Cooks Children's hospital. Nurse Jessica Reaves"

"What do you want on the card?"

"Just something simple like I really appreciate all you did to help us out I look forward to seeing you soon"

"Now is this just a friend or something more?"

"Well"

"OK that answers it you can do better than that. I will help you"

Debbie had known Cowboy for years and not once had he bought flowers for anyone other than a funeral or if someone was in the hospital and normally Bratton would come by and do that.

"OK how about I had a great time and thanks for all your help?"

"Better but what if we say I really enjoyed the time we spent together, and I appreciate everything you did to help out."

"Good enough I aint good with words. You should know that."

"I know that is why I am here to help. So, is this the one that has the whole town talking about?"

"I guess so. You know how it is. They got nothing better to do but watch my every move."

"I know they are all pretty pathetic. I have heard lots of good things about her from the people at the store and around town. Everyone seems to like her"

"She is very likable, but we aren't serious. We are just kind of playing it by ear."

"Well this certainly will not hurt. She is a lucky girl."

Embarrassed by the married ladies' comments "I am not so sure about all that"

"I am you do a lot for this town and most of these people just start rumors about you boys because they don't know you and I don't like that. OK she should get this tomorrow so maybe she will call you. When she comes back into town you need to bring her by so I can meet her."

"We will do that" opening the door and leaving the building. "Well little Tater Bug looks like they will have something to write about in town now. We better get back to the house before the press catches up to us"

He loaded Libby into her seat, and they went back to the house. He enjoyed having Libby with him because he would talk to her like she was an adult and knew she did not understand a word of what he was saying so he could ask or talk to her about anything he wanted and not feel like he was crazy for talking to himself but in reality that is what he was doing. By the time they had made it home Jerry and Gayle were already there, and Jerry was out with Cross working on the fence. Gayle was tidying things up the house just trying to stay busy when Cowboy came in with Libby. Gayle snatched her from his arms and began talking to her and playing with her. She asked Cowboy if there was anything, she needed to do for him and as expected he replied with a no just make yourself at home. So, Gayle made Libby a bottle and fed her to get her ready for her noon nap. Cowboy went out to find Cross and Jerry to see if they needed help and Gayle just went about her business like she had lived there for years Cleaning, dusting and straightening things up. Bratton and Susan were home shortly after she put the baby down and Susan helped her with the house. Bratton saddled up his horse and rode off in the fields looking for the other guys.

Bratton rode up to the other men working on a gate. He dismounted and tied his reins loosely over the saddle horn so the horse could graze while he helped the others repair the gate that had been torn down by their neighbor's bull. While working Bratton asked his father "what were you doing in town today?"

"I was dropping off the tables and chairs"

"Why were you at the flower shop?"

"Oh, I was just up there getting some stuff."

"What kind of stuff."

When I heard he was at the florist he knew what he was doing, and I was put a little at ease because Cowboy had actually listened to my advice.

"Just stuff for the little brat girl to see if they had some decorations for her room to be a little more girly that is all. Don't worry about what I did today you just get this gate mended Cross and I will run back to the house and saddle up the other horses you and Jerry finish up here and we will move the cattle from the west side on out here so we can fertilize the west pasture. Jerry can you ride a horse?"

"It has been years, but I am sure I will pick it back up. Just give me a little time."

Me and Cowboy took off in truck and Jerry and Bratton finished up the gate. While they were waiting on us to return with the horse. Jerry told Bratton" Man you are one lucky kid to get to do this kind of stuff"

"Well to me it is all work and aint much fun, but I am sure you will feel the same if you hang around here. It never ends your fence always has a whole and the tractors always need something done there is no end in sight."

"I know but I have been out in the world for some time and I would rather do this than deal with the idiots elsewhere."

Me and Cowboy rode up on the horses with the old grey mare in tow.

"We will start you off on this one here she don't move real fast but she is dependable and had her head on right, which means she won't do anything stupid to hurt you or her. Jerry crawled up onto the 1200 lb. beast and wiggled around in the saddle a bit. Bratton held the reins and adjusted the stirrups for him, so he was comfortable."

"How's that feel Jerry?"

"Like a million dollar. I feel like I should be paying you boys for letting me be out here"

"Well that will change" I assured him

'Not likely" Jerry said grinning from ear to ear. "I needed something to do but this is more like play to me."

"Come on let's head out and get these cattle moved. Cross I want you and Bratton to stay out on the flank. I will stay back and pickup any stragglers and help Jerry work the back side. Now Jerry don't go off doing anything you're not comfortable with and don't get in a hurry these cows move better at their own pace so don't press on them to hard.

Jerry wrestled with the horse from time to time. The old grey mare was unsure what exactly the inexperienced rider was asking of her so she would wander aimlessly at times. Cowboy would ride up beside him and give him pointers or refresh his skills and ride off to steer a loose calf back to the heard. As time went by Jerry got the hang of riding and was becoming helpful to the others. He would walk slowly in behind the heard meandering from side to side whistling and yelping to keep them moving. He had remembered that Cowboy had told him not to press them to hard so he would back off occasionally not to stress them out. Jerry was working hard to make a hand, so he did not feel like a charity case on the ranch. He was impressed with the way the others rode and handled the livestock. It appeared the horse knew what the rider on his back expected and was trying to achieve. The horses were well trained but from time to time one of them would act up and they would cut them back into the heard and walk them in circles. Jerry knew he was working but he was also having the time of his life. No matter how bad he would mess up he still smiled like a kid at Chuck E. Cheese. This was the life. At one point the cows got spooked going through a gate and the heard split. Cowboy began to holler at everyone and seemed to be upset Jerry figured he had done something wrong and Cowboy would shout out orders from time to time at him like a line boss on a prison ranch. Jerry quickly obeyed his commands and followed them to a "T". Moving the heard took about an hour and half and Jerry had tried to count the cattle as best he could even going as far as to try and figure out how many calves there were and how many of each sex in the event the guys tried to quiz him later on. When it was all said and done the cattle made it to the right pasture and Jerry was worn out. It was hard work riding on a horse for 2 hours when he was not accustomed to doing it. He rode slowly over to Cowboy and noticed he had a calf riding in his lap. He never saw him pick it up and did not know how long he had been there. Jerry inquired about the little calf. Cowboy told him his momma is in the other pasture and he must have gone through the fence. Jerry did not know how he knew that, but he was sure he was right and he was amazed that he had been riding for some time with a 65 pound calf in his lap holding on to him while he worked the cattle. He seen this stuff on TV and even ridden horses before, but these guys were for real they were not movie stars or stunt doubles. This is what they did to survive. The day was coming to an end and the 4 guys rode off to the barn to put up the horses and drop the baby off on the way. Jerry tried a couple of times to open the gate without getting off the horse like the others had done all day long but never could quite figure it out. He leaned down one time and pulled the pin, but he leaned too far off and grabbed the "H" post when the horse walked off Jerry was still on the post and the horse had no rider. Bratton quickly retrieved the mare and led her back to him. He asked Jerry if he would feel more comfortable in a seat belt, but Jerry quickly said no I think I can stay on this time. He fully expected the guys to give him a rash of crap about it, so he just let them poke fun at him and joined in with them. It made him feel like part of the team when they razzed him. By the time they returned to the house Susan and Gayle could hear the 4 men talking loudly and laughing from time to time. They finished feeding and taking care of the horses and went to the front porch but by this time the story had grown into Jerry being bucked off a wild horse while being chased by a rabid bull. The guys all joked around the whole day, but Jerry wanted to make sure and apologize for scattering the heard because he had felt responsible.

"You didn't do that I did. I reached down to grab up that calf and one of the cows tried to kick me. She missed and kicked another momma cow and they split. It happens like that sometimes. Don't mistake me hollering at you for you doing something wrong I just didn't want to have to go back and start all over again. You did a hell of a job out there especially for your first day."

"Well I just want to make sure I am helping out and not in the way, so just tell me and I will go."

"You did a great job. That didn't take us no more time than it normally would have but it was easier having you back there, so I wasn't doing 2 jobs at once. I know Redman appreciated the help he wasn't worn out when we finished up like he normally is when we move them." Redman was Cowboy's working horse. Jerry had come to find out that the men had horses for different kinds of work and for the rodeos much like people have sedans, SUV's and sports cars for driving. He enjoyed the hard day's work and felt a sense of purpose in what he had done unlike many of the factory and distribution centers he had worked at in the past. He was worn out and sore from riding the horse and had trouble walking like a normal person.

Gayle inquired if he was alright and Jerry nodded yes.

"Well you don't look alright you are walking like a silverback gorilla all hunched over and bow legged."

"I am just a little sore from riding is all, I am not used to that part of the job yet, but I will be fine."

I told him "fill up the hot tub by the barn with warm water and to soak" As I pointed at the water trough. "That will ease the pain tonight and we will ride first thing in the morning to loosen you up, so you won't be as sore all day tomorrow. It will hurt like hell for the first 10 minutes or so but after that you will feel much better."

Jerry didn't take the conversation lightly. He knew Cross had more knowledge about this than he did, so he did exactly as he was told to do.

The night went along like a normal night on the ranch everyone ate and sat on the porch talking drinking a cup of coffee or a beer and a few of the guys smoking cigars. Susan and Gayle sat out with them and listened to them rant about the day that had just passed and plan the day ahead of them before retiring to bed the gentlemen would follow shortly behind them. Cowboy lay in his bed trying to sleep but had no one to talk with and for the first time in many years it bothered him.

The next few days went well but Cowboy was growing weary from the lack of sleep. He decided to go into town on Thursday to surprise Jessica and take her to lunch. He had to find a reason to get out of town, so he told the others he was going to get parts for the bailer from Curly's. He went into town and picked up the part then he snuck off into Fort Worth. He made it right around lunch time. Jessica and a few of the other staff members had planned to go out and invited him along. Jess rode with Cowboy" well this is a pleasant surprise. You coming into town to see me and the big teddy bear was adorable. I am going to be spoiled if you don't quit doing this stuff for me." Cowboy just sat in silence through the meal not knowing what to say in a group of women and feeling somewhat embarrassed about sending the candy and teddy bear, then barging in on their lunch he did not want to look like a stalker or a weirdo. Jessica would talk to him and the other ladies to keep anyone from being left out of the conversation. Everyone was done eating and Cowboy went to the waitress to get the bill and paid for Jess and the other 3 ladies' food. Each of them thanked him and assured him he did not have to do that but that is just how he was. He wasn't trying to act like a big shot or a high roller he just didn't like anyone to have to pay when he was around if he could afford it. They all went back to the hospital and Jess sat in the truck for a few minutes talking to Kim about how things were going with her dad and mom out there. Cowboy told her that Jerry was making a good hand and her mother was doing great but cooking too much food for all them to eat, even commenting about his pants getting smaller. She got a kick out of listening to the story about the horse walking out from under her dad and could tell that they were enjoying the time out there from the conversations she had with her mother throughout the week. Cowboy told her he wished she would let them do something around the house even if it was laundry. Her mother was persistent on not letting them do any chores around the house and Susan had been taking care of the flower's beds and garden, so the guys had nothing to do at nighttime. She was relieved that it was going so well and missed being out there around all of them especially since her parents were not around anymore she felt lonely but, she did not dare tell him because she knew it would make him feel bad. Instead she told him" looks like there would be nothing for me to do out there anymore you seem to have it all taken care of"

"I will find something for you to do if you come out there or you can just lay around." They both got out of the truck and stood at the tailgate for a few minutes longer Cowboy held her tight to his chest and told her she had to come back if for nothing else so he could get some sleep and explained to her that he couldn't sleep at night because of her. She assured him that as soon as she got off work on Friday they would be there. She even had their bags already packed and ready to go. The kids had been driving her crazy especially Dylan he was worried about losing his horse. Cowboy felt a little of the weight lifted off his chest when he heard she had already planned on coming out. They embraced one more time and she gripped him tighter taking a deep breath "you smell so good"

"So, do you but, you better get back so you don't lose your job and have to come live with me which, would not be a bad thing in my book"

"I know it is tough on me to, but it will work out."

She moped back into the building and he headed back to the ranch a little refreshed after seeing her. When he made it home, he was in a little better mood told Gayle not to cook anything for dinner that they were all going out to eat for the evening. She did not know why they were going but she acknowledged this request and at dinner time they loaded up and went to the local café for dinner to eat catfish.

It was close to 730 when Jessica and the kids pulled into the drive on Friday evening. The guys were loading up saddles and getting things ready for the roping on Saturday morning and making sure everything was taken care of around the property before they came in for dinner Cowboy was elated to see Jess and she was even more excited to see him she jumped in his arms and kissed him like she had wanted to do when he came to see her at the hospital the day before but neither of them liked to show to much public affection and it would not look good if someone had seen them from the hospital in the truck making out. She was glad to be home she told him, and he replied he was glad to have her home.

Susan came out to greet her from the house," Mom you are home"

Jess just laughed at her. It felt good to be missed by so many people her mother hugged her and grabbed her bag to carry it in the house "I assume you want your stuff in here with Cowboy?"

"Yes, mother I do if that is ok with?"

"I guess it is" she replied sarcastically "but now I have to sleep with your dad in the trailer cuz you are taking my spot" she laughed

"I was sleeping good to with you gone" Jerry snickered

"Now don't you worry Hun she will only be here a couple of days then we can go back to normal when she is gone." Cowboy explained as he put his arm around Gayle

"I am a little worried about all of ya'll now. Is this place safe for kids anymore?" She joked while walking to the porch. "What are ya'll doing with the trailer?"

"We have a roping tomorrow morning I thought Dylan would like to go and it would be a good time for him and Jerry both to get some practice in riding and working cattle. Do you and Cass want to go with us?"

"I really think I would like to just relax around here."

Susan quickly perked up "I will stay with her"

Gayle followed Susan" I will stay home also"

"Good we can have an all-girl day and you boys can go play cowboys and Indians." Jess remarked

Dinner was ready shortly after they arrived, and they all sat around the table eating except Cass and Dylan who sat in the living room eating. It bothered me and the other 2 who had been raised that you all eat together at one table. Cowboy made the comment a few times that he needed a bigger table. No one really paid any attention to it except for Susan. The rest of the night passed just as it always did everyone picking up the kitchen and the reconvening on the front porch to debrief the day's events and plan the next day's endeavors before retiring to their place of slumber.

Jess and cowboy lay side by side in the big bed looking at the ceiling he put his arm under her head and pulled her close to him. She placed her head on his shoulder and put her arm over his chest then she raised up to kiss him good night and nestled her head on to his shoulder. There was no sexual tension but a warm relaxing feeling that quickly fell over the 2 of them and they faded off to sleep. The next morning Cowboy woke up before the dawn like he normally did he laid in bed a few minutes trying to plan an exit strategy that would not wake Jess up. When he removed his arm from below her head. He slowly pulled his arm and she rolled toward him placing her leg over the top of his as if she were afraid to let him go. He let her sleep just a little longer until he could not stay there anymore and just got out of bed. She rolled to her other side and gripped a pillow tightly. He made his way around the bed and kissed her on the forehead. She smiled and opened her eyes slightly. He went into the kitchen to start the coffee for their morning rituals then quietly went into the room with Dylan and Cass to wake Dylan up to get ready for the roping. Dylan walked toward the bathroom rubbing the sleep from his eyes and Cowboy returned to the kitchen to pour a cup of coffee. When he had returned me, Bratton and Jerry were all sitting around the table each sipping a cup of the hot flavorful coffee. Cowboy poured a cup and sat down with them quizzing each of them on their task before heading out.

The men headed for Stephenville. The girls were still in bed. Gayle was the first of them to arrive in the kitchen. Jessica could hear her rustling around in the kitchen with the pots and pans to cook the girls something for breakfast. Jessica got out of bed to join her in the kitchen. The two of them prepared the eggs, bacon and biscuits and sat at the table talking

189

and drinking coffee until Libby woke up. Jessica insisted on taking care of her and her mother argued that it was her job and she should take care of her but she quickly withdrew from the argument because Jess had not gotten to spend any time with her the night before. Jessica changed Libby and brought her to the kitchen. She sat her in her highchair and poured a few Cheerios on her tray while she poured milk into the bottle. Libby was excited to see Jessica and ate very few Cheerios most of them were thrown on the ground around her chair. Jess decided to try and feed the little girl some scrambled eggs at first, she was not too keen on the idea of eating them because of the texture but rapidly adapted to them and ate like a little pig. Susan could here laughter coming from the kitchen and decided to get up and see what was happening. She entered the kitchen to see little miss spoiled rotten, as she called Libby, with a huge mess and feeding herself eggs. "We tried to feed her, but she insisted on feeding herself, she loves eggs" Jessica casually commented about the mess on the floor.

"She is cleaner than I am when I eat" Susan noticed.

"What do we have planned today?" Susan asked as she sat at the table with the remaining women.

"I need to go get groceries in town or we won't have anything to eat" Gayle replied

"Well let's all get dressed and go into town" Jessica told them

So, they did. The three women, Cassie and Libby went into town in Bratton's truck that had been left behind for them to drive. While in town they went to the grocery store and bought food for the next week and picked up some wine and beer. Susan had asked to stop by the furniture store to look around for a table she explained to them that it really bothered them to have the kids sitting in the living room eating. "Oma would have had a heart attack if she had seen them eating alone in there. Lunch was one thing but dinner you always sit together and use that time to bond as a family." So, they shopped around and found a table with 10 chairs that was nice, but it was too expensive for Jessica to pay for and she tried to steer Susan away from it, but she could not do it. Susan told them to load it up in the truck and to charge it to the ranch.

"Is that really all you have to do around here?" Gayle asked

"If you need something you get it and he will pay for it when he comes into town everyone does that here. We still trust people"

"I hope he doesn't mind." Jessica worried

"It will be fine I will tell him I did it and if he doesn't like it, we can bring it back no one will be mad. I just know he does not like to be separated at dinner time."

"Well OK if you say so".

"It will be fine."

"They returned to the ranch and Gayle began putting up the groceries while Susan and Jessica unloaded the boxes that contained all the pieces to the table and chairs they had just purchased. By the time everything was unloaded, and the groceries were put away it was time for lunch. Gayle made sandwiches for everyone and they ate on the front porch because the house was a wreck with all the pieces and parts scattered about. They also purchased a small swing for Libby that they hung from the front porch for her to sit in, so they didn't have to worry so much about her falling down the steps if she decided to start crawling. Libby sat in the swing while everyone ate and talked. Jessica decided to open a bottle of wine while they started reading the directions for the table assembly. A few glasses of wine and 3 pages of instructions later they had the table completed and were working on the chairs. They opened another bottle of wine and began the monotonous chore of assembling the chairs. They had come up with an assembly line Jess would put the base together, Gayle worked on the backs and Susan would put the two together and tighten all the hardware. It seemed to work very well but the wine was going down much smoother than it was when they first started the chore. With Libby and Cass down for a nap the girls had time to let their hair down and enjoy themselves. So, they did just that after it was all put together, they moved the old table and chairs from the kitchen to the barn and put the new furniture in place. The dining area was a little cramped with the additional leaf's in, but it was still easy to navigate around the table if you needed to get up.

Jess had called Cowboy and asked him to stop off and get wine for dinner; little did he know that they had already consumed 2 bottles between the three of them. The men returned home around 4 that afternoon and by that time the ladies were all in an extremely good mood. None of them drank on a regular basis and the two bottles had them feeling frisky. The men unloaded the horses and put the tack in the barn. Dylan fed the horses as they were being unloaded and helped brush them out. The ladies sat

191

on the porch and enjoyed the rest of the day watching the men work and sipping on wine. Me and Jerry retired to their quarters to shower up and Cowboy sent Dylan in to get cleaned up as well. It did not take long for Cowboy and Bratton to figure out the girls had been enjoying there day alone after talking with them about the roping for a few minutes Cowboy recognized the look on Jessica's face from the last time she had a few drinks and her playful mood. Bratton knew by the way Susan was acting that she was drinking. "I see ya'll have been having fun today. What is all the cardboard from?" Cowboy asked

"That is all from this swing we bought Tater Tot" Susan replied pointing toward Libby in her new swing.

"What else is there because there is more trash than that swing weighs" he sneered

"Well don't be mad" Jessica started to say

"What did you do? As he rolled his eyes

"Nothing bad and if you don't like it, we will take it back or I will pay for it"

"What is it?"

"Come here" as she got up out of Cross' rocking chair and walked into the dining area" Ta da" she said swinging her arms open like a magician's assistant "do you like it?"

"It is nice much better than the old one where did you get it?"

"We got it in town. We went to get groceries and stopped by Susan said you wouldn't be upset but I will pay for it we should have asked I am sorry and I would have paid for it but I left my purse here and did not have my card. Please don't be mad at us it was my fault" she stammered.

"I am not mad. I intended on getting one I just forgot, and you are not going to pay for it."

"Yes, I will you would not need it if it wasn't for me and the kids being here so I will pay for it." She really could not afford to pay for the table, but she was willing to find a way to pay for it. That usually meant her dad would pick up the tab for whatever it was but, she did not want him to know that.

"No, you are not paying for it. It is in my house ya'll are all my guest and I will pay for it. How much was it?"

"It was 1200" she whispered sheepishly folding her hands as if praying for forgiveness

"Ok you can pay for it. He joked 1200 dollars for a table dear God that is crazy" he rambled jokingly so she would know he was not serious. He knew she felt bad and he grabbed her by the arm and hugged her. "Thank you and you too Susan and Gayle it is a beautiful table." He spoke loudly. "I am not mad if I didn't like it I would just take it back but it is perfect and if you want to pay for it I will give you the money and you can go pay for it."

"No that is OK, but I really wanted to do something special for you"

"You did you put it together for me. The question is did you start drinking before or after you put it together?"

"Kind of during but it is safe we tested it."

"I guess we will do another test come dinner time."

"I guess we will I better get started on that before it gets late."

"No, I got this we will do dinner I don't trust you 2 cooking right now. Just sit back and relax I will get some steaks out of the freezer and we will grill them up." "Brat get us a fire going in the pit please and I will get the steaks seasoned after I get out of the shower." Bratton scampered off with Susan to gather wood Gayle sat quietly on the porch swing and Jessica plopped down next to her letting out a sigh and resting her head on her mother's shoulder with her hands folded in her lap.," What is wrong Honey?" her mother inquired.

"I don't think he likes it" she said "he is probably mad at me"

"I think you are reading too much into it because you have been drinking, he likes it just fine and I really don't think you can make that man mad. Especially not you. He just doesn't get excited like you and I do over things like this."

"I know I just want him to be excited."

"I think he is excited with you just being here more than anything. I can see the difference in him when you are around than when you are gone in just a week's time"

"How is he different?" She perked up

"He seems to be happier and carefree. During the week they rush around to get things done and when you are here, he acts like it will get done eventually no rush. He really likes you."

193

"I know he does, and I am scared I am going to run him off."

"You cannot worry about stuff like that you have to be yourself because if you aren't then eventually you will show your true colors and you may be too involved to get out"

"You are right I try not to act different around here, but I can't help it. I want to be more like they are. Everyone loves them and they would do anything for a stranger I am just not that trusting."

"Well give it time you will learn to be if you stay around this bunch, Now Come on" she said as she grabbed Libby from the swing "we can pick some tomatoes and potatoes from the garden to have with dinner"

They went out into the garden and pilfered through the fresh vegetables growing there to find the perfect ones for the evening's meal. They talked and played with Libby in the soft soil that was kept clear of weeds by Susan and Gayle throughout the week. They even ran across Herman the snake while out there. The snake had scared Gayle the first time she saw him. She told Jessica the story about walking out there in the morning and screaming when she saw it and running for the barn to get a shovel or hoe to kill it with. Then Susan came out and stopped her explaining to her that the snake, as scary as it is, would not hurt her but it was good for the garden because he ate the mice and other varmints that would come take the ripe veggies. I almost wet my pants when I saw that thing slither across the ground away from me but now he is just a pet you get used to him and she is right I a haven't seen any signs of rabbits or mice anywhere around here. They gathered up what they needed to make a salad and some potatoes to bake and went into the kitchen to rinse them off and get them ready for dinner. Cowboy grilled the steaks, and everyone ate so much they could not move. Bratton leaned back in his chair to stretch out and the back of the chair fell completely off into the floor with Bratton falling on top of the dislodged piece. Everyone laughed.

"We need to check all this to make sure no one gets hurt since the drunk girls put it together" Bratton said lying on the ground beside the table.

"Maybe you shouldn't be leaning back in your chair and that would not happen" Susan quickly replied. Cowboy agreed with her as did everyone else.

"There were never any nuts put on these bolts how is that my fault as he stood up with the chair back in his hand. I guess I will have to check them all."

"You do that" Cowboy said, "I am going to the porch where it is safe to sit." He stood to his feet slowly making sure everyone could see he did not lean on the table or use the chair to stand up and smiling at the ladies just to give them a hard time. He washed off his dishes in the sink and made his way to the porch with a beer in hand Jessica followed behind him after pouring herself another glass of wine and then the others followed suit. Jess and Cowboy sat on the swing, I sat in my chair holding Libby and the rest would lean against the handrail of the porch. Cowboy. Looked at the crowd of people on the porch "I was thinking...." He paused

"What were you thinking?" Jess quizzed him

"Well never mind"

"No what?"

"I don't want to say I am afraid I will go broke if I mention we need to get some furniture and a new meeting spot after dinner. You two will have contractors out in the morning enlarging the front porch cutting down my pecan tree. So, I will just keep silent"

"Ha ha you think you are so funny Mr. smarty pants" Jessica and Susan did not find it as humorous as the rest of the family

"I was just Funnin' with you don't go getting all riled up. But we do need to MAKE another swing or something. Maybe we can just build us a little area out there under the tree to sit at in the evenings. That can be a job for us when we get back from Colorado."

"When are you going to Colorado?"

"Next weekend"

"What for?"

"We are going hunting. We do it every year."

"Well thanks for letting me know. What do you plan to do with Libby during this hunting extravaganza?"

"Well I was hoping that you and your Mom could keep an eye on the place and us guys could go. I was planning on taking Dylan and Jerry if they wanted to go."

"Dylan quickly jumped in I want to go"

"Sit down Dylan. Better yet go get ready for Bed. You too Cassie" Jessica said aggravated

Cowboy could see the look in her eyes, and he knew she was not happy. Bratton had seen this look before at the hospital and her family all threw out life, so they rapidly dispersed. I figured it was not going to be good, so I went with them.

"So, you just automatically assume I am going to come out here and babysit while you go run off to play out of state?"

"No not exactly I figured I would pay you to help out"

"So that is it I am just a weekend nanny to you" as she jumped to her feet with her hands on her hips

"No now wait a minute. Settle down. This trip has been paid for a long time if you don't want to do it that is fine, we will figure it out. I just thought if you wanted to or didn't mind you could but if it is a problem, we will take her a long"

"She is not the problem you can't just go saying stuff like that in front of Dylan without asking me because now I either have to let him go or be the bad person and tell him no.!!"

"Oh!! I am sorry for that I did not think of that. I am sorry you are right. That was wrong of me. You have every right to be upset. It won't happen again I just don't think about stuff like that Bratton never had nobody but me so if I or we wanted to do something we just went. You are gonna have to work with me on this stuff I am a little rusty and unconventional but there is no since running everyone off the porch because you are upset with me. We can discuss it like adults no need to get all pissy."

Chapter 22

BOYS WILL BE BOYS

Stunned to hear him admit he was wrong she sat back down in the rocking chair still in a huff. "Well OK you are right too. I won't do it again. I am a little rusty at this also, actually I have never gone through this, so I am new at it" She had mentally prepared for a huge argument and he did not even get his feathers ruffled.

"Well let's talk about it. What are you worried about?"

"When are you leaving? And for how long?"

"Well we are heading out Thursday evening and we will be back Monday."

"So, he will miss 2 days of school".

"If you are OK with that"

"That is fine he has good enough grades and he will enjoy it but, I am not sure about staying out here alone just me and mom so we will probably stay in town"

"That is fine I can bring her and Libby in with me when I pick up Muscle's. get his work from school and he can work on it while we are driving or at camp in the evenings."

"You promise he will be OK"

"I assure you nothing bad will happen to that boy. He will be with one of us at all times"

197

"OK but I am not going to get to spend any time with you for the next 2 weeks I am not sure I like that."

"It will go by fast and I will make it up to you"

"This is hard for me to do. Raise the kids and being with you. Whatever it is we are doing I don't like being away from you"

"We will get through the rest of school it is only a couple months and we will reevaluate the situation. Unless you want to just move out here, I would love that." He motioned to her to come sit back beside him on the swing, by patting the empty spot next to him with his bare hand.

"I would love that too, but I can't right now it would not be fair"

She sat down with him once again. He pulled her head to his shoulder.

"I know sweetheart I understand."

Her eyes had welled up and began to water she sniffled as if she were going to cry but she fought back the tears. Gayle and Jerry eased their way back up to the porch.

"Is everything alright?" Jerry asked. Jessica nodded her head yes still trying to keep from crying, she could not speak. She wanted to be there with him, and she knew he wanted her there with him, but it just was not fair for the kids to change school at the end of the year. The emotions of doing what was right for her family and what she felt in her heart compounded by the wine she had been drinking was tearing at her insides. She was so afraid that if she was not there with him that he would forget about her or someone else would come a long and take her place. She was put a little at ease with her mother out there every day; at least if another woman was around, she would know ahead of time. She had to clear her mind and think of something else to keep from becoming emotional. She laid her head down in Kim's lap and pulled her feet up on the swing, almost in the fetal position. Cowboy slowly lowered his hand to rub her back as he joked with Jerry "It is fine except all ya'll jumped ship and ran when she got that look in her eyes. You left me Jer I am hurt what if she had killed me or something?"

"You are on your own with her I can't figure out the one I got after 40 years"

"It is all good, so it is settled we are going. Do you get a gun?"

"Yea but I don't think I will be hunting I will just go to help out and so I can get away"

"That is fine by me we will take enough guns if you want to hunt you will have one."

Jessica sat up on the swing still feeling the effects of her emotions and the wine and announced she was heading to bed. Cowboy stayed outside for a little bit talking with Jerry and Gayle and mapping out the week, Telling Jerry everything he would need to bring for the trip, before going in the house for the night. Cowboy cracked the bedroom door open to see Jess laying on the bed gripping a pillow alongside her and her face buried in another. "You still awake?"

"Yes" she sniffled

"We good?" he inquired

"We are fine whatever we are I guess?"

He strolled to her side of the bed and sat on the edge in front of her. Placing his hand on her head and lightly moving the hair from her face and behind her ear then rubbing her ear lightly to console her. "We is you and me! I am sorry if you are mad at me, I did not mean to"

"You did not upset me. It is just I don't like this weekend stuff. I want to be with you, and you are so busy on the weekends I am never going to get to spend any time with you. I know it is selfish and I have no right to think that way because I have only known you for a month or so but I really care about you and I don't want to screw this up so I am trying not to rush thing like we talked about but my heart tells me to jump and my brain tells me that I have done this before."

"This is the stuff I am not good at. I wish I were more like you so I could talk to people. Maybe that is why I haven't found anyone before you. You mean the world to me right now and I have to work to keep my mind off of you. It is not easy for me at all. At least you have tried being in a relationship over the past couple of years. I have avoided them, not because I didn't want to settle down but because I was afraid of what would happen when they got tired of me."

"Right Kim I know you well enough to see that you are not afraid of anything"

"Well I don't like spiders did you know that?"

"That don't count you retard everyone is afraid of spiders"

"Well there you go. I have one thing in common with the vast majority and I am afraid of you."

"Me???"

"I am worried you are in town and you are going to run off with some doctor man or just get tired of the drive or me. I know it sounds crazy, but I haven't done this dating thing for almost 20years now and it scares the living daylights out of me." As he crawled over the top of her to lay on the bed behind her wrapping his long arms around her and pulling the two of them tightly together so she would fit snug inside the arch of his body

"I am not going to get tired" as she shifted around so that their two bodies were perfectly match like pieces of a jigsaw puzzle. She took a long deep breath and exhaled all her fears away while in his warm embrace. "I will get tired of you wearing your boots in my bed" she proclaimed.

"I will get them off." He rolled to his back and started to kick them off. She got out of bed and pulled his boots off, then placed them on the floor by the closet before crawling over the foot of the bed on top of him and kissing him. "I won't get tired of you"

"I don't think I can get tired of you either." He took the remainder of his clothes off except his boxers. They lay side by side until he pulled her back to himself and she nestled herself back to merge together again," This is what I like someone to hold and to spoil"

"I don't need you to spoil me, I just need you to hold me and love me"

"I think I already do ", as they drifted off to sleep. They rested so much better in bed with one another. Their body heat and the security of knowing there would be someone there in the morning to take care of each other put their minds at ease.

Chapter 23

HUNTER'S EXTRAVAGANZA

The next week was extremely busy and sailed by, everyone was busy taking care of their normal duties and trying to get things ready for the trip coming up. Thursday hit and it was time to go. The trucks were loaded, and everyone piled into the vehicles bound for the big city to pick up Dylan and drop off the girls.

They arrived at the house. Dylan had his bags packed and waiting on the curb like garbage bags ready for pick up. He had been pacing the floor since school had let out that day and worrying his mother to death. Bratton and the others unloaded the baby and all her belongings placing them inside at Jessica's house. Cowboy had gone in to see Jess before he left. She motioned him back to her room to talk to him before they had to leave. She knew she would not get a kiss or even a real hug from him with all the others around, so she pulled him back to her room. She wanted to debrief him on Dylan and make sure he knew the ground rules. Really it was just to get a few minutes alone together. They sat and talked briefly before the long kiss and a gentle hug goodbye. Jessica escorted them back to the truck reminding Dylan to mind his manners and never to get out of site from one of the men. She kissed him on the forehead and told him she loved him. Then she went to the other side of the truck where Cowboy stood waiting on Bratton and Jerry to load up. She wrapped her arms around his waist and told him to take care of Dylan. He acknowledged her request and she turned him around to face her. He hugged her tight and she told him she would miss him, and he shocked her by leaning down and kissing her lightly on the lips and telling her he would miss her too. Dumbstruck by the kiss she had no reply. The kiss was just a peck, but it felt like a bolt of lightning running through her, a surge of energy from her lips to her toes. She watched the men load the truck and drive off through the city streets until their taillights became a part of the jumbled lights on the hi-way.

8 hours to drive to the hunting spot Kim suggested that Dylan work on his schoolwork while they were on the road. Dylan fumbled through the tattered old backpack he carried or drug to school each day he pulled out his math book and a spiral notebook. He placed them in his lap and began to read the book. The spiral fell to the ground and Bratton reached down to retrieve it. When he pulled the book up the cover was open, and he could see some cursive writing that looked like it had been done by a girl. Bratton read the name on the book, to give Dylan a hard time about having a girlfriend until he read what it said Jessica Lee. This was even better. "Dad we got problems!!!!!'

"What is it? I am sure one of us can figure it out"

"OK. Here it is she is already signing her name Jessica Lee. Do you know who Jessica Lee is Dylan? Is she your girlfriend?"

"NO, my mom wrote that." He confidently defended him self

"O she did? Huh??"

"Looks like you are in for it now dad you are getting married"

"I am sure she was just doodling girls are crazy like that." Cowboy tried to downplay the conversation

Dylan with a puzzled look asked "Are you and mom getting married?"

"No. Not any time soon buddy"

"Well if ya'll do will that make you my dad?"

"Well...."

Jerry spoke up "don't worry about that stuff just work on your math"

"If we got married it would make me your stepdad. You already have a dad"

"I know but he never comes around"

"Well a stepdad is a dad too"

"Good I want you to be my dad."

Jerry was bewildered by the conversation and somewhat embarrassed he was also amazed at how well Cowboy handled the conversation. The conversation engulfed the first half of the trip until they stopped for gas and something to eat. Bratton had intended to razz his dad about his findings until Dylan started talking about his dad and him wanting Cowboy to be his dad. He had never given much thought to his dad getting married but now it occupied his mind. He had come to grips with the fact that someday it could happen, and it very well could be Jessica so he may have a little stepbrother and sister, he may already have a half-sister, Libby. He felt bad for Dylan not having his dad around Bratton never really missed his mom because he never remembered her, and his dad was all he had growing up. He knew it must be hard on Dylan not having a dad in his life. Bratton knew he would not always be around to look after his dad and thought to himself it may do him some good to have another little boy to help out and run around with after he went to college. The second half of the trip was marred with silence only broken by a subtle snore from one of the passengers and an occasional question if anyone needed to stop for the restroom or something to drink. Cowboy, Jerry and Bratton would all ponder the question what if they did get married. Jerry liked the idea because he liked Cowboy and knew he could take care of his daughter and the kids. This would allow him and Gayle to be able to go and do things they had always wanted too or just to stay around and help on the ranch which Jerry thoroughly enjoyed. Bratton deliberated having them on the ranch to look after his dad and Cross while he was away, and it made his decision of what college to go to easier. For Cowboy it was a surreal moment he had never looked at it as being a parent to someone else's kids until now. Sure, he knew they would come with her, but it never dawned on him that they would be his kids to raise and discipline, especially with their father running out on them. He had come to grips with the reality that was haunting Jessica's mind but he was OK with it he loved the kids being around and it would not be any different than Bratton and Susan running around on the property when they were little. He knew he could handle the task. The trip went fast with the conversation lingering in their heads and they made it to the hunting camp a little after midnight.

Everyone piled out of the truck stretching their arms and legs and breathing the cold air deep into their lungs. Cowboy placed Dylan in the back of the truck to hand the gear to the others so they would not have to crawl in and out and to keep him busy, so he did not wander off in the dark. Cross quickly round up firewood and started the fire. Jerry and Bratton began setting up tents. Cowboy and Dylan hung lanterns and made some sandwiches for everyone to eat. Camp only took a few minutes to set up and everyone quickly retired after eating. The next morning Cowboy and Cross loaded up the fire, put on the coffee and started making breakfast. Bratton, Jerry and Dylan were up shortly after the coffee was done. It was cold outside each of them were bundled up in coveralls and thermal underwear. They ate breakfast and hiked up the hillside for about 45 minutes to the first blind which was a ground blind Cross hunted out of every year. They had discussed before leaving camp that it would be safer to have Dylan hunt with Cross because he was the closest to camp and he was on the ground. The next 2 stands were tree stands set up for bow hunting. Cowboy put Jerry in the first one and Bratton in the next before making his way further up the mountain to find him a spot to bed down. Cowboy preferred to hunt from the ground and use natural cover, as opposed to setting up feeders and a blind. He said it made it more of a sport. He also liked to hunt with a Bow, so they had to come in closer to him for him to get a good shot off. Cowboy sat in the woods until night fall and started his journey back to camp along the way he would stop at each stand to pick up each hunter it was a system they had worked out to make sure none of them were left behind or got shot. Bratton was the first one and Cowboy signaled him to come down. He made his descent from the tree and hiked down the path asking if Cowboy had seen anything neither of them had seen anything worth taking a shot on. The next stand was Jerry and after waking him up he scaled down the tree to meet them at the base of it. He had seen a nice size bull and 3 cows. They went to get Cross and Dylan. When they got to the stand Dylan was asleep on the floor, so Cross picked him up and carried him back to camp. Cross had seen a few but nothing too big. He would have shot one, but he did not want to wake Dylan up, so he let the elk live another day, as he put it. They got back to camp it was very dark that night. The stars were close enough to touch and the cold temperature was made colder by the howling wind. The forecast for snow the next day and the wind blowing that night meant the elk would bed down and that a morning hunt was sure to have them up and moving to stay warm. The next morning, they repeated the same path they had the day before except this time Bratton and Jerry traded places. Cowboy made it back to the same spot he was at the day before and had just gotten comfortable when he heard a gunshot echo through the trees. The men knew to stay in their spots until dark so it would not mess up one of the other hunter's chance of shooting an elk. Cowboy left his spot a little before dark in the event they had to track down a wounded animal. He picked up Jerry. Jerry inquired if he had heard the shot and he acknowledged that he had, Bratton asked the same and they all figured that Cross had killed something. Cross was waiting with Dylan outside the blind when the others arrived.

"Did you kill it?" Cowboy hollered out.

"I shot him!!!" Dylan hollered out holding a small 45 caliber rifle in the air

"Ok good deal what did you shoot?"

"A big bull he is over there somewhere we saw him take a few steps, but Cross said he didn't go far."

Cowboy and Bratton knew something was not right because the gun they heard go off was a much more powerful riffle than a 45 and a 45 would not have killed an elk at that range. They walked to where he was pointing into the trees just to appease the young hunter both of them assuming they would not find anything. Cross led them in a direction he thought the large animal had traveled and Dylan would direct them also. Sure, enough it was a descent size bull laying on the ground in a small ravine. They tied a rope around its hind legs and drug it back to camp to field dress him. Cowboy and Bratton were baffled by the elk shot by the 45. Something just was not right about the whole thing. They pulled the carcass up in a tree just outside of camp and gutted him. Dylan was in the middle of all it. His excitement had his adrenaline flowing and wanted to know what every part they took out of the elk was and asked a million questions. They took pictures of him holding the elks head up, with help from a rope and some people not in the picture then they took a few funny ones of the elk on top of him just to play around. The excited little boy rejuvenated the camp everyone reminisced over their first kill some had revised the stories to add entertainment value. Cross had mixed up a batch or Cherry Jell-O and grape juice to make it look like blood and told Dylan he had to drink it to honor the animal he had just shot. A trick they had not done in years but enjoyed pulling on a naïve little hunter. Dylan drank the blood like liquid with caution at first until he realized it was not real blood then he started playing with it letting it run out of the sides of his mouth and smearing it on his cheeks like the Indians used to do. The guys all got a kick out of him and enjoyed watching him talk about his kill. Bratton had carved off a chunk of meat from the elk's back strap and had cooked it over the open flame for them all to enjoy. After hesitantly eating the meat, he knew was real, Dylan's abundant energy quickly faded, and he fell asleep by the fire. Jerry picked him up and moved him into the tent where he would be warm through the night. With a pot of coffee on the campfire, the beautiful night sky the men sat and talked. Cowboy could not believe the boy had shot the elk with a 45 so he asked Cross "OK enough bull shit what happened?"

"What do you mean?" I replied with a suspicious grin.

"You and I both know he did not kill that elk with a 45 and the gun I heard sounded more like a 300 mag so what happened?"

"OK well he doesn't know either. We saw the bull out there and I knew his gun would not take him down, so I lined him up on it and told him not to shoot until I told him. I sighted him in, and he cleared a tree where I had a clean shot. Then I counted to 3 and we shot at the same time. Don't tell him because he thinks I was just looking at him through my scope. It would break that boy's heart if he knew that."

"That sounds more like what had happened, but he hit him in the shoulder with that 45. I seen the bullet whole going in we will dig it out tomorrow"

"I don't know how he hit him shaking like he was but that is funny that he did."

They sat around the fire joking about what had happened and all of them agreed to keep it quiet. They went to bed and the next morning repeated the same thing they had the 2 days before. None of them even saw an elk the next day. After returning to camp they started packing all the things they did not need in the truck so they could get on the road home first thing in the morning. Dylan had tried to wash his face off but the grape juice and cherry Jell-O concoction I had made stained his skin. He would have to wear the badge of his kill until it wore off. The next morning, they packed their tents and the rest of their gear in the cold and ensured the fire was out by pouring all the water they had left on it. The elk was placed in the back and they headed down the hill for the long drive home. Dylan and Bratton spent most of the trip doing Dylan's homework. Jerry slept and I sat quiet as usual until Bratton and Dylan fell asleep. Then I started talking to Cowboy about the ranch and the things we had to get done, mapping out the next few weeks, prior to hay season. Before talking about what was really on his mind. "You know ole Brat boy back there will be heading off to college here pretty soon. What are we gonna do about replacing him? Our two old asses can't keep that place up alone."

"Well I am hoping Jerry will want to stay on with us. He seems like he will work out pretty good when he learns the ropes."

"He is a good hand, but he is just as old as we are."

"You are right but that is what we are going with for now. Why what is on your mind? I know you got something up there in them cobwebs bugging you."

"Why don't you see if the boy can come out during the summer and we can start training him. His grand pa will be there."

Cowboy could see that I missed having all the little helpers on the ranch too and the hunting trip just made me miss the kids that much more." That aint a bad idea, so long as Jess aint fed up with me by then"

"I don't think you got much to worry about with her she is too sweet to let something as rotten as you ruin her."

"She is a good woman. I actually thought about, if everything works out through the end of school, seeing if they all wanted to spend the summer with us. You think that is too much?"

"Not if that is what you want. We always adapt to whatever comes up. You know that. I also think we could let Jerry and Gayle have my little place and I would sleep in the trailer. It would be more comfortable for them."

"Cross I am not gonna ask you to give up your house. That aint fair we can build them something or they can sleep inside and I will sleep in the trailer."

"You didn't ask and it aint an option. It will be fine I don't need a lot of room just a bed and a closet and it has both of them."

"We can talk about it all later, but we will work it out one way or another."

I had come to like the company on the ranch as of late. I enjoyed having Jerry around to talk with and Gayle's cooking. I even liked all the kids but having Dylan around to look up to me made me feel good and reminded me of Bratton when he was just a kid.

The trip home seemed to take much longer than the trip up but, we still made good time. With most everyone sleeping, we only stopped 2 times once for breakfast and the other to fill up with fuel and restroom break. We were all worn out from hiking in the high altitude and not getting much sleep on the hard-cold ground. We also had not had a real shower since we had been gone. Just a washcloth to wipe the dirt off the surface or baby wipes to clean up and sterilize their hands before we ate, so we were smelling pretty ripe as, Cowboy would say. After stopping by the local processing plant to drop the elk off we pulled into the driveway at Jessica's around 2. The only people home were Gayle and Libby, Cass was at school, Jess at work and Susan had gone back to the ranch for school and to check on the animals. Gayle could see the men had not bathed and could also smell them. Jerry took their car home to shower and change. Cowboy did not hesitate to use Jessica's shower to get cleaned up and change clothes Bratton jumped in next not being able to tolerate the stench of his body odor any longer, like normal he took a long shower. By the time he was out Jess had come home from work and picking up Cassie. Cowboy was enlightening Jess on the trip when Dylan told her he had shot an Elk. Jessica was not happy when she heard the news about her boy shooting an animal and as his story went on about the blood and eating the meat, she was really not happy. The stains still on his face she commanded him to get in the shower as soon as Bratton was out to wash it off. He knew by the tone of her voice that she was not joking with him and thought he was in trouble. Cowboy quickly came to his defense and the two of them began a heated discussion. Cowboy told Dylan to run get cleaned up and assured him he was not in trouble. When he left the room, Jessica was able to speak freely. "You let him shoot an animal with a gun? He has blood on his face he looks like an orphan. What will his teacher think tomorrow at school when he tells everyone?"

"Slow down there Jess we went hunting. What did you think we were going to do? We weren't going to take pictures. You knew we were taking guns. Did you think we were going to throw rocks at them and stone them to death?"

"No but I did not think you would let him shoot something."

"Well he did."

"Why did you make him drink the blood?"

It wasn't blood it was a joke Cross played on him it was a grape juice and Jell-O mixture he made up to look like blood and the kid had fun with it. I didn't know it would not wash off but it aint that big a deal."

"Well it is to me. We don't live out in the sticks. People around here will get offended if he tells them that story."

"Well they need to get over it and you need to quit worrying about what other people think. We did nothing wrong and he should be proud of what he did. If you want to be mad, be mad at me he didn't do anything wrong and he was excited to get home and tell you about it and you made him feel bad."

"OK then I will be mad at you"

"Fine and you will tell him you are sorry?"

"Yes, I will, and he is not allowed to shoot anything else."

"Now that aint fair he needs to learn how to handle a gun the right way and know what is capable of doing."

"I don't like him being around guns do you know how many kids die each year from playing with guns?"

"The problem is they are playing with them, not using them and they were not taught how to handle them safely. How many of the kids that were killed had ever been hunting?? I bet less than 1% or none. I know what I am talking about and we will teach him the right way, but you have to trust me on this it is better for him to learn about them than to be curious about them."

"AHHH!! I really hate you because you are always so convincing, and I am sure you are right but if something happens, I am blaming you."

"Fair enough. The other good thing about it is, if he isn't doing good in school or gets in trouble you have more leverage on him."

"I guess you are right it just worries me."

"It will be fine. Let me get the camera and I will show you the pictures we took." Cowboy ran out to the truck and grabbed the camera. He saw Dylan's bag in the back seat and remembered the signature she had been practicing in his spiral notebook so he thought he would have fun with it. He carried the camera and the bag into the house and sat on the couch next to Jessica. Cowboy scanned through the pictures slowly and narrated what all was going on behind the scenes. She got a kick out of the one with the elk laying on Dylan and the blood running out of his mouth. She commented several times about how big it was and was still in disbelief that her baby boy had shot the large creature. Cowboy told her he would have the antlers mounted for him and wanted her to find a few pictures of him in the camera for him to blow up and put on the base of the mount so he would remember the trip. He asked her for a pen and paper so he could write the pictures down. Looking at the camera she nonchalantly told him to get some out of Dylan's bag. Exactly what he wanted her to say. "Can I just rip a page out of this spiral I don't see any loose paper."

"I don't care. Sure, that is fine. I like this one."

Kim opened the book with the back cover exposing her writings "OK what number is it?"

"It is number 112 what do you think?" Glancing toward the paper she realized that the book he had was the one she had written on. She grabbed it up thinking he had not seen the scribble and said "I will write them down"

"I can write it down give it back to me." He reached across her for the tablet and she leaned away from him

"No, I will do it" she screamed laughing loudly "Cassie help"

Cass ran to assist her mother

"Take this and don't let Cowboy have it"

Cass grabbed the book from her mother's extended arm while Cowboy lay on top of her. The two of them, acting like preschoolers fighting over a toy. He sat up on the couch and Jess got up to get the book from Cass. She ripped a blank piece of paper from the book and handed it to him "There now you can do it."

"What is in that book I am not supposed to see?"

"None of your business it is." She thought for a second "well if you must know it is Dylan's diary"

"What you are crazy boys don't have diaries"

"Well that is why he is so protective of it." She placed it behind her back, out of breath and clearing the strands of her hair from her face. "So, I will just go put this in his room somewhere safe and come back to help with the pictures. She turned and walked into the room."

"Jess!!!" he hollered loudly

"What??" She sweetly replied

"That is your room not Dylan's

"O Yea right. So, she scampered over to his room and came back empty handed"

"So where were we." She sat on the couch and Cowboy just looked at her shaking his head.

"Well I was writing down the numbers to the picture when Mrs. Jessica Lee took the paper from me." His voice elevated with each word

"You are an ass"

"I know."

"How did you know?"

"Bratton saw it when they were working on Dylan's homework and you know that was the topic of conversation for the trip up"

"O MY GOD are you serious I am sooo embarrassed. Everyone knows?"

"YEP" she heard from over her shoulder.:" Me, Cross, Dad and your dad too. Everybody knows." Bratton leaned down to whisper in her ear.

"So, what I was just bored talking to mom on the phone. I's Just Funnin' Ay Bout" dragging her words out with her hands on her hips and shaking them from side to side and acting sassy, as she pronounced each syllable with a Texas draw to mock Cowboy.

"Just admit it you are in love with me and you want to marry me"

"You are such a conceded pig" she joked with him. They joked for a few minutes until the conversation faded the men had to get on the road for the house so they could get the truck unloaded before dark. Me and Bratton climbed back in the truck and Kim said his goodbye and confirmed that Jess would be back out the next weekend.

Chapter 24

LET'S GET MOVING

The next few weeks went by as planned Jess and the kids would come out and stay and Cowboy would sneak into town to see her during the week every once in a while. It was becoming too predictable and Cowboy was never comfortable being complacent. One weekend he actually took Jess out of town for the night just to spend some time alone with her. Even though they would get time together it was not the same they felt like they were not getting to see each other except when they laid down to sleep. Cowboy rented a small cabin on Possum Kingdom Lake that was only 45 minutes away and he took her out to dinner at a restaurant on a bluff overlooking the water. They sat on the patio that evening looking over the lake and gazing at the stars. The dimly lit patio was a perfect spot to sit and talk. She thanked him for bringing her to such a beautiful spot. His reply was "Well I think you deserve to be taken out on a real date. The way all this started between us, you kind of got the short end of the stick and I did not think it is fair to you. Not getting to enjoy all that when we first met, stuff like a normally relationship."

"You are too good to me. I wouldn't change any of it. I am just happy I met you."

"Me too I wish it would have been different circumstances, but I will take it any way I can."

"Not me because if we had met in passing you might have talked to me but, it would not have lasted with me living in town you way out here. We never would have even gotten to really know each other. We might have gone out a time or two but neither of us would have let our guard down that quick had we not been thrown into it like this. So, I will keep everything just the same. I would not want to chance not being with you."

"You are probably right. I guess it is better this way."

They went to the cabin and sat on the back-patio side by side not talking not kissing just enjoying the peace and quiet of the evening and one another's company. Cowboy liked the fact that he had someone to share this with and did not have to go out catting around for what he used to fill the void in his life temporarily. Now he felt like the void did not exist anymore. The whole thing was still just a dream to her, and she would sit and pray that she did not wake up if it was. School would be over in a few weeks and she was debating what to do about the kids and so she broke the stillness of the night by sighing and saying "School will be over soon"

"Yep. It won't be long, and Bratton and Susan will be off to Tarleton" he lowered his head shaking it in disbelief "they sure grow up quick."

"I know. How are you gonna handle them not being around all the time?"

"Not sure to be honest with you he and I aint been apart more than 2 days his whole life. I try not to think about it. I wonder how Cross will handle it more than me."

"I know he thinks the world of that boy."

"Well I have been meaning to talk to you since the hunting trip. Cross brought up a good point. He thought it would be good to get Dylan out here for the summer and he could start helping out if you were OK with it. That kid makes him feel young and he likes having him around."

"Well they have to do something this summer, but I can't leave Cassie at home alone."

"Oh I figure she would come too."

"Then you leave me with nobody you would have my whole family out here and I would be all alone."

"You are right I need to start looking at the whole picture"

"No, you are fine they can come out I will deal with it. It will be better for them. Mom can keep Cass occupied they will enjoy it better than sitting at home waiting on me to get there."

"I wish you could take a few months off and spend out here."

"Me too but we burned all those days up when Libby came into the picture. This is still hard on me being away from you all week I just learned to cover it up and not think about it, but I want to be out here."

"Why don't you look around out here for a job?"

"Well I have to be able to pay for the house. Out here the pay just would not be enough for me to do that."

"Can you not rent that house out for what you pay on it? You won't have rent or anything out here"

"I know but I don't want to force my way in your house and impose on you."

"You are not imposing I wish you had never left the first time. I just did not want to pressure you into staying because it wasn't the right thing for the kids at the time. Now they are out of school and they can go here next year. It would even help us out. I am sure your mom and dad would like a break from this place, and I would need help with Libby after Susan leaves. It will be fine. We all discussed it on the trip when we went hunting. Everyone agreed it would be better for us all."

"But what if I can't find a job?"

"That won't matter we can make it work." His eyes lit up because she was actually considering the move this time unlike the other times, she just shot it down because the kids. He was truly excited." I can build a house for ya'll if you want and you can stay in it."

"UHH no! If we move, I am sleeping in our room" she said with determination. "If we move out here it won't be just for the kids it will be more about me for a change."

He smiled and grabbed her up out of the chair holding her up with her feet off the ground "So that is a yes you are gonna move out here with me." The date paid off he finally had her convinced to make the move after 3 months she was ready, and he could not have been happier.

"I have never seen you like this before what has gotten into you?" She asked with her remaining breath before he let her down.

"It will be nice to have you with me every day instead of just on the weekends".

"I am glad you feel that way. I was scared you were just being polite."

"Let's get to bed it is getting late we can work out the particulars in the morning."

The next morning when they returned home, they discussed their decision with the rest of the family. Most everyone had expected them to move in eventually, but they were not for sure when they would. The kids were especially excited, Dylan more so than Cassie. She knew it would be better because Cowboy always bought her what she wanted. Dylan wanted to be able to ride the horses and help Cross work. It made Bratton feel a little better about leaving because he knew the other kids would occupy his dad and Cross while he was gone so he would not feel guilty for leaving.

The next week Jessica talked with her boss and put her 2 weeks' notice in at work. Cowboy spent most of his time at her house during those two weeks packing up things she did not have to have and getting ready for the move. The kids would come home from school to help him out. By the time the last day of school came around they only had their beds and a few boxes to move. Susan and Gayle spent their spare time unpacking things and getting everything organized at the ranch so Jessica and Cowboy would not have to deal with it when they got there. Jerry mainly worked on the equipment in the shop while Cross and Bratton cut and baled the hay and the three of them would work the cattle on the weekends giving shots and separating them out. When Jessica got back to the house, she was relieved to be there and to find everything was already put away. The only problem she and Cowboy had, was trying to locate their things since it had all be rearranged. Everything seemed to be working out like they had planned the summer went by without any problems. Jerry had proven to be an asset and was doing much better on his riding. Dylan would help his grand pa in the shop and work the herd with the other men. Having 5 riders work the heard wasn't much work and it was the time the guys all spent together every weekend and gave the girls their time alone also. With the summer coming to a close it was time for Bratton and Susan to go off to school. Jess could see that Cowboy was a little emotional about his boy leaving but knew it was what was best for him. Cowboy hugged him several times as did Cross and patted him on the back telling him "make me proud son". All three men were a little watery eyed during the long goodbye, but all were too proud to shed a tear. The next few days they were all in a funk trying to function missing two hands around the farm, but the hay season was just about over and between Jerry and Cowboy they picked up the slack for Bratton being gone on the tractor. The ladies managed and Cassie started helping out more with Libby who was walking and getting into everything. She was growing up to fast.

Occasionally Cowboy and Jess would wonder what happened with the mother, but the curious times kept getting further and further apart. Jess had the kids enrolled in school and they spent the first day with them only leaving for a few minutes between lunch and recess. Jess loved the small-town school and could see that Dylan would fit in just fine.

Chapter 25

HOLDING A GRUDGE

At the café in town Jess and Cowboy had sat down for lunch waiting to pick the kids up from school when the Sherriff approached Cowboy. "We need to talk"

"About what"

"It might be better in private. Ma'am" He tilted his hat to Jessica and stepped outside to wait on Kim. Jess waited inside looking through the large picture window at the two men trying to read their lips to see what was going on.

Cowboy returned shortly after the Sherriff pulled away in his vehicle. Cowboy was holding an envelope and had a bewildered look on his face. Jess was curious to what had happened. "What was that all about?"

"I am not sure"

"What is in the envelope?"

"I am being summoned to court for something."

"What?? Why??"

"Not real sure Charlie wouldn't say, and he was acting awful strange."

"Open the package and let's see if there is something in there." He opened the envelope and handed the papers to Jessica to look at. As she read thru the papers, she realized it was about Libby and someone had done an inquiry about her. "Who would do that?"

"What?"

"It is Libby someone is looking for her"

"Do you think it is her mother? What should we do?"

"I am not sure we need to have someone look at these and translate what it is all about. I can take them to my cousin he will look them over for us."

"If it is the mother why would she not just come back to the place she left her? This sounds fishy and Charlie acted about half scared to deliver them papers to me."

"This is strange I will run by and see if Lee will take a look at them for me" They finished their lunch or at least picked at it and Jessica left to see Jack at his law office while Cowboy went to pick up the kids from school.

Jessica walked into the law office with the papers in her hand and asked Shelly if Jack was busy. Jack was in court in Weatherford and would not be back until after dark, so she let Shelly look over the paperwork.

"Do you know what this is about?" she asked

"Well it looks like the county has made an inquiry about the baby and her wellbeing.?"

"Why would they do that?"

"I am not sure."

"CPS has already cleared the house and everyone and the adoption papers are being filed why would the county care?"

"Someone had to have made an inquiry about the baby and they are setting this up for a court hearing":

"Really this is strange. Almost 6 months and now they have an inquiry? Kim will be upset over this. When is the court date and where?"

"It is on the 23rd in Palo Pinto county court. If you want, I can make copies and have Jack look them over and give you a call back."

"Please if you don't mind that would be great."

Shelly made the copies and brought the originals back to her. "I am sorry I don't know anymore. If nothing else I will make sure that Jack clears his schedule that day to be there."

"That will be great. I am not sure how that will go over with Kim, but he will just have to get over it."

"Jack will not be too thrilled to be there either. I am looking at his calendar and he already has court that day in Palo Pinto, so it won't be any trouble for him to look into this."

"Thank you, Shelly, I will see you next time maybe we can do lunch next week."

"Sounds good"

Jess left the building and was uneasy about telling Kim that she had asked Jack to be at court with them and did not want to break the news to him. She walked down the road to the feed store to meet up with Cowboy and the kids and pondered how to break the new. When she arrived, the kids were in the truck, so she did not want to discuss it in any great detail in front of them. Cowboy asked when the court date was, and she told him. He got on his cell phone and made a call to his lawyer and gave him the case number and date so he could be there. Jessica was not going to tell him that Jack would already be there because she knew how the two men felt about one another. She was not sure why they disliked each other so much and was hesitant to ask because even the sight of Jack made Kim's blood boil. She just let him handle it his own way.

After speaking to his lawyer and getting to the house she asked what the lawyer said.

"He said that the county had brought the case up and that there was not much information about it because it involved a minor."

"Why would the county bring this up?"

"He told me that it had to be someone filing a complaint."

"Who would do that I wonder?"

"Anyone could have done it according to him we will just have to wait it out and see."

This was the worst thing that could happen. Everything was going great and now this. Why? Who? The questions they pondered for hours. What will this do to them? Tear them apart? Make them stronger, so many questions unanswered and they would get no answers until they went to court. For the next 2 weeks there were many sleepless nights. Cowboy's lawyer came out to visit a few nights before the hearing but he was no help just telling them what to expect and the whole situation was just like with CPS if it was not the mother or the father of the baby coming forward than they would have an investigation and do a case study but that was all he could tell them at that time. Cowboy was a nervous wreck that whole week before the hearing.

The morning of the hearing Jerry took the kids to school and would pick them up if the hearing took too long. Kim, Jess and Gayle went to the courthouse to meet up with the lawyer about an hour before the hearing began. The Lawyer told all of them to let him do all the talking they were only to answer questions asked directly to them by the judge if that were to happen. When they entered the court room Jessica saw Jack talking with the judge. *Thank god he is here maybe he will help us out* she thought to herself. Each of them entered the court room and slowly walked to the front to sit on the right side of the room facing the judge. Kim sat down with his hands clasped together and patting his foot nervously anticipating the event. Jess tried to soothe the tension by whispering in his ear "It will be fine they have no reason to take her for us. She is your blood and the only way they can take her is if the mother comes forward and if she does then we will work with her to make sure we get to see Libby as much as possible. Don't get too worked up. I know this is hard on you because it is hard on me too."

He shook his head to acknowledge her and then looked to the ground. She was just as nervous as he was but knew it was her job to calm him down. The court proceeded with all the formalities. "All rise. Judge Durant presiding "and all that other stuff. The small and old Court house was built back in the 50's with wood railing and big windows that had been blocked out to let the light in but so no one could see in it smelled old but was a true work of art constructed by craftsman who worked with hand tools mostly and knew their trade very well. Kim knew the place very well from his younger years and when he had gotten divorced from Stacy, he had to go file custody paperwork for Bratton there. When the actual hearing began it did not dawn on either of them that Jack was sitting on the opposite side of the room from them. *That means he is against us. That son of a bitch how did he know about her and why would he do this* Kim wandered. He could hear the judge and his lawyer talking back and forth but none of it was registering with him he was so mad at the situation knowing Jack was behind the whole thing. What kind of person would put a child through this? The lawyer leaned over to Cowboy and whispered in his ear "the county wants to do a case study on your place because they think it is unfit for a child."

"That is bull shit and they know it!" his volume increases the more he spoke "the county don't give a shit it is that bastard over there"

"Mr. LEE!!!! I will not have that kind of disrespect in my court you can either keep it down or I will hold you in contempt."

"Your Honor I apologize but, we have already done this through the CPS, and they determined that our establishment was fine for rearing children. He" Pointing toward Jack "is just trying to cause problems because we don't see eye to eye."

"Mr. Lee I am well aware of the CPS case study being performed. The court is concerned that the study may have been swayed by your relationship with one Jessica Caldwell and her close ties to the CPS office that performed the study."

"That is Bull" Cowboy started to rant when his Lawyer and Jessica pulled him back down to his seat

"Your honor what my client is trying to say is we would like to post pone this hearing to another date so we can be better prepared. Now that we know what all the accusations are." His lawyer quickly uttered.

"Counsel I will postpone the hearing, but I will not put off the Case study. The case study will be performed with in one week from today not to be shared with the party in question because we want a true and accurate snapshot of the residence not a dog and pony show. We will reconvene in two weeks to determine the outcome of the hearing. Keep in mind should the officials find your place unfit the child will be placed in foster care immediately. I am making provisions for her to stay in place because Miss Caldwell is a trained professional and the child is not to leave her sight until after the hearing." Slap of the gavel. "Court dismissed!"

Cowboy and the rest feverishly left the court room to discuss the case outside. Jessica was discussing what needed to be done with the lawyer when Jack opened the door to exit the court room. He was surprised to see Kim still there in front of the door. Kim scampered over to him before Jessica and the lawyer knew what was going on. "You low life son of a bitch" Jessica and the lawyer separated the 2 of the Jessica pushing back Jack and the lawyer holding Kim back.

"You better get your sorry ass out of here"

"Or what? Are you threatening me Kim?" antagonizing Cowboy "I am sure the judge would love to hear this." As he strutted by Cowboy "you better settle down there boy before you get hurt. See Jess just like I told you the day you met him he is no good and that temper will get the best of him he is just like a pit bull hope he don't turn his anger toward you."

"Jack just shut up and leave. You are scum. I cannot believe you had the gall to do this to us"

"I am not doing it to ya'll. It is all about him. I will bury you under paperwork until you screw up and they lock you in prison BOYEE!" As he closed his car door and drove away. "he rolled down the window as he passed by "You are playing in my home field now"

"I will kill him" Kim was to mad to talk his face was blood red and his body trembling with anger.

They calmed Kim down and managed to get him in the truck. The lawyer scheduled to come to the house the next day with a game plan of what to do about the situation. On the ride home Jessica called her cousin Shelly on the phone. "Shelly? How could you?"

"How could I what?"

"You knew this was Jack doing this to us. Why would you not tell me?

"What?! Jack is the one behind all of this? I had no Idea. I swear Jess you know I would never do this to you or Cowboy. I am so sorry. He is a piece of work. I will get to the bottom of this, I am so sorry."

"Well someone needs to get a handle on him this is out of control" she hung up the phone.

Cowboy never spoke a word on the way home. He was in a daze the whole drive back to the ranch. When they arrived at the house Cowboy still never said a word he just went inside, changed clothes, then to the barn saddled his horse and took off into the field.

Jessica sat on the couch and started crying. Her mother laid Libby in her bed and came to console Jessica." Honey it will all work out"

"This is all my fault"

"No, it is not"

"Yes, it is I am the one who asked Jack to help with the legal stuff for Libby otherwise he would not have even known about her."

"That does not make this your fault"

"No one would have ever thought he would do this. He is just a real jerk. What did Shelly say when you talked with her"?

"She had no Idea he was doing this"

"Well maybe she can talk some sense into him."

"I doubt it they have not gotten along for about 3 years now. She was waiting for Case to graduate so she could leave him."

"Well it will be fine."

"Where is Kim?"

"He left on the horse probably to go work. That is what he does."

"I need him." She left the couch and climbed in the truck and took off through the field to find Kim. She drove through the first field and realized he probably wanted to be alone so she took the truck to the top of old baldy and to her surprise he was sitting there on the alter picking up rocks and pitching them down the hill. "Sorry I ran out on you like that. I hate when I get all worked up."

"That is OK I am a little upset myself. This is all my fault. If I had not stuck my nose in this would all be behind, you."

"How can you say that? This is not your fault. This is all him."

"No Kim I talked to him about the adoption paperwork and if I had not told him about her, he would have never known."

"Jess you had no way of knowing he would pull a stunt like this. He is doing it to get back at me."

"Why does he hate you so much?"

"He was always second fiddle to me in school. Football, girls, you name it I was better. We were best friends for a while, and we did a lot of roping together. We did pretty good. He met up with Shelly at the bar one night and they kind of started dating. We all knew each other after a couple of weeks of running around from one rodeo to the next with me and Jack we were at the bar and I was not in the party mood, so I went out the trailer to lay down. Jack was not ready to go so, they stayed in the Bar. I guess Shelly had enough to drink and decided to come to the trailer with me. I was asleep when she came in the camper with nothing on but her coat and crawled on top of me and started kissing me. When I realized who it was it was too late because Jack had come in and seen her on top of me kissing me and he blew up. He was drunk and She was drunk, so I got her clothes on her and went to find Jack. Well I found him hitting on a girl I had been out with a couple of times and it all came to a head. We got into a fight and he did not fare so well, and we never talked again. Him and Shelly got married and me and Stacy got married and that was it. It was a bad deal. I couldn't tell him that the girl he loved was doing that to me, so I just let him think it was all me"

"Shelly never told me that she always said he was jealous of you, but it was because you were better than him."

I don't think she would have done that had she not been drinking but I still could not break it to him that was her and not me.

What are we going to do? About this situation?

I am going to wait for him to leave his house and beat his ass

That will not solve anything

I know but it will make me feel better.

I think we just wait and see what happens with the case study if it does not go well then, we can get Shirley involved she will know how to handle it and will testify on our behalf. This is rough. Everything was clicking along like clockwork and now this. She sat beside him in silence they sat for an hour or more hoping an answer would just fall from the sky or be delivered by FedEx, but it never did it never comes easy. They went about their days like they normally would Thursday come around and no County people came by.

Chapter 26

MAMA KNOWS

Cowboy and the other hands were out cutting a field on a Friday afternoon Jess had gone to town for an interview and to pick up a few supplies they had needed. On her way back home, she was behind a small sports car she could tell was not from around the area. She had come to know all the vehicles on the road to the way property and she had never seen this one before. The car turned right, and she turned right the car turned left and she turned left. It looked like she was following the car, but the car was heading to their house. Surely, they are not going to our place, but the car turned down the long driveway and preceded toward the house a cautious speed. She assumed it was the CPS officials. Jess was right behind it and when they stopped in the drive Jess got out of the car with two bags of groceries in her hand. The windows on the car were tinted so she could only see an image of what appeared to be a lady in the driver seat, but the driver did not get out right away. After the dust had settled, she noticed the license plate was from California. She thought it was odd and went in to put the groceries in the kitchen and a gun by the door just in case. She stepped out on the porch about the same time the door of the car opened up. "Can I help you?" she asked loudly

"I am looking for Kim Lee. Does he live here?"

"Yes, but he is out in the field right now he should be home before too long are you with the county?

"No"

"Do you want to wait on him?"

"No, I don't want to be a bother."

"It is no problem. Come on in." she walked down the steps and toward the lady who clearly was not from around the area. She looked familiar to her but could not place the face. She was wearing what appeared to be a Catholic School girl outfit. It was not a real short skirt, but it still looked a little trashy. She figured the girl was around 20 years old, but it was hard to tell with all her makeup. She didn't figure she was a past fling of Cowboys but maybe a friend's kid or someone who knew Bratton.

"Hi!! I am Jessica most everyone just calls me Jess."

"My name is Breanne."

"Nice to meet you. I just need to grab a few more things out of the truck. Go ahead and go inside." She still could not figure out why she looked so familiar. She was positive she had not seen her in town, and it was bugging her.

Breanne offered to help with the groceries and Jessica handed her a bag and thanked her for the help. The two of them lugged the groceries up the steps and into the house. "So, are you from around here?"

"No, I am from California."

"Well that must have been a long drive from there to here."

"Yes, it was"

"Would you like a something to drink? I have tea or water."

"If you don't mind, I will have some tea."

The girl was soft spoken and seemed to be well mannered she also had an air about her like she was from a wealthy family. "So, what brings you to Texas Breanne?"

"Oh, I just came to visit some people."

"OK" something was bothering the girl, but she could see she did not want talk to Jessica about it. Gayle came in with the Libby from the bunk house where they had been taking a nap together. "Hey baby did the interview go well?"

"I am not sure it was part time at the clinic just during the day three days a week. I am sorry how rude of me. Mom this is Breanne. Breanne this is my mother Gayle."

"Who is this little cutie?"

"That is Libby she is a spoiled rotten mess".

"I bet she is. Can I hold her?"

Sure, as Gayle passed her across the table to her.

"Wow she is a little chunk" Breanne started playing with her and talking to her. She would talk to Gayle and Jessica while playing with her. As she waited around for Kim to get home. It was getting late and she was going to leave but Jessica and Gayle talked her into staying for dinner. Jess was trying to get information from her without being to nosey, but she would avoid questions or change the subject each time. Cassie and Dylan came up the drive from the school bus stop. Dylan headed for the barn to take care of the horses and to play with the newborn calves. Cassie stayed inside to herself playing Barbie dolls with Libby.

Breanne told her she was a beautiful little girl and asked her name.

"I am Cassie who are you"

"My name is Breanne. I think I have something in my car you might like. As she turned to Jessica. "Is it OK if I give her another doll? And some makeup?"

"I don't see why not."

She went to the car and while she was gone, she asked Cassie if she knew who the girl was, and she said "that is the girl from the Disney Channel mom"

"No, it isn't." living on the ranch they did not have cable TV or Satellite, so they did not get anything but local channels. They rarely watched TV at all unless it was raining.

"Yes, it is you ask her."

When Breanne returned to the house, she did ask her." Breanne you look so familiar. Where have I seen you before?"

"I am sure that Cassie can tell you. I was on Disney show for a few years. The life of Bree. I am Breanne Keaton"

"That is right I remember that show."

"I try to avoid it when I can, but I love little kids and I have a bunch of stuff from the show if she wants it, she can have it."

"Sure, she can have it I apologize for not recognizing you earlier."

"It is quite ok I prefer to be treated like a person and not a movie star that is why I was being vague to you with all your questions."

"I understand it must be hard going into public being a movie star."

"It is in California you get no breaks you have to get away from it or it will drive you crazy."

"Well we won't hassle you too much."

Breanne sat on the floor with Libby and Cass playing and enjoying the peaceful ranch. Cass took her around the house and the barn showing her everything. Breanne made her promise not to tell anyone she was there because it would cause problems.

Cowboy and the others drove up on the tractors to the shop. Breanne and Cass went back into the house. Cowboy came into the house dusting himself off with his hat and Jerry and Cross shortly behind him. He saw Breanne holding Libby and stuck his hand out. "I am Cowboy how are you doing?"

"I am fine."

He went to the kitchen and made himself a glass of tea. "So how did it go today?"

"It went fine they had a few more people to talk to and they said they would call me back if they were interested. We will see!" Jess cheerfully explained.

"Well that is good. How are you Sassy? Did you have fun at school?"

"Yes, I did. We learned about a tadpole and frogs. It was gross."

"Oh, that sounds fun. How are you doing there Tater bug?" As he reached out for Libby and she leaned out to him smiling. He grabbed her up and tossed her up a little in the air and she started laughing and reaching for his face. He held on to her rubbing his whiskers on her hand and making her giggle.

"Where is Kim?" Breanne interrupted.

Jess even more puzzled by the girl because Kim had no clue who she was either. Jess said, "That is Kim right there." The girl did not even know who he was. This was weird to her.

"I am Kim what can I do for you."

"Can we talk?"

"Sure, what do you got?"

"Well can we talk somewhere more private. No offense to you it will only take a few seconds and I will be on my way". Her eyes begin to well up with tears and she looked scared to death. Jess had been worried about her and now she was concerned about her. "You two go ahead we will get dinner ready."

Kim motioned to her to step outside and she turned around to Jess and mouthed "Thank You" Jess just motioned her on out as if it was no bother to her, but it was a huge bother. It was eating her up inside not knowing what was going on out there. Kim walked slowly to the barn and placed one foot on the bottom rung of the fence looking out into the field. "What is bothering you?"

"You have a beautiful place here. I have heard about it and seeing it in real life it is so much prettier."

"So, what was your name I didn't catch it?"

"I am Breanne." She paused as he quickly turned his head toward her in shock.

"Breanne who?"

"Breanne Keaton. It's me dad."

"How did you find us here? Why did you not just call?"

"Mom told me where you lived so I used my GPS for directions are you mad? I probably should not have come. I feel bad."

"No, I am glad you are here I am just a little shocked is all. He turned to look at her again, removed his hat, and rubbed his head with his free hand. He took a deep breath. Does your mom know you are here?"

"No not here she knows I am in Texas but not out here"

"Wow. What I mean gosh. I don't know what to say. You are so beautiful, and all grown up. So, what did your mom tell you?"

"Nothing really except you lived here and your name. She did tell me you were a big cowboy and handsome man. She was right."

"Wow you look just like her too. I am stunned. She did not tell you anything else?"

"No that is it. Well come on in. You are here might as well meet everyone and I will fill you in. This will be a shocker to everyone else too."

"I don't want to disturb your family you all look so happy I will just go. I just wanted to meet you."

"No, you are not doing any such thing we are going in there together and I will explain this all to them."

Bratton pulled in the drive with Susan while they were on the fence. He ran to the porch to greet everyone. He could see Jess peeking around the door from time to time. "What is going on? Who is that out there talking to dad?"

"Shhh!! I don't know. Here they come everyone act natural."

"Jess you are the only one acting weird" her mother replied

"Oh, just hush."

Breanne and Kim walked back up the steps. "Hey everyone, this is Breanne. She is gonna stay the night or two with us. This old guy here is Cross, the other old guy is Jerry, that is Bratton and Susan I reckon you know the rest of them already."

"Luckily we have an empty seat at the table for you, so you don't have to eat on the porch". All of them sat at the table and ate dinner. During dinner Susan look at her. "I know you. You are Breanne Keaton, right? Your mother is Stacy Keaton I used to watcher shows all the time."

"Yep that is me"

"Well glad to meet you. How is your mother?"

"She is. Hmm. Can you pass me the salt?"

Sure, and Susan handed her the salt and the conversation never came back to her. After dinner they all worked their way through the kitchen cleaning off their dishes and then out to the enlarged porch with 3 swings and the rocking chair for Cross. As tired as they all appeared to be, no one went to bed early that night. They were all curious as to why Breanne Keaton had shown up on their doorstep. The mood was somber, and no one spoke a word for the first few seconds, they all settled into their respected seats and waited with anticipation. Cowboy, not being one for small talk, got straight to the point. "For those of you who have not figured this out, this is Breanne Keaton. She is my daughter." Everyone's jaw dropped to the floor. Stunned by what they had just heard.

"WHAT!!" Bratton was caught off guard by his statement

"Hold on and let me finish before you go any further. She is also your twin sister." Breanne was unaware that she had a brother much less a twin. She did not even know what was going on now. All her mother had told her was that her father's name was Kim and he was an All-Around Cowboy for the PRCA before she was born. "You have got to be kidding me I have a twin?? Oh MY God."

"Yes, you do" Bratton and Breanne both speechless just looked at one another in awe of their new discovery. Each of them angry, that they were never told about the other, and excited to find out about the other.

Jessica now knew why the young girl looked so familiar to her. After hearing the news form Cowboy, she looked at the two of them and realized they looked exactly alike. She looked toward Cross to see him sitting on the edge of his seat with his elbows on his knees hanging on every word that was said, he had no clue what was going on or who she was until just then. This was weird that no one knew about her not even Cross. It was apparent by the way Cowboy acted that he had not seen her in many years.

"Dad you better be explaining this pretty quick and if this is a joke it aint funny"

"I have a brother. Why would she not tell me that?"

"I am not sure why it all happened like it did, but we were out on the circuit after you two were born. It was my last circuit and I was gonna hang it up. You two were a hand full on the road and it was tough on all of us. I wanted to bring ya'll back here to raise you with the family. Your mother just never could bring herself to moving away from Hollywood. One morning I heard one of you crying and I got up to check on ya'll. Bratton was the only one there with a note. Saying a bunch of stuff and that she would take Breanne and I could have Bratton. That is when we packed up and headed home. I am sorry you had to find out this way. I wanted to tell you son but by time you were old enough to understand I figured you would be mad at me and I did not know if your mother wanted you to know about her or what so I figured at this age it would never come up. I guess I should have told you I am sorry." He hung his head down in shame. Disappointed in himself and knowing now that he was wrong for not telling him. He did not say another word except "it was not my decision. I would have never walked out on any of you." Jess rubbed his back and saw the pain in his eyes. Bratton with angered look on his face just stared in his direction and shook his head in disbelief. Breanne was not as upset as Bratton. She was mostly excited that she had a twin brother and curious why her mother had done what she did. Many thoughts occupied her brain and she sat in awkward silence with the rest of her newly found family. Before realizing she had created this mess by coming to see him.

"Maybe I should go I am sorry" her eyes filled with tears and her voice cracking she turned to walk off the porch.

In unison Bratton, Cowboy and Jess all asked her to stay. Jess knew she had to stifle the situation before it got out of hand and she did not want Breanne to think she was not welcome there "We can work this out. It is all new to everyone. There is a lot of emotions and tempers going on right now. Let's just all take the night to think about it and process what we have just learned before jumping to conclusions. I am sure your father will answer any questions you have but he is a little overwhelmed right now too. Breanne it took a lot for you to come here. You are very brave. A trait I am sure you inherited from your father. So please stay the night and we can talk more tomorrow."

"She is right. Bratton, I know you are mad at me son." Cowboy raised his head with tears in his eyes. "I love you and I know I screwed up. So be mad if you have to, I understand. When you want to talk about it either of you, I will be more than happy to tell you everything I know." Cowboy stood up and walked to Breanne and gave her a hug whispering in her ear "you are always welcome here" stepped to the side to Bratton and wrapped his arms around him. Bratton still standing with arms crossed and a scowl on his face he did not reciprocate the gesture "I love you son". Cowboy went into the house. Bratton just stayed on the porch leaning back on the handrail Susan stood up beside him and put her arm around him and rubbed his back

"I know you are mad. But your dad is really hurting right now." He turned his head slightly looking down toward her

"I need to get away from here for a minute."

"OK let's go for a ride."

He nodded his head yes while trying to fight back tears of his own and walked off the porch toward his truck. Jess followed behind him stopping him under the big pecan tree. "He knows he was wrong, but he is more upset that he hurt you." She wrapped her arms around him and held him for a few minutes like a mother would a son and he cried on her shoulder. "I know you feel betrayed and I would to. But give him a chance to explain when you cool off." again he nodded yes, and she told him she loved him and reiterated what she had always told him. "I am hear if you need to talk or just vent."

Susan stepped down off the porch and turned back to see Breanne sitting on the swing alone and crying. "Breanne come on you can go with us. Is that OK Brat?" Jess softly whispered "I think that would be good. If you are OK with it." He nodded his head and went to the passenger side of the truck to get in. "Come on you two"

Jess told Breanne she would move Cass into the room with Dylan and she would sleep in her room. "Don't move her I can sleep on the floor or I can just sleep with her if it is OK with you."

"Well you are not sleeping on the floor and I am sure she would not mind sleeping with you if you are ok with it"

"That is fine." She walked to the truck. Susan hopped in the driver's seat and Breanne climbed in the back. The three of them took off down the driveway. Jess went back on to the porch and sat on the empty swing Cross was still in his rocking chair looking and listening to the whole chain of events. Jess still had not taken it all in "wow"

"You can say that again"

"What just happened? Bratton has a twin sister; Cowboy has another kid?"

"That is what I gather, and I knew nothing about it. That must have been eating him up keeping that inside all these years."

It never even dawned on Jess that Cross was taken back by the whole thing and felt a little betrayed himself. She could see he was a little perturbed as was Bratton.

"Are you OK"

"I am fine just a little taken off guard by the whole deal"

"I am sure you are. I haven't been around as long as you and I am little taken back myself."

"Well I reckon I am going to bed I have had enough of this for the day"

"I think I will do the same"

They went their separate ways. Jess went in the house. Her mother was cleaning the dining room and kitchen from the evening meal and her dad was setting at the table sipping on a cup of coffee. "Well is everything OK?" Her mother asked

"I am not sure. I think it will be fine when everyone has a little time to think."

233

"I hope so Sugar. We are gonna call it a night unless you need me to stay up?"

"No, I am fine. I am going to the bedroom to see how Kim is doing."

"OK we will see you in the morning."

Jess put some more coffee on and went to the restroom before stopping at the room and peaking her head in the door. Kim was setting in his rocking chair in the dark staring at the wall. "I am going back out to the porch to have some coffee do you want to come out with me. Everyone has left or gone to bed."

He said nothing and she went to the kitchen confident he would come out eventually. With 2 cups of coffee in hand she went to the front porch and sat in the swing with a blanket over her legs. She took one sip of coffee before he strolled out to sit beside her. Placing her arm around his head, rubbing his ear, she pulled his head down to her shoulder." Do you want to talk about it?"

"Not really!!! There aint much to talk about. The cat is out of the bag."

"I am sure there is a little relief getting that off your chest"

"Yea!! It did feel better for a second until I seen the way Bratton looked at me."

"He will settle down and it will be fine"

"There just aint no good time to tell someone they have a sister or brother. One day they are too young and the next day it is too late."

"I know you did not mean to keep it from him, and he will understand if you tell him that."

He sighed and sat up pulling her head over into his lap and slowly running his fingers through her hair. "I don't want to talk about it anymore tonight"

She just laid there with him playing with her hair until they both started to nod off to sleep. The three kids came back later that night Susan woke the two sleeping in the swing up and told them to go to bed. She showed Breanne where everything was in the house and they went to bed.

Kim unable to sleep that night went to the kitchen and started coffee around 4 in the morning. He sipped a few cups and started Breakfast he heard Libby wake up crying and went to her room to get her out of bed. She sat in her highchair listening to him talk and watching him cook. When he was troubled by a problem cooking helped take his mind off of it. Breanne heard the rustling around in the kitchen, so she got out of bed and went into the kitchen. She immediately pulled the baby from the highchair and held her in her lap talking to Kim. She told him she was not mad at him and she figured that it was not his idea to split her and her brother up because she knew how her mother acted. Kim didn't really talk much to her but listened to her talk and play with Libby. Jessica tried to stay in bed and get some sleep after Kim had gotten up, but she could not get any rest either, so she went into the kitchen. She rounded the corner to see Breanne and Libby playing in the kitchen and it hit her like a ton of bricks maybe she was the mother. Jessica did not say anything but watched her closely while she played with the little girl. Kim left the kitchen for a brief moment to use the restroom so Jess decide to seize the moment and ask her in a polite way " I don't want to offend you but there is something I need to ask you but I do not want you to get mad at me for asking."

"You can ask me anything what is it?"

"Do you know who Libby's mother is?"

She stammered for a moment, embarrassed, "Yes"

"Is she yours?"

"Yes"

"Why didn't you say anything?"

Kim overheard the tail end of the question on his way back from the restroom. It all made sense now why they could not determine by the DNA who the father was because, the baby belonged to his daughter. He had not even thought about who Libby's mother was for a few months but now he knows. He came into the room when she was talking to Jessica

"I was going to tell you, but everything last night was just so overwhelming, and I did not want ya'll to think I was a bad person."

"A bad person? For what?" Kim asked.

"For leaving Libby on your doorstep, I didn't leave her there. I waited until Bratton took her inside before I left. I knew ya'll would take care of her. Please don't hate me."

"I don't hate you but why did you come all the way here and leave her with us? Why not take her to your mother or someone closer to you?"

"Mom is in no shape to care for a baby. I was in some trouble and managed to hide being pregnant from the media and I did not want her to be raised in that life like I was. So, I checked into a rehab after I left here, in Dallas, and I got out about a 2 months ago. I wanted to make sure I could stay clean before I came back here. I had intended on talking to you that night, but I was in no condition to do that."

"Well that is good to know." With a concerned look on his face

"I don't want her to go to California. She is happy here, but I don't want to burden any of you."

"She is not a burden. You are not a burden so don't ever think that way. What are you planning on doing?"

"I have to go back to California for a few weeks. I have some contracts that I have to fulfill, so I can get out of there."

"Then what?"

"I was hoping I might find a place in this area to buy and I could live out here and just do a movie here and there."

Jess listened to her talk in disbelief, concerned she would take the baby away from them and they would never see her again. Jess quickly spoke up "well there is no sense in dragging her around until you get settled in. We will take care of her until you get back."

Cowboy looked bewildered at what she was saying. Jessica had become a little defensive about the situation and was trying to protect Libby.

"I hoped you would say that. She is getting so big and she is so happy."

Kim, reminded of her mother, asked her "you think you will be able to make it here? You are from the city and your mother wanted no part of this."

"Well we are totally different. I hate it there and that is no place for a family. Mom is slowly killing herself one pill at a time, and I don't want Libby to be around that stuff."

"I understand that, and we will be more than happy to help you out with anything you need." Kim assured her. They spoke for a little bit about her mother and how she was not doing well. It had just dawned on Jessica that Cowboy had been married to Stacy Keaton an actress she always emulated, and thought was absolutely beautiful. She knew her family was very wealthy and with all the movie she had been in and then Breanne being on the Disney channel and movies also they had to be very well off. She knew she was not here for the money and she was not trying to get the baby back. She must have really been telling the truth. She still could not get past the fact that Cowboy was married to a movie star, now she felt she was really not up to his standards. She did not say anything to him about his marriage before and she knew he did not like to talk about it from what brief moments it came up in the past.

Breanne was relieved to hear that they wanted to keep Libby with them and expressed her gratitude to them for their help and support. Kim told her it was a big relief knowing who her mother was and that neither Bratton nor he was the father. He also told her that Libby was the reason he and Jessica were together and if it had not been for her leaving Libby there that night they would have never met. Jessica was flattered to hear him talk that way about their relationship and her. She sat in his lap and they told Breanne the story from start to finish and Jessica showed her the scrap book she had started for Libby. Breanne had come clean and was not so reserved around them anymore. They sat and talked until the rest of the family had come in for Breakfast. Breanne enjoyed being around a true family for a change she liked that they all ate at the table together and actually liked one another. Everyone was so thoughtful and caring. She loved Susan. The two of them were a lot alike she told Bratton the reason he was with her is because he was trying to replace his missing sister from his life, they managed to get him to laugh and smile the night before on their drive around town. She was already beginning to feel like she was part of the family. Susan was relieved to find out that Bratton was not the father more so than Bratton, not that she did not like Libby because she loved that little girl but, because she wanted to be the mother of any baby of his. Breanne spent most of the day playing with Libby and Cassie who just adored her. Susan took her for a ride around the property and showed her all the main sights telling her about things she and Bratton had done growing up.

Bratton went most of the day avoiding his father but before he loaded the truck to head back to school, he gave him a hug and told him "I love you too dad but I am still mad at you."

Cowboy conceded "I love you too. And you have every right to be mad at me."

Jess was glad to see Bratton hug his father. She knew that Cowboy was pretty tore up over Bratton not talking to him especially since he had been off to college and not around much anymore. She went around the truck and gave Bratton a big hug because she had missed him being around also and did not feel like she had even gotten to spend any time with him since they had all the drama that weekend. She had become his adopted mother over the past few months and she treated him like she would if she had a son his age. Susan interrupted the two of them by jumping on his back just to aggravate him and then said her goodbye to Jess as well.

They left and Breanne stayed for a few days. She had decided to stay around and fly back instead of drive back so she could spend more time with Libby and get to know her father a little better. She never really knew what to expect of him, but she had imagined him being a rough, dirty, and old cowboy. He looked a lot like what she imagined but he did not act anything like she had expected. Instead of being a hard-callused old man she noticed he was very reserved and thoughtful of other people. He did not say a whole lot, but his actions spoke volumes. She thought they might have been a poor family scraping to get by and would want money from her but she was pleased to know that they were not hurting either but did not have some of the things she treasured in life like air conditioning and cable TV. She was acclimating to ranch life pretty quickly; she even rode a horse inside the area for the first time in her life.

Monday came around and another strange vehicle came down the drive. Jess and Breanne were in the kitchen baking cookies and saw the car through the window.

"Are you expecting company?" Breanne asked Jess

"No none that I know of why?"

"A black car just came down the drive with 3 people in it. I hope it is not the media following me."

"Well you just stay in here and I will see who it is" Jessica walked through the open screen door to the porch and 3 men in suits stepped out of the vehicle. "Can I help you?"

"Yes, is this the Lee estate?"

"It is"

"We are with the county and come to do a case study on your residence."

"O yes I forgot all about you coming out. Come on up"

"We will just need to take a look around if you don't mind, I am sure it won't be long." Two of the men inspected the house while the other wandered around the cars and the barn. They appeared to be looking for something specific when they were there and never really asked about the baby or anything. The one that was outside came and whispered something to one of the men inside and they left without a word. It was really strange, so Jess called Cowboy and he came straight in from the field. "So, they just left without a word? What did they look at?"

Jess told him everything and everywhere they went, and he called the Sheriff's' department to make sure it was all on the up and up. Breanne asked them what was going on and Jessica filled her in on the whole baby situation.

"Oh, my goodness I had no idea I was going to create this much trouble."

"It was not you it is the crazy idiot who is doing this" referring to Lee. After being debriefed on the situation she thought it might be best to take Libby back with her to California until the dust could settle. Jessica and Cowboy talked her out of taking her and asked her to write a letter about the situation and have it notarized so they could take it to court with them on Thursday. She obliged them and had it taken care of for them so the court would not give them any more trouble. Cowboy didn't talk much so the conversations normally were with Jessica and Cowboy would chime in from time to time. Tuesday came around and she had to leave for the airport. She left most everything there because she had planned on coming back in a couple of weeks. Cowboy helped her load her car and she came back in to kiss Libby and tell everyone bye. Cowboy walked her out to the car, and they had a little talk. He wanted to make sure she was going to be OK going back. He was concerned about her lifestyle in California after listening to her talk about her mother and the trouble she had been in and having the baby by herself. He wanted her to know he was glad she came out and made her promise she would come back. It was the longest conversation they had the whole time she was there, but it did put her mind at ease knowing he cared about her. They had discussed her coming back for Thanksgiving and planned to go to California over Christmas break to pick up her stuff and move her to Texas if everything went to plan.

She left and Cowboy went back up to the porch and turned to see her drive off with his arm around Jess they waved at her until she could no longer see them. Then they turned around and sat down on the swing looking out over the property. "Well now we know who the mother is." Jess stated.

"Yep we sure do"

"You don't think she will try to take Libby away with her, do you?"

"I don't know. I don't think she will, but you never know. I hope she comes back here like she talked about, but I am not sure she can adapt to this lifestyle."

"I know. She sure seems like a sweet girl. I hope she gets her life straightened out."

"I am sure she will. She is a brave girl. She will be fine. I hope. I feel bad not ever meeting her. I went to see her a few times but with all her mother's entourage around her I never got the chance."

"It had to be hard on you"

'It was and it is now.'

'I am here if you want to talk about it".

"I know you are, and I am glad you are but let's not talk about it anymore. She is my daughter and she is welcome here anytime and we will help her out anyway we can."

"I think that is the best way to look at it." She leaned over and kissed him on the cheek and hugged him tight.

Wednesday rolled around Kim, Jessica and Libby went to visit the lawyer and sign some papers before court the next day. Kim tried to pay him for his services but before Breanne left town she went by and took care of all his fees and a little more in the event there was more trouble. She wanted me to make sure you knew she was coming back, and that Jack would never try to get his baby from you again. Kim felt a little better after hearing that she had been to the lawyer and spoken with him and even paid him for his trouble.

That next morning, they came to the court room early as they had done before and sat in the same seats as the last time, but Kim was not as nervous about the situation this time as he was the last. He sat between the lawyer and Jessica so they could keep him quiet. The judge entered the room and they went through the all the mumbo jumbo that courts do and took their seats. The judge looked to Jack and asked him what his findings were on the case study. Jack had a report from the social worker that said the place was unfit. Kim rose to his feet and slammed his hands on the table in front of him "you have got to be kidding me" Jess and their lawyer coaxed him back into his seat. His lawyer leaned over to whisper in his ear "sit down you are going to love this". Jack continued to bash and taunt Kim recommending the state take the baby immediately into their custody and have Kim arrested on a 48 hour no bond until the baby is in a secure place making him look like a convicted felon. Kim looked to his defense attorney "you better do something". All he did was sit back and smile.

As Jack finished up his personal assault on Kim the judge asked if the defense had a rebuttal to his argument. Kim's lawyer stood to his feet and said "yes we do your Honor. I have heard in my possession a signed affidavit from the mother of the child awarding temporary custody of the child to Kim Lee and Jessica Caldwell. Your Honor I think we are done here". As he sat back down in his seat with confidence

The Judge said" now hold on just one second I do not have to allow this in my court. Seeing as how the mother was nowhere to be found 2 weeks ago and now, we have a signed document from her. I will not allow this to be admitted into evidence."

"We had a feeling you would say that, so she sent her lawyers to represent her." He walked to the back of the room and opened the doors to the court to allow an entourage of legal advisors and lawyers followed by several reporters into the court room. Your Honor will you please explain to Miss Breanne Keaton's, the daughter of Stacy Keaton, legal team and the press why you will not allow this document to be admitted into evidence? We would also like to bring Jack Barrett up on slandering charges and miss use of public officials' charges for using the Social Works Department to benefit himself."

The judge had never seen so many people in the court room he had no choice but to admit the document into evidence and therefor they had no case. Or he would risk not being re-elected next year. He also did not want to drag this out in the public eye and have all the reporters investigating him and his side business that he was using to filter money given to him by Jack to sway in his favor. Kim was surprised that Breanne had set this all up and was laughing at poor Jack because he could not win against him even in the court room or his "Home Field".

Chapter 27

BRIGHT LIGHTS BIG CITY

$\mathcal{B}$y the time Breanne had made it back Libby was walking and talking. Halloween was that weekend and they all went into town for the fall festival dressed up in their costumes. Bratton and Susan had come into town also and went with the rest of the family to the festival Susan and Breanne dressed up with Cassie as Cinderella and the two stepsisters with Bratton dressed as the prince and Libby as the little mouse. Everyone had a great time and the tension between Bratton and his dad had let up, but Bratton still had a little dissention towards him. Cowboy understood and was OK with him being upset. Cowboy told him about moving Breanne from California to Texas so she could be closer to all of them and the baby and asked if he and Susan would help mover her. Bratton agreed to help, and Susan was excited to get to go to California. Thanksgiving had passed and school let out for the semester. The plan was for Bratton and Susan to fly out with Breanne to help her pack everything up. Kim and Jessica would drive so they could pull a trailer for all of her things back. Dylan and Cass would stay home with the others to keep an eye on the ranch.

By this time Breanne felt like part of the family. She would talk to her dad and Jess on the phone and video chat with Susan and Bratton on the computer, so she was pretty comfortable with everyone. That Friday Kim dropped them off at the Airport and picked Jessica up to head West toward California. Breanne picked them up from the airport and took them back to her house to meet Bratton's mother. Breanne tried to warn them that she was not in her right state of mind before they got there and did not want to tell her that Bratton was the son she had walked out on. Bratton was not excited to meet the woman because of what she had done and placed most of the blame on her after finding out how she was and from what his father had told him. Breanne drove them to a mansion overlooking the valley below. The place was huge with everything you could imagine. Susan did not understand why she would want to move away from such a beautiful house but knew from talking to her that she was doing the right thing. They unpacked their bags and took a tour of the house. Breanne took them into meet her mother who never even knew they had been there for a few hours. They walked into her bedroom/ living quarters it was decorated like a king's castle with a big huge bed and large throne like chair. Fruit on the table it was just like walking on to a movie set. Her mother sat at the desk with a drink in her hand and on the computer. She introduced Bratton and Susan as friends when her mother talked Susan understood why she had to leave. Her speech was slurred from the pills she had been taking and the mixture of the alcohol and pills made her loopy. It was a depressing sight for Susan especially because she had idolized her growing up and to see her in this condition made her sick. She did not stay long. Stacy's assistant Diane, the person who raised Breanne, followed them out of the room. "Is this your brother?"

"Yes, this is Bratton. My twin"

"It is so nice to meet you Bratton I had no ideal you were twins until after Breanne told me. You are very handsome. I am sorry you had to meet her like this. She is having some issues and we are trying to get her help."

"It is nice to meet you too. Bree told me she would be like this so we kind of expected it. I just wanted to see her in person."

"Breanne are you leaving this week?"

"Yes, I am moving down there. I will give you the address so you can visit and meet Libby. She is a doll."

"Well you all be careful and thank you for taking care of Breanne it means a lot to me that she has a good family, and this is no place for that baby to be raised. I need to go take care of her so I must go but it was a pleasure meeting you both."

She disappeared behind the door and the three of them walked through the big house to Breanne's side once again. Bratton and Susan got settled into their room. Most of the stuff had been packed and Breanne wanted to take them out for dinner. So, the girls got dressed and they went out on the town. Susan was excited to see Hollywood and get dressed up. She borrowed some of Bree's clothes so she would fit in. Susan was wearing a short black dress that hugged her body close, with the sides' open and high heels. Bratton looked at her and his jaw dropped to the ground as she came down the winding staircase from the second floor. She looked like royalty or a model in a magazine. "Are you wearing that?"

"Yes. Why does it not look good?

"Oh, it looks better than good. You look amazing in that. I am going to be beating guys off you all night."

"Stop it Brat. You really like it?

"I love it!!"

Breanne gave her an emerald pendant and earrings that matched to wear with the outfit. Bratton was gawking at her the whole way to the restaurant. They went to a vineyard for dinner and had some food and wine looking out over the fields of grapes at sundown. The picturesque view was more than words could describe and the bill for the food was more than enough to pay for it. Breanne was not worried about the money she paid the tab and they walked through the vineyard to see how the wine was made and to sample several different varieties of wine made there. They left the vineyard and went to a private club where most of the actors and actresses went to stay away from the media and the normal people. The club was down an alley way in the basement of a high-rise office building. It was not advertised on the radio or TV because the owner wanted to keep his elite clients from being bothered. Breanne walked right in with Susan and Bratton in tow. The door man made Bratton remove his hat and leave it at the door to claim when he left. Bratton did not like the idea of leaving his hat, but his sister assured him it was fine. Bratton knew when he entered the club that this was not his type of place. He went along because he knew Susan wanted to go and Breanne was excited to introduce them to her friends. They were escorted to a round booth at the back of the dance floor. Girls had been hired to dance in cages elevated above the floor and on speakers that were surrounding the dance floor. The dimly lit club was illuminated every few seconds by the strobe's lights reflecting off the disco ball centered above the dance floor. They sat down at the table. Bratton offered to go get everyone a drink, but Breanne quickly explained to him that it did not work that way in this kind of night club. The waitress walked to their table with her tray in her hand. "What are you drinking today Breanne?"

"What do you want guys?"

"I will take a beer. Miller Lite if you have it."

"I want a vodka and cranberry." Susan requested.

"They only sell bottles here. You buy a bottle of whatever you want, and they will bring it to your table, and you can mix it with whatever you want. Bring us a bottle of Kettle One Vodka and whatever he wants."

"Ok I will take a bottle of Crown Black with coke."

"No. No. no. Not coke. You cannot say that here because you might get COCAINE. He means cola"

"Really? It is that easy here?"

"Yes, it is. And in a place like this where you are protected from the media, they are not shy about it."

"I understand now why you would want to get away." Susan said with remorse.

"Well it is not bad if you have no family, but I don't want to be in that scene anymore."

They sat and had a few drinks and the club began to fill up with "A" lister's and other TV stars. Susan and Breanne went to the restroom together and Bratton stayed at the table. Feeling a little out of place he kept to himself. A girl came over and asked him if he liked to party and he just ignored her. He watched Susan come out of the restroom being drug across the dance floor by Breanne. Several guys grabbed their arms and tried to dance with them, but they danced their way back to the table. Bratton could feel the tension building inside of him he did not like this place at all. One of the guys that had grabbed Susan came to the table and tried to get Susan to go back and dance with him and she respectfully declined and slid closer to Bratton holding his arm. Bratton was getting angry but did not want to spoil the fun for the two girls, so he just sat and kept to himself but became more and more infuriated each drink he consumed. Several other guys tried to get the girls to go dance but the first guy Tom kept coming back until finally Bratton had enough. "She don't want to dance with your goofy ass now leave her alone."

"Who are you?" the Tom guy replied?

"It don't matter who I am. You need to go away before I lose my patience with you."

"Bratton don't worry about it is OK" Susan said, "I am not going to dance with anyone."

"Sorry Breanne I am just not used to this stuff. I did not mean to make your friend mad."

"Tom?? He damn sure aint my friend, he is a freak. Just because his family owns half of Hollywood, he thinks he can get any girl he wants. I don't like him. He will leave you alone."

"I hope he does cuz I can't take much more of his crap."

They sat there for a few minutes and some of Breanne's friends came over and sat with them. Most of them were other girls who had been on the Disney shows with her. Some of them barely had any clothes on and the others had less on. Bratton was sure to stay close to Susan and try not to stare. He leaned over to whisper in her ear. "is it just me or do they need to get some clothes on?" Susan shook her head yes to the beat of the music. Tom lingered around the table and stalked all the girls. Bratton would catch him staring at Susan and Breanne from time to time and Tom would quickly look away. The night was coming to a close and Tom had an entourage with him when Breanne decide to leave. They stood up from the table and began walking across the crowded dance floor. There was no way around the group of people Tom was entertaining, so Breanne walked through them. Tom grabbed Bree's arm. "Where are you going this early?"

"We are going home let go of me TOM.", annoyed by his actions. She jerked her arm away. He made a motion to grab her again

Bratton grabbed his arm. "Let it be buddy. I don't know you and I don't want to cause a scene, so just let us leave and everybody will stay in one piece" as he tightened the grip on his arm and made him grimace with pain.

"Who is this? Your new body guards?"

"He is my brother and you might want to leave him alone."

Tom was putting on a show and acting tough because he had all his buddies behind him. Bratton did not know how many people were on his side, so he just wanted to get out without fighting.

"Your brother?" puzzled by her response.

Breanne broke through the crowd and Bratton followed her pulling Susan through behind her.

"Well is this your sister?", as he lifted Susan's skirt up. Susan screamed at him and then turned and punched him in the face. Bratton had turned around to see what happened and Bratton followed her hit with a much more powerful punch knocking Tom to the ground on the dance floor. He got on top of him and hit him several times another guy hit Bratton in the back of the head and Susan took off her heels and hit him over the head. Then she began fighting the crowd with Bratton. After hitting 2 bouncers and beating down half the people in the club they were politely asked to leave. Breanne grabbed their hands and pulled them out as if she were a mother breaking up two kids from fighting. "I knew that would happen. That is why I wanted to leave."

"I am sorry Bree he just needed his ass beat."

"I know I was not your fault"

When they walked out the door to the street all they could see was camera flashes and lenses in their face. People were hollering out questions and Breanne's name. Bratton walked ahead of the girls and they each buried their heads in his shoulder as he pushed his way through the crowd of media. One of the guys was too persistent and Bratton pushed him down and kicked his camera. A cop nearby who was called about the disturbance in the bar went to defuse the situation. After separating them from the crowd he began to write Bratton a ticket. Bratton argued with the officer and refused to sign the ticket until Breanne told him to sign it before they hauled him to jail. They finally left the bar and went home. The next morning when they woke up it was all on the news about Breanne and her Brother starting a fight in a local club. They showed footage of them in the bar fighting and interviewed Tom about the situation. They made it out like Bratton had started the whole thing.

That afternoon Kim and Jessica showed up at the house to load up. Bratton, Susan and Breanne were moving very slow. Kim could see that

Brat had scratch marks on his neck and he inquired about where he had gotten them.

"It is a long story Dad; I don't really care to go into it right now. Let's just get this stuff loaded and get out of this town."

"Well does it have anything to do with the bar fight last night. "He asked facetiously

"So, you know about that?"

"It is all on the news. You are the Rocky of Hollywood." Jabbing at the air like a boxer

"Let's just load up and leave. I obviously don't belong here."

Cowboy was glad to hear Bratton had come to the realization that he did not belong in a place like that and that Susan had the same opinion as he did. The rest of the day was spent loading the truck. Cowboy and Jessica spent most of their time outside placing the boxes and furniture in the trailer so it would not shift and so Cowboy would have less of a chance of running into Stacy. They had no idea that she was watching them from her window. As messed up in the head as she was, she recognized him and remised on her decision that she had made so many years ago. Seeing Cowboy there made her worse and she knew she was in no shape to see him, but she had never forgotten him. She knew she would never find another person who would treat her the way he did or make her feel the way he did. She had always known she made a mistake but seeing him with another woman loading up all of Breanne's things made her realize the consequences of that rash decision.

It was late when they finished loading the truck, but Cowboy insisted on leaving that night. He said he wanted to get a head start on the trip home but in reality, he was uncomfortable being there because it brought back a lot of memories and heart ache from the past. Cowboy and Bratton rode in the truck and the girls followed them in Breanne's escalade. Bothe vehicles were loaded down with just enough room for passengers. They drove off a little before dark and never looked back. Jessica was a little upset that she was not able to see the town or visit any restaurants, but she could feel the uneasy tension from Bratton and Cowboy being in a the crowded city around Cowboy's ex-wife and Bratton's mother he had never seen before.

Cowboy and Bratton sat in silence for the first few hours. Cowboy asked Bratton how he liked being out there knowing the answer to the question but wanting to start a conversation since their relationship as of late had not been as strong as it had in the past 18 years. Bratton replied" I hope I never have to come back to this place."

"Other than the little confrontation in the bar was it really that bad?"

"Dad we don't belong here. The people are rude and always in a hurry. The scenery is beautiful, but it is not worth all the other crap you have to deal with."

"I agree with you. So did you get a chance to meet Stacy?" not wanting to call her his mother because she had never been around and did not want to make him feel like he was obligated to visit her or take care of her. He tips toed into the subject that had created the dispute they had been in for the last few months.

"Yes, I met her"

"How was that for you?"

With disappointment Bratton muttered "It wasn't. She did not know who I was because she was hopped up on pills and/or drunk, probably both."

"I hate that, she used to be very fun, levelheaded, and independent girl at one time."

"Not anymore she has someone do everything for her and Bree said she never leaves the house unless she has to go for an interview or something. She is really skinny and white as a ghost. She had no idea who I was and did not even care. Bree just said we were friends of hers' there to help her move. So, she would not go off the deep end."

"I had heard she was in bad shape and wasn't doing well. I never told you this but I came out here about 8 years ago because I wanted to see Breanne and try to get her to come see us so I could introduce the 2 of you to each other but they would not let me in the gate for one reason or another. I saw your mother and had read a few articles about her and knew she was up to no good back then. That is when I decided to not say anything because I didn't know if she even wanted to see you or have anything to do with you and I did not want you to get hurt."

"I know you were just trying to protect me. I get that but you still should have told me about her or at least about Breanne. I am not mad at you. I never really was, I was just disappointed and felt like I had been betrayed. After coming out here and seeing her I understand a little better why you did it."

"She wasn't always this way. When we met, she was beautiful and full of life? She loved being on the go and all the attention from the media and I would sit back and watch her smile for the camera. She was something and way above my pay grade. I figured it would not last long with her. Not because of me but because she never really fit in with my kind of people and I didn't fit in with her crowd. When it was just the 2 of us together it was special."

"So, what really happened? Why did she leave?"

Cowboy was not comfortable going that deep into the conversation, so he pulled the truck into and IHOP restaurant and parked it. He killed the engine and told Bratton "let's get a bite to eat."

Are you going to tell me?

"Son that is a story for another day."

The End

CPSIA information can be obtained
at www.ICGtesting.com
Printed in the USA
LVHW022041210221
679522LV00004B/282